# Just The Facts 101
## Textbook Key Facts

Slovenia Immigration Laws and Regulations Handbook: Strategic Information and Basic Laws

by Cram101
Textbook NOT Included

**Table of Contents**

Title Page

Copyright

Foundations of Business

Management

Business law

Finance

Human resource management

Information systems

Marketing

Manufacturing

Commerce

Business ethics

Accounting

Index: Answers

# Just The Facts101

Exam Prep for

Slovenia Immigration Laws and Regulations Handbook: Strategic Information and Basic Laws

Just The Facts101 Exam Prep is your link from the textbook and lecture to your exams.

**Just The Facts101 Exam Preps are unauthorized and comprehensive reviews of your textbooks.**

All material provided by CTI Publications (c) 2019

Textbook publishers and textbook authors do not participate in or contribute to these reviews.

Just The Facts101 Exam Prep

Copyright © 2019 by CTI Publications. All rights reserved.

eAIN 438786

# Foundations of Business

A business, also known as an enterprise, agency or a firm, is an entity involved in the provision of goods and/or services to consumers. Businesses are prevalent in capitalist economies, where most of them are privately owned and provide goods and services to customers in exchange for other goods, services, or money.

---

:: Business law ::

A _____ is an arrangement where parties, known as partners, agree to cooperate to advance their mutual interests. The partners in a _____ may be individuals, businesses, interest-based organizations, schools, governments or combinations. Organizations may partner to increase the likelihood of each achieving their mission and to amplify their reach. A _____ may result in issuing and holding equity or may be only governed by a contract.

Exam Probability: **Medium**

1. *Answer choices:*

(see index for correct answer)

- a. Oppression remedy
- b. Limited partnership
- c. Unfair competition
- d. United States labor law

*Guidance:* level 1

---

:: Stock market ::

A _____ , equity market or share market is the aggregation of buyers and sellers of stocks , which represent ownership claims on businesses; these may include securities listed on a public stock exchange, as well as stock that is only traded privately. Examples of the latter include shares of private companies which are sold to investors through equity crowdfunding platforms. Stock exchanges list shares of common equity as well as other security types, e.g. corporate bonds and convertible bonds.

Exam Probability: **Medium**

2. *Answer choices:*

(see index for correct answer)

- a. China Concepts Stock
- b. Stock market
- c. CNBC Ticker
- d. Secondary shares

*Guidance:* level 1

:: Management ::

A _____ is when two or more people come together to discuss one or more topics, often in a formal or business setting, but _____ s also occur in a variety of other environments. Many various types of _____ s exist.

Exam Probability: **Medium**

3. *Answer choices:*

(see index for correct answer)

- a. Operations management
- b. Supply management
- c. Supplier relationship management
- d. Meeting

*Guidance:* level 1

:: Meetings ::

An _____ is a group of people who participate in a show or encounter a work of art, literature, theatre, music, video games, or academics in any medium. _____ members participate in different ways in different kinds of art; some events invite overt _____ participation and others allowing only modest clapping and criticism and reception.

Exam Probability: **Low**

4. *Answer choices:*
(see index for correct answer)

- a. Salon
- b. Audience
- c. Ex officio member
- d. Parley

*Guidance:* level 1

:: Legal terms ::

_____ , a form of alternative dispute resolution, is a way to resolve disputes outside the courts. The dispute will be decided by one or more persons, which renders the " _____ award". An _____ award is legally binding on both sides and enforceable in the courts.

Exam Probability: **High**

5. *Answer choices:*
(see index for correct answer)

- a. Arbitration
- b. Querulant
- c. Misfeasance
- d. Incorporation of international law

*Guidance:* level 1

:: Investment ::

In finance, the benefit from an _____ is called a return. The return may consist of a gain realised from the sale of property or an _____, unrealised capital appreciation, or _____ income such as dividends, interest, rental income etc., or a combination of capital gain and income. The return may also include currency gains or losses due to changes in foreign currency exchange rates.

Exam Probability: **High**

6. *Answer choices:*

(see index for correct answer)

- a. Investment
- b. Value premium
- c. Fund of funds
- d. Lehman scale

*Guidance:* level 1

:: Supply chain management ::

_____ is the process of finding and agreeing to terms, and acquiring goods, services, or works from an external source, often via a tendering or competitive bidding process. _____ is used to ensure the buyer receives goods, services, or works at the best possible price when aspects such as quality, quantity, time, and location are compared. Corporations and public bodies often define processes intended to promote fair and open competition for their business while minimizing risks such as exposure to fraud and collusion.

Exam Probability: **Low**

7. *Answer choices:*

(see index for correct answer)

- a. Institute for Supply Management
- b. Procurement
- c. Calculating demand forecast accuracy
- d. Corporate sourcing

*Guidance:* level 1

:: International trade ::

An _____ is a good brought into a jurisdiction, especially across a national border, from an external source. The party bringing in the good is called an _____ er. An _____ in the receiving country is an export from the sending country. _____ ation and exportation are the defining financial transactions of international trade.

Exam Probability: **High**

8. *Answer choices:*

(see index for correct answer)

- a. Import
- b. Gas Exporting Countries Forum
- c. Global financial system
- d. Market access

*Guidance:* level 1

:: Stock market ::

A _____, securities exchange or bourse, is a facility where stock brokers and traders can buy and sell securities, such as shares of stock and bonds and other financial instruments. _____ s may also provide for facilities the issue and redemption of such securities and instruments and capital events including the payment of income and dividends. Securities traded on a _____ include stock issued by listed companies, unit trusts, derivatives, pooled investment products and bonds. _____ s often function as "continuous auction" markets with buyers and sellers consummating transactions via open outcry at a central location such as the floor of the exchange or by using an electronic trading platform.

Exam Probability: **Medium**

9. *Answer choices:*

(see index for correct answer)

- a. All or none
- b. Stock market index
- c. Delivery versus payment
- d. Chip

*Guidance:* level 1

:: Social security ::

_____ is "any government system that provides monetary assistance to people with an inadequate or no income." In the United States, this is usually called welfare or a social safety net, especially when talking about Canada and European countries.

Exam Probability: **High**

10. *Answer choices:*

(see index for correct answer)

- a. Social Security System
- b. SNILS
- c. Social security
- d. Welfare in Finland

*Guidance:* level 1

:: ::

Some scenarios associate "this kind of planning" with learning "life skills". Schedules are necessary, or at least useful, in situations where individuals need to know what time they must be at a specific location to receive a specific service, and where people need to accomplish a set of goals within a set time period.

Exam Probability: **Medium**

11. *Answer choices:*

(see index for correct answer)

- a. co-culture
- b. surface-level diversity
- c. deep-level diversity
- d. Scheduling

*Guidance:* level 1

:: Energy and fuel journals ::

In physics, energy is the quantitative property that must be transferred to an object in order to perform work on, or to heat, the object. Energy is a conserved quantity; the law of conservation of energy states that energy can be converted in form, but not created or destroyed. The SI unit of energy is the joule, which is the energy transferred to an object by the work of moving it a distance of 1 metre against a force of 1 newton.

Exam Probability: **Medium**

12. *Answer choices:*

(see index for correct answer)

- a. Energy-Safety and Energy-Economy
- b. The Energy Journal
- c. Journal of Renewable and Sustainable Energy
- d. Oil Shale

*Guidance:* level 1

:: Packaging ::

In work place, _____ or job _____ means good ranking with the hypothesized conception of requirements of a role. There are two types of job _____ s: contextual and task. Task _____ is related to cognitive ability while contextual _____ is dependent upon personality. Task _____ are behavioral roles that are recognized in job descriptions and by remuneration systems, they are directly related to organizational _____ , whereas, contextual _____ are value based and additional behavioral roles that are not recognized in job descriptions and covered by compensation; they are extra roles that are indirectly related to organizational _____ . Citizenship _____ like contextual _____ means a set of individual activity/contribution that supports the organizational culture.

Exam Probability: **Low**

13. *Answer choices:*

(see index for correct answer)

- a. Reel
- b. Optical disc packaging
- c. Lid
- d. Performance

*Guidance:* level 1

:: Statistical terminology ::

_____ es can be learned implicitly within cultural contexts. People may develop _____ es toward or against an individual, an ethnic group, a sexual or gender identity, a nation, a religion, a social class, a political party, theoretical paradigms and ideologies within academic domains, or a species. _____ ed means one-sided, lacking a neutral viewpoint, or not having an open mind. _____ can come in many forms and is related to prejudice and intuition.

Exam Probability: **Low**

14. *Answer choices:*
(see index for correct answer)

- a. Concentration parameter
- b. Raw score
- c. Bias
- d. Burstiness

*Guidance:* level 1

:: Systems theory ::

A _____ is a group of interacting or interrelated entities that form a unified whole. A _____ is delineated by its spatial and temporal boundaries, surrounded and influenced by its environment, described by its structure and purpose and expressed in its functioning.

Exam Probability: **Low**

15. *Answer choices:*
(see index for correct answer)

- a. decentralized system
- b. transient state
- c. equifinality
- d. management system

*Guidance:* level 1

:: ::

A _____ is any person who contracts to acquire an asset in return for some form of consideration.

Exam Probability: **Medium**

16. *Answer choices:*
(see index for correct answer)

- a. hierarchical perspective
- b. levels of analysis
- c. functional perspective
- d. imperative

*Guidance:* level 1

:: Business models ::

_____ es are privately owned corporations, partnerships, or sole proprietorships that have fewer employees and/or less annual revenue than a regular-sized business or corporation. Businesses are defined as "small" in terms of being able to apply for government support and qualify for preferential tax policy varies depending on the country and industry. _____ es range from fifteen employees under the Australian Fair Work Act 2009, fifty employees according to the definition used by the European Union, and fewer than five hundred employees to qualify for many U.S. _____ Administration programs. While _____ es can also be classified according to other methods, such as annual revenues, shipments, sales, assets, or by annual gross or net revenue or net profits, the number of employees is one of the most widely used measures.

Exam Probability: **Medium**

17. *Answer choices:*
(see index for correct answer)

- a. Gratis
- b. European Cooperative Society
- c. Utility computing
- d. Small business

*Guidance:* level 1

:: ::

_____ is the administration of an organization, whether it is a business, a not-for-profit organization, or government body. _____ includes the activities of setting the strategy of an organization and coordinating the efforts of its employees to accomplish its objectives through the application of available resources, such as financial, natural, technological, and human resources. The term "_____" may also refer to those people who manage an organization.

Exam Probability: **Low**

18. *Answer choices:*
(see index for correct answer)

- a. cultural
- b. process perspective
- c. hierarchical perspective
- d. corporate values

*Guidance:* level 1

:: ::

_____ is an abstract concept of management of complex systems according to a set of rules and trends. In systems theory, these types of rules exist in various fields of biology and society, but the term has slightly different meanings according to context. For example.

Exam Probability: **Medium**

19. *Answer choices:*
(see index for correct answer)

- a. co-culture
- b. Regulation
- c. empathy
- d. Character

*Guidance:* level 1

:: Marketing ::

A _____ is a group of customers within a business's serviceable available market at which a business aims its marketing efforts and resources. A _____ is a subset of the total market for a product or service. The _____ typically consists of consumers who exhibit similar characteristics and are considered most likely to buy a business's market offerings or are likely to be the most profitable segments for the business to service.

Exam Probability: **High**

20. *Answer choices:*

(see index for correct answer)

- a. Pharmaceutical marketing
- b. Cultural consumer
- c. Boston matrix
- d. Target market

*Guidance:* level 1

---

:: Business planning ::

_____ is an organization's process of defining its strategy, or direction, and making decisions on allocating its resources to pursue this strategy. It may also extend to control mechanisms for guiding the implementation of the strategy. _____ became prominent in corporations during the 1960s and remains an important aspect of strategic management. It is executed by strategic planners or strategists, who involve many parties and research sources in their analysis of the organization and its relationship to the environment in which it competes.

Exam Probability: **Medium**

21. *Answer choices:*

(see index for correct answer)

- a. Business war games
- b. Customer Demand Planning
- c. Stakeholder management
- d. Joint decision trap

*Guidance:* level 1

---

:: Management ::

In business, a _____ is the attribute that allows an organization to outperform its competitors. A _____ may include access to natural resources, such as high-grade ores or a low-cost power source, highly skilled labor, geographic location, high entry barriers, and access to new technology.

Exam Probability: **Low**

22. *Answer choices:*
(see index for correct answer)

- a. Identity formation
- b. Intelligent customer
- c. Economic order quantity
- d. Competitive advantage

*Guidance:* level 1

:: Regression analysis ::

A _____ often refers to a set of documented requirements to be satisfied by a material, design, product, or service. A _____ is often a type of technical standard.

Exam Probability: **High**

23. *Answer choices:*
(see index for correct answer)

- a. Guess value
- b. Explained sum of squares
- c. Bayesian linear regression
- d. Specification

*Guidance:* level 1

:: Unemployment ::

In economics, a _____ is a business cycle contraction when there is a general decline in economic activity. Macroeconomic indicators such as GDP , investment spending, capacity utilization, household income, business profits, and inflation fall, while bankruptcies and the unemployment rate rise. In the United Kingdom, it is defined as a negative economic growth for two consecutive quarters.

Exam Probability: **High**

24. *Answer choices:*

(see index for correct answer)

- a. Phillips curve
- b. Unemployment Convention, 1919
- c. Recession
- d. JobBridge

*Guidance:* level 1

---

:: Market research ::

_____ is "the process or set of processes that links the producers, customers, and end users to the marketer through information used to identify and define marketing opportunities and problems; generate, refine, and evaluate marketing actions; monitor marketing performance; and improve understanding of marketing as a process. _____ specifies the information required to address these issues, designs the method for collecting information, manages and implements the data collection process, analyzes the results, and communicates the findings and their implications."

Exam Probability: **Medium**

25. *Answer choices:*

(see index for correct answer)

- a. Ad Tracking
- b. Industry analyst
- c. Marketing research
- d. Confidence interval

*Guidance:* level 1

---

:: Globalization-related theories ::

_____ is the process in which a nation is being improved in the sector of the economic, political, and social well-being of its people. The term has been used frequently by economists, politicians, and others in the 20th and 21st centuries. The concept, however, has been in existence in the West for centuries. "Modernization, "westernization", and especially "industrialization" are other terms often used while discussing _____ . _____ has a direct relationship with the environment and environmental issues. _____ is very often confused with industrial development, even in some academic sources.

Exam Probability: **High**

26. *Answer choices:*

(see index for correct answer)

- a. post-industrial
- b. postmodernism
- c. Capitalism

*Guidance:* level 1

:: Semiconductor companies ::

_____ Corporation is a Japanese multinational conglomerate corporation headquartered in Konan, Minato, Tokyo. Its diversified business includes consumer and professional electronics, gaming, entertainment and financial services. The company owns the largest music entertainment business in the world, the largest video game console business and one of the largest video game publishing businesses, and is one of the leading manufacturers of electronic products for the consumer and professional markets, and a leading player in the film and television entertainment industry. _____ was ranked 97th on the 2018 Fortune Global 500 list.

Exam Probability: **Medium**

27. *Answer choices:*

(see index for correct answer)

- a. Freescale Semiconductor
- b. Ingenic Semiconductor
- c. VeriSilicon
- d. Sony

*Guidance:* level 1

:: Materials ::

A _____, also known as a feedstock, unprocessed material, or primary commodity, is a basic material that is used to produce goods, finished products, energy, or intermediate materials which are feedstock for future finished products. As feedstock, the term connotes these materials are bottleneck assets and are highly important with regard to producing other products. An example of this is crude oil, which is a _____ and a feedstock used in the production of industrial chemicals, fuels, plastics, and pharmaceutical goods; lumber is a _____ used to produce a variety of products including all types of furniture. The term "_____" denotes materials in minimally processed or unprocessed in states; e.g., raw latex, crude oil, cotton, coal, raw biomass, iron ore, air, logs, or water i.e. "...any product of agriculture, forestry, fishing and any other mineral that is in its natural form or which has undergone the transformation required to prepare it for internationally marketing in substantial volumes."

Exam Probability: **Low**

28. *Answer choices:*
(see index for correct answer)

- a. Raw material
- b. LRPu
- c. Nanophase
- d. Auxetics

*Guidance:* level 1

:: Public relations ::

_____ is the public visibility or awareness for any product, service or company. It may also refer to the movement of information from its source to the general public, often but not always via the media. The subjects of _____ include people, goods and services, organizations, and works of art or entertainment.

Exam Probability: **Low**

29. *Answer choices:*

(see index for correct answer)

- a. Mobile Public Affairs Detachment
- b. Defense Video %26 Imagery Distribution System
- c. Publicity
- d. African Press Organization

*Guidance:* level 1

---

:: Private equity ::

_____ is a type of private equity, a form of financing that is provided by firms or funds to small, early-stage, emerging firms that are deemed to have high growth potential, or which have demonstrated high growth. _____ firms or funds invest in these early-stage companies in exchange for equity, or an ownership stake, in the companies they invest in. _____ ists take on the risk of financing risky start-ups in the hopes that some of the firms they support will become successful. Because startups face high uncertainty, VC investments do have high rates of failure. The start-ups are usually based on an innovative technology or business model and they are usually from the high technology industries, such as information technology, clean technology or biotechnology.

Exam Probability: **Medium**

30. *Answer choices:*
(see index for correct answer)

- a. Earnout
- b. Private equity in the 1990s
- c. Rollup
- d. Leveraged buyout

*Guidance:* level 1

---

:: Income ::

_____ is a ratio between the net profit and cost of investment resulting from an investment of some resources. A high ROI means the investment's gains favorably to its cost. As a performance measure, ROI is used to evaluate the efficiency of an investment or to compare the efficiencies of several different investments. In purely economic terms, it is one way of relating profits to capital invested. _____ is a performance measure used by businesses to identify the efficiency of an investment or number of different investments.

Exam Probability: **Medium**

31. *Answer choices:*

(see index for correct answer)

- a. Total personal income
- b. Creative real estate investing
- c. Return on investment
- d. Mandatory tipping

*Guidance:* level 1

:: Customs duties ::

A _____ is a tax on imports or exports between sovereign states. It is a form of regulation of foreign trade and a policy that taxes foreign products to encourage or safeguard domestic industry. _____ s are the simplest and oldest instrument of trade policy. Traditionally, states have used them as a source of income. Now, they are among the most widely used instruments of protection, along with import and export quotas.

Exam Probability: **Low**

32. *Answer choices:*

(see index for correct answer)

- a. Canadian import duties
- b. Tariff
- c. Cochin Duty Free
- d. Duty-free shop

*Guidance:* level 1

:: Management accounting ::

In economics, _____ s, indirect costs or overheads are business expenses that are not dependent on the level of goods or services produced by the business. They tend to be time-related, such as interest or rents being paid per month, and are often referred to as overhead costs. This is in contrast to variable costs, which are volume-related and unknown at the beginning of the accounting year. For a simple example, such as a bakery, the monthly rent for the baking facilities, and the monthly payments for the security system and basic phone line are _____ s, as they do not change according to how much bread the bakery produces and sells. On the other hand, the wage costs of the bakery are variable, as the bakery will have to hire more workers if the production of bread increases. Economists reckon _____ as a entry barrier for new entrepreneurs.

Exam Probability: **Medium**

33. *Answer choices:*
(see index for correct answer)

- a. Backflush accounting
- b. Entity-level controls
- c. Fixed cost
- d. Responsibility center

*Guidance:* level 1

---

:: Scientific method ::

In the social sciences and life sciences, a _____ is a research method involving an up-close, in-depth, and detailed examination of a subject of study , as well as its related contextual conditions.

Exam Probability: **Medium**

34. *Answer choices:*
(see index for correct answer)

- a. pilot project
- b. Causal research
- c. Preference test
- d. Case study

*Guidance:* level 1

---

:: Elementary arithmetic ::

In mathematics, a _____ is a number or ratio expressed as a fraction of 100. It is often denoted using the percent sign, "%", or the abbreviations "pct.", "pct"; sometimes the abbreviation "pc" is also used. A _____ is a dimensionless number .

Exam Probability: **Medium**

35. *Answer choices:*

(see index for correct answer)

- a. Significance arithmetic
- b. Chunking
- c. Parity
- d. Percentage

*Guidance:* level 1

---

:: Production economics ::

In microeconomics, _____ are the cost advantages that enterprises obtain due to their scale of operation , with cost per unit of output decreasing with increasing scale.

Exam Probability: **Medium**

36. *Answer choices:*

(see index for correct answer)

- a. Foundations of Economic Analysis
- b. Economic batch quantity
- c. Marginal product of labor
- d. Sectoral output

*Guidance:* level 1

---

:: International trade ::

_____ or globalisation is the process of interaction and integration among people, companies, and governments worldwide. As a complex and multifaceted phenomenon, _____ is considered by some as a form of capitalist expansion which entails the integration of local and national economies into a global, unregulated market economy. _____ has grown due to advances in transportation and communication technology. With the increased global interactions comes the growth of international trade, ideas, and culture. _____ is primarily an economic process of interaction and integration that's associated with social and cultural aspects. However, conflicts and diplomacy are also large parts of the history of _____ , and modern _____ .

Exam Probability: **Medium**

37. *Answer choices:*
(see index for correct answer)

- a. Globalization
- b. Trade commissioner
- c. Arab Chamber of Commerce
- d. Northwest Cattle Project

*Guidance:* level 1

:: Evaluation ::

A _____ is an evaluation of a publication, service, or company such as a movie, video game, musical composition, book ; a piece of hardware like a car, home appliance, or computer; or an event or performance, such as a live music concert, play, musical theater show, dance show, or art exhibition. In addition to a critical evaluation, the _____ 's author may assign the work a rating to indicate its relative merit. More loosely, an author may _____ current events, trends, or items in the news. A compilation of _____ s may itself be called a _____ . The New York _____ of Books, for instance, is a collection of essays on literature, culture, and current affairs. National _____ , founded by William F. Buckley, Jr., is an influential conservative magazine, and Monthly _____ is a long-running socialist periodical.

Exam Probability: **High**

38. *Answer choices:*

(see index for correct answer)

- a. Quality assurance
- b. Transferable skills analysis
- c. Problem
- d. Review

*Guidance:* level 1

:: Quality management ::

_____ ensures that an organization, product or service is consistent. It has four main components: quality planning, quality assurance, quality control and quality improvement. _____ is focused not only on product and service quality, but also on the means to achieve it. _____ , therefore, uses quality assurance and control of processes as well as products to achieve more consistent quality. What a customer wants and is willing to pay for it determines quality. It is written or unwritten commitment to a known or unknown consumer in the market. Thus, quality can be defined as fitness for intended use or, in other words, how well the product performs its intended function

Exam Probability: **High**

39. *Answer choices:*

(see index for correct answer)

- a. Dana Ulery
- b. Bureau Veritas
- c. Institute of Standards and Industrial Research of Iran
- d. European Quality in Social Services

*Guidance:* level 1

:: Television commercials ::

_____ is a characteristic that distinguishes physical entities that have biological processes, such as signaling and self-sustaining processes, from those that do not, either because such functions have ceased, or because they never had such functions and are classified as inanimate. Various forms of _____ exist, such as plants, animals, fungi, protists, archaea, and bacteria. The criteria can at times be ambiguous and may or may not define viruses, viroids, or potential synthetic _____ as "living". Biology is the science concerned with the study of _____ .

Exam Probability: **Medium**

40. *Answer choices:*
(see index for correct answer)

- a. Hotel Hell Vacation
- b. CM Yoko
- c. Life
- d. St George

*Guidance:* level 1

:: Fraud ::

In law, _____ is intentional deception to secure unfair or unlawful gain, or to deprive a victim of a legal right. _____ can violate civil law, a criminal law, or it may cause no loss of money, property or legal right but still be an element of another civil or criminal wrong. The purpose of _____ may be monetary gain or other benefits, for example by obtaining a passport, travel document, or driver's license, or mortgage _____, where the perpetrator may attempt to qualify for a mortgage by way of false statements.

Exam Probability: **Low**

41. *Answer choices:*
(see index for correct answer)

- a. Fraud
- b. Mussolini diaries
- c. Sham marriage
- d. Pharma fraud

*Guidance:* level 1

:: Information technology ::

_____ is the use of computers to store, retrieve, transmit, and manipulate data, or information, often in the context of a business or other enterprise. IT is considered to be a subset of information and communications technology. An _____ system is generally an information system, a communications system or, more specifically speaking, a computer system – including all hardware, software and peripheral equipment – operated by a limited group of users.

Exam Probability: **High**

42. *Answer choices:*
(see index for correct answer)

- a. Normalized Systems
- b. SPAN Infotech
- c. Infocommunications
- d. Omniview technology

*Guidance:* level 1

:: Project management ::

_____ is the right to exercise power, which can be formalized by a state and exercised by way of judges, appointed executives of government, or the ecclesiastical or priestly appointed representatives of a God or other deities.

Exam Probability: **High**

43. *Answer choices:*
(see index for correct answer)

- a. NetPoint
- b. Cost-benefit
- c. Authority
- d. The Transformation Project

*Guidance:* level 1

:: Treaties ::

An _____ is a relationship among people, groups, or states that have joined together for mutual benefit or to achieve some common purpose, whether or not explicit agreement has been worked out among them. Members of an _____ are called allies. _____ s form in many settings, including political _____ s, military _____ s, and business _____ s. When the term is used in the context of war or armed struggle, such associations may also be called allied powers, especially when discussing World War I or World War II.

Exam Probability: **High**

44. *Answer choices:*

(see index for correct answer)

- a. Full Powers
- b. Alliance
- c. Treaty
- d. Bilateral treaty

*Guidance:* level 1

:: Competition regulators ::

The _____ is an independent agency of the United States government, established in 1914 by the _____ Act. Its principal mission is the promotion of consumer protection and the elimination and prevention of anticompetitive business practices, such as coercive monopoly. It is headquartered in the _____ Building in Washington, D.C.

Exam Probability: **Low**

45. *Answer choices:*

(see index for correct answer)

- a. Federal Antimonopoly Service
- b. Competition Appeal Tribunal
- c. Australian Competition and Consumer Commission
- d. Federal Trade Commission

*Guidance:* level 1

:: Marketing ::

A _____ is the quantity of payment or compensation given by one party to another in return for one unit of goods or services.. A _____ is influenced by both production costs and demand for the product. A _____ may be determined by a monopolist or may be imposed on the firm by market conditions.

Exam Probability: **Low**

46. *Answer choices:*

(see index for correct answer)

- a. Price
- b. Digital omnivore
- c. Market share
- d. Analyst relations

*Guidance:* level 1

:: Logistics ::

_____ is generally the detailed organization and implementation of a complex operation. In a general business sense, _____ is the management of the flow of things between the point of origin and the point of consumption in order to meet requirements of customers or corporations. The resources managed in _____ may include tangible goods such as materials, equipment, and supplies, as well as food and other consumable items. The _____ of physical items usually involves the integration of information flow, materials handling, production, packaging, inventory, transportation, warehousing, and often security.

Exam Probability: **Low**

47. *Answer choices:*

(see index for correct answer)

- a. Logistics
- b. Menlo Worldwide Logistics
- c. International Society of Logistics
- d. Hubs and Nodes

*Guidance:* level 1

:: National accounts ::

An _____ is a relationship among people, groups, or states that have joined together for mutual benefit or to achieve some common purpose, whether or not explicit agreement has been worked out among them. Members of an _____ are called allies. _____ s form in many settings, including political _____ s, military _____ s, and business _____ s. When the term is used in the context of war or armed struggle, such associations may also be called allied powers, especially when discussing World War I or World War II.

Exam Probability: **High**

44. *Answer choices:*

(see index for correct answer)

- a. Full Powers
- b. Alliance
- c. Treaty
- d. Bilateral treaty

*Guidance:* level 1

:: Competition regulators ::

The _____ is an independent agency of the United States government, established in 1914 by the _____ Act. Its principal mission is the promotion of consumer protection and the elimination and prevention of anticompetitive business practices, such as coercive monopoly. It is headquartered in the _____ Building in Washington, D.C.

Exam Probability: **Low**

45. *Answer choices:*

(see index for correct answer)

- a. Federal Antimonopoly Service
- b. Competition Appeal Tribunal
- c. Australian Competition and Consumer Commission
- d. Federal Trade Commission

*Guidance:* level 1

:: Marketing ::

A _____ is the quantity of payment or compensation given by one party to another in return for one unit of goods or services.. A _____ is influenced by both production costs and demand for the product. A _____ may be determined by a monopolist or may be imposed on the firm by market conditions.

Exam Probability: **Low**

46. *Answer choices:*

(see index for correct answer)

- a. Price
- b. Digital omnivore
- c. Market share
- d. Analyst relations

*Guidance:* level 1

:: Logistics ::

_____ is generally the detailed organization and implementation of a complex operation. In a general business sense, _____ is the management of the flow of things between the point of origin and the point of consumption in order to meet requirements of customers or corporations. The resources managed in _____ may include tangible goods such as materials, equipment, and supplies, as well as food and other consumable items. The _____ of physical items usually involves the integration of information flow, materials handling, production, packaging, inventory, transportation, warehousing, and often security.

Exam Probability: **Low**

47. *Answer choices:*

(see index for correct answer)

- a. Logistics
- b. Menlo Worldwide Logistics
- c. International Society of Logistics
- d. Hubs and Nodes

*Guidance:* level 1

:: National accounts ::

_____ is a monetary measure of the market value of all the final goods and services produced in a period of time, often annually. GDP per capita does not, however, reflect differences in the cost of living and the inflation rates of the countries; therefore using a basis of GDP per capita at purchasing power parity is arguably more useful when comparing differences in living standards between nations.

Exam Probability: **Low**

48. *Answer choices:*

(see index for correct answer)

- a. capital formation
- b. National Income
- c. Fixed capital

*Guidance:* level 1

---

:: Decision theory ::

A _____ is a deliberate system of principles to guide decisions and achieve rational outcomes. A _____ is a statement of intent, and is implemented as a procedure or protocol. Policies are generally adopted by a governance body within an organization. Policies can assist in both subjective and objective decision making. Policies to assist in subjective decision making usually assist senior management with decisions that must be based on the relative merits of a number of factors, and as a result are often hard to test objectively, e.g. work-life balance _____. In contrast policies to assist in objective decision making are usually operational in nature and can be objectively tested, e.g. password _____.

Exam Probability: **High**

49. *Answer choices:*

(see index for correct answer)

- a. Policy
- b. There are known knowns
- c. Business rules engine
- d. New Approach to Appraisal

*Guidance:* level 1

:: Workplace ::

_____ is a systematic determination of a subject's merit, worth and significance, using criteria governed by a set of standards. It can assist an organization, program, design, project or any other intervention or initiative to assess any aim, realisable concept/proposal, or any alternative, to help in decision-making; or to ascertain the degree of achievement or value in regard to the aim and objectives and results of any such action that has been completed. The primary purpose of _____, in addition to gaining insight into prior or existing initiatives, is to enable reflection and assist in the identification of future change.

Exam Probability: **High**

50. *Answer choices:*
(see index for correct answer)

- a. Evaluation
- b. Workplace incivility
- c. Work etiquette
- d. Staff turnover

*Guidance:* level 1

---

:: Commerce ::

_____ relates to "the exchange of goods and services, especially on a large scale". It includes legal, economic, political, social, cultural and technological systems that operate in a country or in international trade.

Exam Probability: **High**

51. *Answer choices:*
(see index for correct answer)

- a. Straw purchase
- b. Oniomania
- c. Commerce
- d. Hong Kong Mercantile Exchange

*Guidance:* level 1

---

:: Payments ::

A _____ is the trade of value from one party to another for goods, or services, or to fulfill a legal obligation.

Exam Probability: **High**

52. *Answer choices:*

(see index for correct answer)

- a. Thirty pieces of silver
- b. Payment
- c. Direct Payments
- d. Tuition payments

*Guidance:* level 1

:: ::

_____ is the production of products for use or sale using labour and machines, tools, chemical and biological processing, or formulation. The term may refer to a range of human activity, from handicraft to high tech, but is most commonly applied to industrial design, in which raw materials are transformed into finished goods on a large scale. Such finished goods may be sold to other manufacturers for the production of other, more complex products, such as aircraft, household appliances, furniture, sports equipment or automobiles, or sold to wholesalers, who in turn sell them to retailers, who then sell them to end users and consumers.

Exam Probability: **High**

53. *Answer choices:*

(see index for correct answer)

- a. Manufacturing
- b. co-culture
- c. hierarchical perspective
- d. personal values

*Guidance:* level 1

:: Statistical terminology ::

_____ is the ability to avoid wasting materials, energy, efforts, money, and time in doing something or in producing a desired result. In a more general sense, it is the ability to do things well, successfully, and without waste. In more mathematical or scientific terms, it is a measure of the extent to which input is well used for an intended task or function. It often specifically comprises the capability of a specific application of effort to produce a specific outcome with a minimum amount or quantity of waste, expense, or unnecessary effort. _____ refers to very different inputs and outputs in different fields and industries.

Exam Probability: **Low**

54. *Answer choices:*

(see index for correct answer)

- a. Gompertz function
- b. Law of large numbers
- c. Polykay
- d. Efficiency

*Guidance:* level 1

---

:: Generally Accepted Accounting Principles ::

Expenditure is an outflow of money to another person or group to pay for an item or service, or for a category of costs. For a tenant, rent is an _____. For students or parents, tuition is an _____. Buying food, clothing, furniture or an automobile is often referred to as an _____. An _____ is a cost that is "paid" or "remitted", usually in exchange for something of value. Something that seems to cost a great deal is "expensive". Something that seems to cost little is "inexpensive". "_____ s of the table" are _____ s of dining, refreshments, a feast, etc.

Exam Probability: **Medium**

55. *Answer choices:*

(see index for correct answer)

- a. Expense
- b. Cost principle
- c. Gross sales
- d. AICPA Statements of Position

*Guidance:* level 1

:: ::

Competition arises whenever at least two parties strive for a goal which cannot be shared: where one's gain is the other's loss .

Exam Probability: **Low**

56. *Answer choices:*

(see index for correct answer)

- a. surface-level diversity
- b. functional perspective
- c. Competitor
- d. open system

*Guidance:* level 1

:: Financial accounting ::

_____ is a financial metric which represents operating liquidity available to a business, organisation or other entity, including governmental entities. Along with fixed assets such as plant and equipment, _____ is considered a part of operating capital. Gross _____ is equal to current assets. _____ is calculated as current assets minus current liabilities. If current assets are less than current liabilities, an entity has a _____ deficiency, also called a _____ deficit.

Exam Probability: **Medium**

57. *Answer choices:*

(see index for correct answer)

- a. Hidden asset
- b. Convenience translation
- c. Controlling interest
- d. Advance payment

*Guidance:* level 1

:: Planning ::

_____ is a high level plan to achieve one or more goals under conditions of uncertainty. In the sense of the "art of the general," which included several subsets of skills including tactics, siegecraft, logistics etc., the term came into use in the 6th century C.E. in East Roman terminology, and was translated into Western vernacular languages only in the 18th century. From then until the 20th century, the word "_____" came to denote "a comprehensive way to try to pursue political ends, including the threat or actual use of force, in a dialectic of wills" in a military conflict, in which both adversaries interact.

Exam Probability: **Low**

58. *Answer choices:*
(see index for correct answer)

- a. BLUF
- b. Counterplan
- c. Strategy
- d. Implementation intention

*Guidance:* level 1

---

:: Occupations ::

An _____ is a person who has a position of authority in a hierarchical organization. The term derives from the late Latin from officiarius, meaning "official".

Exam Probability: **High**

59. *Answer choices:*
(see index for correct answer)

- a. Officer
- b. Gaonburha
- c. Signwriter
- d. Blacksmith

*Guidance:* level 1

## Management

Management is the administration of an organization, whether it is a business, a not-for-profit organization, or government body. Management includes the activities of setting the strategy of an organization and coordinating the efforts of its employees (or of volunteers) to accomplish its objectives through the application of available resources, such as financial, natural, technological, and human resources.

---

:: ::

_____ is both a research area and a practical skill encompassing the ability of an individual or organization to "lead" or guide other individuals, teams, or entire organizations. Specialist literature debates various viewpoints, contrasting Eastern and Western approaches to _____, and also United States versus European approaches. U.S. academic environments define _____ as "a process of social influence in which a person can enlist the aid and support of others in the accomplishment of a common task".

Exam Probability: **High**

1. *Answer choices:*
(see index for correct answer)

- a. Leadership
- b. corporate values
- c. interpersonal communication
- d. process perspective

*Guidance: level 1*

---

:: Cash flow ::

_____ s are narrowly interconnected with the concepts of value, interest rate and liquidity. A _____ that shall happen on a future day tN can be transformed into a _____ of the same value in t0.

Exam Probability: **Medium**

2. *Answer choices:*
(see index for correct answer)

- a. Factoring
- b. Cash flow
- c. Discounted cash flow
- d. Free cash flow

*Guidance: level 1*

:: Human resource management ::

_____ is a core function of human resource management and it is related to the specification of contents, methods and relationship of jobs in order to satisfy technological and organizational requirements as well as the social and personal requirements of the job holder or the employee. Its principles are geared towards how the nature of a person's job affects their attitudes and behavior at work, particularly relating to characteristics such as skill variety and autonomy. The aim of a _____ is to improve job satisfaction, to improve through-put, to improve quality and to reduce employee problems.

Exam Probability: **High**

3. *Answer choices:*
(see index for correct answer)

- a. Job enrichment
- b. Adecco Group North America
- c. Job design
- d. Human resource policies

*Guidance: level 1*

:: Leadership ::

_____/Management is a part of a style of leadership that focuses on supervision, organization, and performance; it is an integral part of the Full Range Leadership Model. _____ is a style of leadership in which leaders promote compliance by followers through both rewards and punishments. Through a rewards and punishments system, transactional leaders are able to keep followers motivated for the short-term. Unlike transformational leaders, those using the transactional approach are not looking to change the future, they look to keep things the same. Leaders using _____ as a model pay attention to followers' work in order to find faults and deviations.

Exam Probability: **Low**

4. *Answer choices:*

(see index for correct answer)

- a. Motivational Leadership
- b. Consideration and Initiating Structure
- c. Inspired Leadership Award
- d. Transactional leadership

*Guidance:* level 1

---

:: Management ::

_____ is a process by which entities review the quality of all factors involved in production. ISO 9000 defines _____ as "A part of quality management focused on fulfilling quality requirements".

Exam Probability: **Low**

5. *Answer choices:*

(see index for correct answer)

- a. Situational crisis communication theory
- b. Visual learning
- c. Quality control
- d. Telescopic observations strategic framework

*Guidance:* level 1

---

:: ::

_____ refers to the overall process of attracting, shortlisting, selecting and appointing suitable candidates for jobs within an organization. _____ can also refer to processes involved in choosing individuals for unpaid roles. Managers, human resource generalists and _____ specialists may be tasked with carrying out _____, but in some cases public-sector employment agencies, commercial _____ agencies, or specialist search consultancies are used to undertake parts of the process. Internet-based technologies which support all aspects of _____ have become widespread.

Exam Probability: **Medium**

6. *Answer choices:*

(see index for correct answer)

- a. process perspective
- b. Recruitment
- c. hierarchical perspective
- d. co-culture

*Guidance:* level 1

:: ::

An _____ is a contingent motivator. Traditional _____s are extrinsic motivators which reward actions to yield a desired outcome. The effectiveness of traditional _____s has changed as the needs of Western society have evolved. While the traditional _____ model is effective when there is a defined procedure and goal for a task, Western society started to require a higher volume of critical thinkers, so the traditional model became less effective. Institutions are now following a trend in implementing strategies that rely on intrinsic motivations rather than the extrinsic motivations that the traditional _____s foster.

Exam Probability: **Low**

7. *Answer choices:*

(see index for correct answer)

- a. functional perspective
- b. Incentive
- c. cultural
- d. surface-level diversity

*Guidance:* level 1

:: ::

In mathematics, a _____ is a relationship between two numbers indicating how many times the first number contains the second. For example, if a bowl of fruit contains eight oranges and six lemons, then the _____ of oranges to lemons is eight to six . Similarly, the _____ of lemons to oranges is 6:8 and the _____ of oranges to the total amount of fruit is 8:14 .

Exam Probability: **Low**

8. *Answer choices:*

(see index for correct answer)

- a. hierarchical
- b. Ratio
- c. interpersonal communication
- d. deep-level diversity

*Guidance:* level 1

:: ::

_____ is the moral stance, political philosophy, ideology, or social outlook that emphasizes the moral worth of the individual. Individualists promote the exercise of one's goals and desires and so value independence and self-reliance and advocate that interests of the individual should achieve precedence over the state or a social group, while opposing external interference upon one's own interests by society or institutions such as the government. _____ is often defined in contrast to totalitarianism, collectivism, and more corporate social forms.

Exam Probability: **Medium**

9. *Answer choices:*

(see index for correct answer)

- a. levels of analysis
- b. Character
- c. information systems assessment
- d. empathy

*Guidance:* level 1

:: Rhetoric ::

_____ is the pattern of narrative development that aims to make vivid a place, object, character, or group. _____ is one of four rhetorical modes, along with exposition, argumentation, and narration. In practice it would be difficult to write literature that drew on just one of the four basic modes.

Exam Probability: **Medium**

10. *Answer choices:*
<sub>(see index for correct answer)</sub>

- a. Synonymia
- b. Master suppression techniques
- c. Description
- d. Praegnans constructio

*Guidance:* level 1

:: ::

In business strategy, _____ is establishing a competitive advantage by having the lowest cost of operation in the industry. _____ is often driven by company efficiency, size, scale, scope and cumulative experience. A _____ strategy aims to exploit scale of production, well-defined scope and other economies, producing highly standardized products, using advanced technology. In recent years, more and more companies have chosen a strategic mix to achieve market leadership. These patterns consist of simultaneous _____, superior customer service and product leadership. Walmart has succeeded across the world due to its _____ strategy. The company has cut down on exesses at every point of production and thus are able to provide the consumers with quality products at low prices.

Exam Probability: **Medium**

11. *Answer choices:*
<sub>(see index for correct answer)</sub>

- a. levels of analysis
- b. open system
- c. corporate values
- d. Cost leadership

*Guidance:* level 1

:: Project management ::

A _____ is a type of bar chart that illustrates a project schedule, named after its inventor, Henry Gantt, who designed such a chart around the years 1910–1915. Modern _____ s also show the dependency relationships between activities and current schedule status.

Exam Probability: **High**

12. *Answer choices:*
(see index for correct answer)

- a. Gantt chart
- b. Advanced Integrated Practice
- c. Flexible product development
- d. RationalPlan

*Guidance:* level 1

:: Quality management ::

_____ ensures that an organization, product or service is consistent. It has four main components: quality planning, quality assurance, quality control and quality improvement. _____ is focused not only on product and service quality, but also on the means to achieve it. _____ , therefore, uses quality assurance and control of processes as well as products to achieve more consistent quality. What a customer wants and is willing to pay for it determines quality. It is written or unwritten commitment to a known or unknown consumer in the market . Thus, quality can be defined as fitness for intended use or, in other words, how well the product performs its intended function

Exam Probability: **High**

13. *Answer choices:*
(see index for correct answer)

- a. China Quality Course
- b. Test bay
- c. Quality management
- d. Institute of Standards and Industrial Research of Iran

*Guidance:* level 1

:: Production and manufacturing ::

_____ is a set of techniques and tools for process improvement. Though as a shortened form it may be found written as 6S, it should not be confused with the methodology known as 6S.

Exam Probability: **Medium**

14. *Answer choices:*

(see index for correct answer)

- a. Pegging report
- b. Six Sigma
- c. Business Planning and Control System
- d. Material requirements planning

*Guidance:* level 1

:: ::

_____ is the exchange of capital, goods, and services across international borders or territories.

Exam Probability: **Medium**

15. *Answer choices:*

(see index for correct answer)

- a. co-culture
- b. levels of analysis
- c. process perspective
- d. International trade

*Guidance:* level 1

:: Workplace ::

A _____ is a process through which feedback from an employee's subordinates, colleagues, and supervisor, as well as a self-evaluation by the employee themselves is gathered. Such feedback can also include, when relevant, feedback from external sources who interact with the employee, such as customers and suppliers or other interested stakeholders. _____ is so named because it solicits feedback regarding an employee's behavior from a variety of points of view. It therefore may be contrasted with "downward feedback", or "upward feedback" delivered to supervisory or management employees by subordinates only.

Exam Probability: **High**

16. *Answer choices:*

(see index for correct answer)

- a. Rat race
- b. 360-degree feedback
- c. Staff turnover
- d. Workplace deviance

*Guidance:* level 1

:: Human resource management ::

_____ are the people who make up the workforce of an organization, business sector, or economy. "Human capital" is sometimes used synonymously with "_____", although human capital typically refers to a narrower effect. Likewise, other terms sometimes used include manpower, talent, labor, personnel, or simply people.

Exam Probability: **Medium**

17. *Answer choices:*

(see index for correct answer)

- a. Human resources
- b. Human resource accounting
- c. Contractor management
- d. Corporate Equality Index

*Guidance:* level 1

:: ::

_____, known in Europe as research and technological development, refers to innovative activities undertaken by corporations or governments in developing new services or products, or improving existing services or products. _____ constitutes the first stage of development of a potential new service or the production process.

Exam Probability: **High**

18. *Answer choices:*

(see index for correct answer)

- a. interpersonal communication
- b. open system
- c. Research and development
- d. deep-level diversity

*Guidance:* level 1

:: Business models ::

A _____ is "an autonomous association of persons united voluntarily to meet their common economic, social, and cultural needs and aspirations through a jointly-owned and democratically-controlled enterprise". _____ s may include.

Exam Probability: **Low**

19. *Answer choices:*

(see index for correct answer)

- a. Subscription business model
- b. What if chart
- c. Cooperative
- d. Entreship

*Guidance:* level 1

:: Project management ::

A _____ is a team whose members usually belong to different groups, functions and are assigned to activities for the same project. A team can be divided into sub-teams according to need. Usually _____ s are only used for a defined period of time. They are disbanded after the project is deemed complete. Due to the nature of the specific formation and disbandment, _____ s are usually in organizations.

Exam Probability: **Medium**

20. *Answer choices:*
(see index for correct answer)

- a. Transport Initiatives Edinburgh
- b. Project team
- c. Collaborative project management
- d. Pre-construction services

*Guidance:* level 1

:: Product design ::

_____ as a verb is to create a new product to be sold by a business to its customers. A very broad coefficient and effective generation and development of ideas through a process that leads to new products. Thus, it is a major aspect of new product development.

Exam Probability: **High**

21. *Answer choices:*
(see index for correct answer)

- a. Rodney Fitch
- b. Product design
- c. The Handle
- d. Rubbot

*Guidance:* level 1

:: ::

_____ is a kind of action that occur as two or more objects have an effect upon one another. The idea of a two-way effect is essential in the concept of _____ , as opposed to a one-way causal effect. A closely related term is interconnectivity, which deals with the _____ s of _____ s within systems: combinations of many simple _____ s can lead to surprising emergent phenomena. _____ has different tailored meanings in various sciences. Changes can also involve _____ .

Exam Probability: **Medium**

22. *Answer choices:*
(see index for correct answer)

- a. information systems assessment
- b. Character
- c. cultural
- d. Interaction

*Guidance: level 1*

---

:: Strategic alliances ::

A _____ is an agreement between two or more parties to pursue a set of agreed upon objectives needed while remaining independent organizations. A _____ will usually fall short of a legal partnership entity, agency, or corporate affiliate relationship. Typically, two companies form a _____ when each possesses one or more business assets or have expertise that will help the other by enhancing their businesses. _____ s can develop in outsourcing relationships where the parties desire to achieve long-term win-win benefits and innovation based on mutually desired outcomes.

Exam Probability: **Low**

23. *Answer choices:*
(see index for correct answer)

- a. Bridge Alliance
- b. Strategic alliance
- c. Cross-licensing
- d. Management contract

*Guidance: level 1*

---

:: Legal terms ::

_____ is a type of meaning in which a phrase, statement or resolution is not explicitly defined, making several interpretations plausible. A common aspect of _____ is uncertainty. It is thus an attribute of any idea or statement whose intended meaning cannot be definitively resolved according to a rule or process with a finite number of steps.

Exam Probability: **Medium**

24. *Answer choices:*
(see index for correct answer)

- a. Ambiguity
- b. Preliminary injunction
- c. Curator bonis
- d. Direct examination

*Guidance:* level 1

:: Marketing ::

_____ or stock is the goods and materials that a business holds for the ultimate goal of resale.

Exam Probability: **Low**

25. *Answer choices:*
(see index for correct answer)

- a. Marketing warfare strategies
- b. Albuquerque Craft Beer Market
- c. elaboration likelihood model
- d. Product planning

*Guidance:* level 1

:: Information science ::

_____ is the resolution of uncertainty; it is that which answers the question of "what an entity is" and thus defines both its essence and nature of its characteristics. _____ relates to both data and knowledge, as data is meaningful _____ representing values attributed to parameters, and knowledge signifies understanding of a concept. _____ is uncoupled from an observer, which is an entity that can access _____ and thus discern what it specifies; _____ exists beyond an event horizon for example. In the case of knowledge, the _____ itself requires a cognitive observer to be obtained.

Exam Probability: **High**

26. *Answer choices:*

(see index for correct answer)

- a. Information
- b. SIRCA
- c. Information access
- d. Interviewer effect

*Guidance:* level 1

:: Human resource management ::

_____ is the strategic approach to the effective management of people in an organization so that they help the business to gain a competitive advantage. It is designed to maximize employee performance in service of an employer's strategic objectives. HR is primarily concerned with the management of people within organizations, focusing on policies and on systems. HR departments are responsible for overseeing employee-benefits design, employee recruitment, training and development, performance appraisal, and Reward management . HR also concerns itself with organizational change and industrial relations, that is, the balancing of organizational practices with requirements arising from collective bargaining and from governmental laws.

Exam Probability: **Medium**

27. *Answer choices:*

(see index for correct answer)

- a. Voluntary redundancy
- b. Human resource management
- c. Professional employer organization

- d. Labour is not a commodity

*Guidance:* level 1

---

:: Production economics ::

In microeconomics, _____ are the cost advantages that enterprises obtain due to their scale of operation, with cost per unit of output decreasing with increasing scale.

Exam Probability: **Medium**

28. *Answer choices:*
(see index for correct answer)

- a. Economies of scale
- b. Sectoral output
- c. Marginal product
- d. HMI quality

*Guidance:* level 1

---

:: ::

_____ is the assignment of any responsibility or authority to another person to carry out specific activities. It is one of the core concepts of management leadership. However, the person who delegated the work remains accountable for the outcome of the delegated work. _____ empowers a subordinate to make decisions, i.e. it is a shifting of decision-making authority from one organizational level to a lower one. _____, if properly done, is not fabrication. The opposite of effective _____ is micromanagement, where a manager provides too much input, direction, and review of delegated work. In general, _____ is good and can save money and time, help in building skills, and motivate people. On the other hand, poor _____ might cause frustration and confusion to all the involved parties. Some agents, however, do not favour a _____ and consider the power of making a decision rather burdensome.

Exam Probability: **High**

29. *Answer choices:*
(see index for correct answer)

- a. information systems assessment
- b. similarity-attraction theory
- c. levels of analysis
- d. open system

*Guidance:* level 1

:: Systems thinking ::

In business management, a _____ is a company that facilitates the learning of its members and continuously transforms itself. The concept was coined through the work and research of Peter Senge and his colleagues.

Exam Probability: **Low**

30. *Answer choices:*
(see index for correct answer)

- a. Bioterrorism
- b. Business continuity planning
- c. Learning organization
- d. Club of Rome

*Guidance:* level 1

:: Poker strategy ::

_____ is any measure taken to guard a thing against damage caused by outside forces. _____ can be provided to physical objects, including organisms, to systems, and to intangible things like civil and political rights. Although the mechanisms for providing _____ vary widely, the basic meaning of the term remains the same. This is illustrated by an explanation found in a manual on electrical wiring.

Exam Probability: **Medium**

31. *Answer choices:*
(see index for correct answer)

- a. Steal
- b. Bluff
- c. Q-ratio
- d. Fold equity

*Guidance:* level 1

:: Income ::

_____ is a ratio between the net profit and cost of investment resulting from an investment of some resources. A high ROI means the investment's gains favorably to its cost. As a performance measure, ROI is used to evaluate the efficiency of an investment or to compare the efficiencies of several different investments. In purely economic terms, it is one way of relating profits to capital invested. _____ is a performance measure used by businesses to identify the efficiency of an investment or number of different investments.

Exam Probability: **Medium**

32. *Answer choices:*
(see index for correct answer)

- a. Trinity study
- b. bottom line
- c. Return on investment
- d. Per capita income

*Guidance:* level 1

---

:: Management ::

_____ is an area of management concerned with designing and controlling the process of production and redesigning business operations in the production of goods or services. It involves the responsibility of ensuring that business operations are efficient in terms of using as few resources as needed and effective in terms of meeting customer requirements. _____ is primarily concerned with planning, organizing and supervising in the contexts of production, manufacturing or the provision of services.

Exam Probability: **High**

33. *Answer choices:*
(see index for correct answer)

- a. Local management board
- b. Management fad
- c. Planning
- d. Operations management

*Guidance:* level 1

:: Critical thinking ::

In psychology, _____ is regarded as the cognitive process resulting in the selection of a belief or a course of action among several alternative possibilities. Every _____ process produces a final choice, which may or may not prompt action.

Exam Probability: **Medium**

34. *Answer choices:*
(see index for correct answer)

- a. Association for Informal Logic and Critical Thinking
- b. Precising definition
- c. Decision-making
- d. Evidence

Guidance: level 1

:: ::

_____ or accountancy is the measurement, processing, and communication of financial information about economic entities such as businesses and corporations. The modern field was established by the Italian mathematician Luca Pacioli in 1494. _____, which has been called the "language of business", measures the results of an organization's economic activities and conveys this information to a variety of users, including investors, creditors, management, and regulators. Practitioners of _____ are known as accountants. The terms "_____" and "financial reporting" are often used as synonyms.

Exam Probability: **Low**

35. *Answer choices:*
(see index for correct answer)

- a. process perspective
- b. information systems assessment
- c. interpersonal communication
- d. deep-level diversity

Guidance: level 1

:: Human resource management ::

_____ is the corporate management term for the act of reorganizing the legal, ownership, operational, or other structures of a company for the purpose of making it more profitable, or better organized for its present needs. Other reasons for _____ include a change of ownership or ownership structure, demerger, or a response to a crisis or major change in the business such as bankruptcy, repositioning, or buyout. _____ may also be described as corporate _____, debt _____ and financial _____.

Exam Probability: **Low**

36. *Answer choices:*
(see index for correct answer)

- a. Person specification
- b. Organizational culture
- c. Restructuring
- d. Functional job analysis

*Guidance:* level 1

---

:: Employee relations ::

_____ ownership, or employee share ownership, is an ownership interest in a company held by the company's workforce. The ownership interest may be facilitated by the company as part of employees' remuneration or incentive compensation for work performed, or the company itself may be employee owned.

Exam Probability: **High**

37. *Answer choices:*
(see index for correct answer)

- a. Employee engagement
- b. Employee stock
- c. Fringe benefit
- d. Employee motivation

*Guidance:* level 1

---

:: Financial risk ::

_____ is a type of risk faced by investors, corporations, and governments that political decisions, events, or conditions will significantly affect the profitability of a business actor or the expected value of a given economic action. _____ can be understood and managed with reasoned foresight and investment.

Exam Probability: **Low**

38. *Answer choices:*
(see index for correct answer)

- a. Political risk
- b. Investment management
- c. Tail risk
- d. Credit scorecards

*Guidance:* level 1

---

:: Business models ::

_____ es are privately owned corporations, partnerships, or sole proprietorships that have fewer employees and/or less annual revenue than a regular-sized business or corporation. Businesses are defined as "small" in terms of being able to apply for government support and qualify for preferential tax policy varies depending on the country and industry. _____ es range from fifteen employees under the Australian Fair Work Act 2009, fifty employees according to the definition used by the European Union, and fewer than five hundred employees to qualify for many U.S. _____ Administration programs. While _____ es can also be classified according to other methods, such as annual revenues, shipments, sales, assets, or by annual gross or net revenue or net profits, the number of employees is one of the most widely used measures.

Exam Probability: **Medium**

39. *Answer choices:*
(see index for correct answer)

- a. Organizational architecture
- b. Data as a service
- c. Small business
- d. Brainsworking

*Guidance:* level 1

:: Project management ::

A _____ is a source or supply from which a benefit is produced and it has some utility. _____ s can broadly be classified upon their availability—they are classified into renewable and non-renewable _____ s. Examples of non renewable _____ s are coal, crude oil natural gas nuclear energy etc. Examples of renewable _____ s are air, water, wind, solar energy etc. They can also be classified as actual and potential on the basis of level of development and use, on the basis of origin they can be classified as biotic and abiotic, and on the basis of their distribution, as ubiquitous and localized. An item becomes a _____ with time and developing technology. Typically, _____ s are materials, energy, services, staff, knowledge, or other assets that are transformed to produce benefit and in the process may be consumed or made unavailable. Benefits of _____ utilization may include increased wealth, proper functioning of a system, or enhanced well-being. From a human perspective a natural _____ is anything obtained from the environment to satisfy human needs and wants. From a broader biological or ecological perspective a _____ satisfies the needs of a living organism.

Exam Probability: **High**

40. *Answer choices:*
(see index for correct answer)

- a. Resource
- b. Work package
- c. Elemental cost planning
- d. Problem domain analysis

*Guidance:* level 1

:: Market research ::

_____ is an organized effort to gather information about target markets or customers. It is a very important component of business strategy. The term is commonly interchanged with marketing research; however, expert practitioners may wish to draw a distinction, in that marketing research is concerned specifically about marketing processes, while _____ is concerned specifically with markets.

Exam Probability: **Medium**

41. *Answer choices:*
(see index for correct answer)

- a. Cambashi
- b. Confidence interval
- c. Product Intelligence
- d. Market research

*Guidance:* level 1

---

:: ::

_____ is an evaluative or corrective exercise that can occur in any area of human life. _____ can therefore take many different forms. How people go about criticizing, can vary a great deal. In specific areas of human endeavour, the form of _____ can be highly specialized and technical; it often requires professional knowledge to appreciate the _____. For subject-specific information, see the Varieties of _____ page.

Exam Probability: **Low**

42. *Answer choices:*
(see index for correct answer)

- a. Criticism
- b. personal values
- c. Character
- d. deep-level diversity

*Guidance:* level 1

---

:: ::

_____ is the practice of protecting the natural environment by individuals, organizations and governments. Its objectives are to conserve natural resources and the existing natural environment and, where possible, to repair damage and reverse trends.

Exam Probability: **High**

43. *Answer choices:*
(see index for correct answer)

- a. interpersonal communication
- b. corporate values

- c. Environmental protection
- d. levels of analysis

*Guidance:* level 1

---

:: Management accounting ::

In economics, _____ s, indirect costs or overheads are business expenses that are not dependent on the level of goods or services produced by the business. They tend to be time-related, such as interest or rents being paid per month, and are often referred to as overhead costs. This is in contrast to variable costs, which are volume-related and unknown at the beginning of the accounting year. For a simple example, such as a bakery, the monthly rent for the baking facilities, and the monthly payments for the security system and basic phone line are _____ s, as they do not change according to how much bread the bakery produces and sells. On the other hand, the wage costs of the bakery are variable, as the bakery will have to hire more workers if the production of bread increases. Economists reckon _____ as a entry barrier for new entrepreneurs.

Exam Probability: **High**

44. *Answer choices:*
(see index for correct answer)

- a. Notional profit
- b. Entity-level controls
- c. Chartered Institute of Management Accountants
- d. Fixed cost

*Guidance:* level 1

---

:: Costs ::

In economics, _____ is the total economic cost of production and is made up of variable cost, which varies according to the quantity of a good produced and includes inputs such as labour and raw materials, plus fixed cost, which is independent of the quantity of a good produced and includes inputs that cannot be varied in the short term: fixed costs such as buildings and machinery, including sunk costs if any. Since cost is measured per unit of time, it is a flow variable.

Exam Probability: **High**

45. *Answer choices:*
(see index for correct answer)

- a. Total cost
- b. Implicit cost
- c. Incremental cost-effectiveness ratio
- d. Cost per paper

*Guidance:* level 1

:: ::

_____ is a means of protection from financial loss. It is a form of risk management, primarily used to hedge against the risk of a contingent or uncertain loss

Exam Probability: **Medium**

46. *Answer choices:*
(see index for correct answer)

- a. similarity-attraction theory
- b. interpersonal communication
- c. cultural
- d. personal values

*Guidance:* level 1

:: Organizational behavior ::

_____ is the term now used more commonly in business management, particularly human resource management. _____ refers to the number of subordinates a supervisor has.

Exam Probability: **High**

47. *Answer choices:*
(see index for correct answer)

- a. Group behaviour
- b. Affective events theory
- c. Ownership
- d. Counterproductive norms

*Guidance:* level 1

:: Business law ::

A _____ is a group of people who jointly supervise the activities of an organization, which can be either a for-profit business, nonprofit organization, or a government agency. Such a board's powers, duties, and responsibilities are determined by government regulations and the organization's own constitution and bylaws. These authorities may specify the number of members of the board, how they are to be chosen, and how often they are to meet.

Exam Probability: **Low**

48. *Answer choices:*

(see index for correct answer)

- a. Security interest
- b. Time-and-a-half
- c. Board of directors
- d. Partnership

*Guidance:* level 1

:: Business terms ::

A _____ is a short statement of why an organization exists, what its overall goal is, identifying the goal of its operations: what kind of product or service it provides, its primary customers or market, and its geographical region of operation. It may include a short statement of such fundamental matters as the organization's values or philosophies, a business's main competitive advantages, or a desired future state—the "vision".

Exam Probability: **Low**

49. *Answer choices:*

(see index for correct answer)

- a. customer base
- b. strategic plan
- c. Mission statement
- d. back office

*Guidance:* level 1

:: Business models ::

A _____, _____ company or daughter company is a company that is owned or controlled by another company, which is called the parent company, parent, or holding company. The _____ can be a company, corporation, or limited liability company. In some cases it is a government or state-owned enterprise. In some cases, particularly in the music and book publishing industries, subsidiaries are referred to as imprints.

Exam Probability: **High**

50. *Answer choices:*
<sub>(see index for correct answer)</sub>

- a. Interactive contract manufacturing
- b. What if chart
- c. Premium business model
- d. Subsidiary

*Guidance:* level 1

---

:: Critical thinking ::

An _____ is someone who has a prolonged or intense experience through practice and education in a particular field. Informally, an _____ is someone widely recognized as a reliable source of technique or skill whose faculty for judging or deciding rightly, justly, or wisely is accorded authority and status by peers or the public in a specific well-distinguished domain. An _____, more generally, is a person with extensive knowledge or ability based on research, experience, or occupation and in a particular area of study. _____ s are called in for advice on their respective subject, but they do not always agree on the particulars of a field of study. An _____ can be believed, by virtue of credential, training, education, profession, publication or experience, to have special knowledge of a subject beyond that of the average person, sufficient that others may officially rely upon the individual's opinion. Historically, an _____ was referred to as a sage . The individual was usually a profound thinker distinguished for wisdom and sound judgment.

Exam Probability: **Low**

51. *Answer choices:*

(see index for correct answer)

- a. Source credibility
- b. Expert
- c. Decidophobia
- d. Succinctness

*Guidance:* level 1

---

:: Project management ::

Some scenarios associate "this kind of planning" with learning "life skills". _____ s are necessary, or at least useful, in situations where individuals need to know what time they must be at a specific location to receive a specific service, and where people need to accomplish a set of goals within a set time period.

Exam Probability: **High**

52. *Answer choices:*

(see index for correct answer)

- a. Milestone
- b. Time horizon
- c. Operational bill
- d. Schedule

*Guidance:* level 1

---

:: Human resource management ::

An organizational chart is a diagram that shows the structure of an organization and the relationships and relative ranks of its parts and positions/jobs. The term is also used for similar diagrams, for example ones showing the different elements of a field of knowledge or a group of languages.

Exam Probability: **High**

53. *Answer choices:*

(see index for correct answer)

- a. Income bracket
- b. Expense management
- c. Skill mix
- d. Talascend

*Guidance:* level 1

:: Teams ::

A _____ usually refers to a group of individuals who work together from different geographic locations and rely on communication technology such as email, FAX, and video or voice conferencing services in order to collaborate. The term can also refer to groups or teams that work together asynchronously or across organizational levels. Powell, Piccoli and Ives define _____ s as "groups of geographically, organizationally and/or time dispersed workers brought together by information and telecommunication technologies to accomplish one or more organizational tasks." According to Ale Ebrahim et. al. , _____ s can also be defined as "small temporary groups of geographically, organizationally and/or time dispersed knowledge workers who coordinate their work predominantly with electronic information and communication technologies in order to accomplish one or more organization tasks."

Exam Probability: **Medium**

54. *Answer choices:*

(see index for correct answer)

- a. Virtual team
- b. Team-building

*Guidance:* level 1

:: ::

A _____ is a problem offering two possibilities, neither of which is unambiguously acceptable or preferable. The possibilities are termed the horns of the _____ , a clichéd usage, but distinguishing the _____ from other kinds of predicament as a matter of usage.

Exam Probability: **High**

55. *Answer choices:*

(see index for correct answer)

- a. Dilemma
- b. hierarchical perspective
- c. levels of analysis

- d. open system

*Guidance: level 1*

---

:: Time management ::

_____ is the process of planning and exercising conscious control of time spent on specific activities, especially to increase effectiveness, efficiency, and productivity. It involves a juggling act of various demands upon a person relating to work, social life, family, hobbies, personal interests and commitments with the finiteness of time. Using time effectively gives the person "choice" on spending/managing activities at their own time and expediency.

Exam Probability: **High**

56. *Answer choices:*
(see index for correct answer)

- a. Time management
- b. Sufficient unto the day is the evil thereof
- c. Time Trek
- d. Getting Things Done

*Guidance: level 1*

---

:: ::

The _____ or just chief executive, is the most senior corporate, executive, or administrative officer in charge of managing an organization especially an independent legal entity such as a company or nonprofit institution. CEOs lead a range of organizations, including public and private corporations, non-profit organizations and even some government organizations. The CEO of a corporation or company typically reports to the board of directors and is charged with maximizing the value of the entity, which may include maximizing the share price, market share, revenues or another element. In the non-profit and government sector, CEOs typically aim at achieving outcomes related to the organization's mission, such as reducing poverty, increasing literacy, etc.

Exam Probability: **High**

57. *Answer choices:*

(see index for correct answer)

- a. information systems assessment
- b. levels of analysis
- c. Chief executive officer
- d. process perspective

*Guidance:* level 1

:: Reputation management ::

_____ or image of a social entity is an opinion about that entity, typically as a result of social evaluation on a set of criteria.

Exam Probability: **High**

58. *Answer choices:*

(see index for correct answer)

- a. Sybil attack
- b. The Economy of Esteem
- c. Star
- d. Reputation

*Guidance:* level 1

:: Training ::

_____ is action or inaction that is regulated to be in accordance with a particular system of governance. _____ is commonly applied to regulating human and animal behavior, and furthermore, it is applied to each activity-branch in all branches of organized activity, knowledge, and other fields of study and observation. _____ can be a set of expectations that are required by any governing entity including the self, groups, classes, fields, industries, or societies.

Exam Probability: **Medium**

59. *Answer choices:*

(see index for correct answer)

- a. Discipline
- b. ActivePresenter
- c. Boardcast
- d. Effective safety training

*Guidance:* level 1

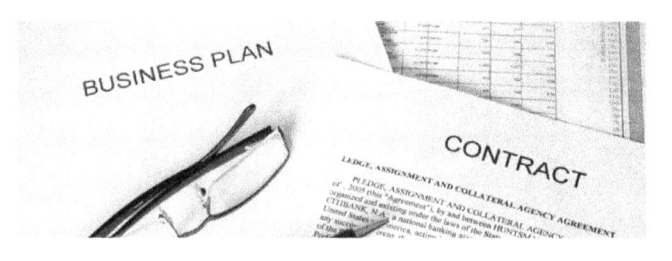

## Business law

Corporate law (also known as business law) is the body of law governing the rights, relations, and conduct of persons, companies, organizations and businesses. It refers to the legal practice relating to, or the theory of corporations. Corporate law often describes the law relating to matters which derive directly from the life-cycle of a corporation. It thus encompasses the formation, funding, governance, and death of a corporation.

:: Promotion and marketing communications ::

In everyday language, _____ refers to exaggerated or false praise. In law, _____ is a promotional statement or claim that expresses subjective rather than objective views, which no "reasonable person" would take literally. _____ serves to "puff up" an exaggerated image of what is being described and is especially featured in testimonials.

Exam Probability: **High**

1. *Answer choices:*
(see index for correct answer)

- a. Puffery
- b. Dumb Ways to Die
- c. Direct mail
- d. Aeroplan

*Guidance:* level 1

:: Mereology ::

_____ , in the abstract, is what belongs to or with something, whether as an attribute or as a component of said thing. In the context of this article, it is one or more components , whether physical or incorporeal, of a person's estate; or so belonging to, as in being owned by, a person or jointly a group of people or a legal entity like a corporation or even a society. Depending on the nature of the _____ , an owner of _____ has the right to consume, alter, share, redefine, rent, mortgage, pawn, sell, exchange, transfer, give away or destroy it, or to exclude others from doing these things, as well as to perhaps abandon it; whereas regardless of the nature of the _____ , the owner thereof has the right to properly use it , or at the very least exclusively keep it.

Exam Probability: **High**

2. *Answer choices:*

(see index for correct answer)

- a. Mereotopology
- b. Mereology
- c. Gunk
- d. Property

*Guidance:* level 1

:: Advertising ::

In law, _____ is speech or writing on behalf of a business with the intent of earning revenue or a profit. It is economic in nature and usually attempts to persuade consumers to purchase the business's product or service. The Supreme Court of the United States defines _____ as speech that "proposes a commercial transaction".

Exam Probability: **Low**

3. *Answer choices:*

(see index for correct answer)

- a. Commercial speech
- b. Accepted pairing
- c. Taykey
- d. Advertising management

*Guidance:* level 1

:: ::

A concept of English law, a _____ is an untrue or misleading statement of fact made during negotiations by one party to another, the statement then inducing that other party into the contract. The misled party may normally rescind the contract, and sometimes may be awarded damages as well.

Exam Probability: **Low**

4. *Answer choices:*

(see index for correct answer)

- a. Misrepresentation
- b. open system
- c. co-culture
- d. personal values

*Guidance:* level 1

:: Auctioneering ::

An _____ is a process of buying and selling goods or services by offering them up for bid, taking bids, and then selling the item to the highest bidder. The open ascending price _____ is arguably the most common form of _____ in use today. Participants bid openly against one another, with each subsequent bid required to be higher than the previous bid. An _____ eer may announce prices, bidders may call out their bids themselves, or bids may be submitted electronically with the highest current bid publicly displayed. In a Dutch _____, the _____ eer begins with a high asking price for some quantity of like items; the price is lowered until a participant is willing to accept the _____ eer's price for some quantity of the goods in the lot or until the seller's reserve price is met. While _____ s are most associated in the public imagination with the sale of antiques, paintings, rare collectibles and expensive wines, _____ s are also used for commodities, livestock, radio spectrum and used cars. In economic theory, an _____ may refer to any mechanism or set of trading rules for exchange.

Exam Probability: **Low**

5. *Answer choices:*

(see index for correct answer)

- a. Auction
- b. Dutch auction
- c. Estate sale
- d. National Auctioneers Association

*Guidance:* level 1

---

:: Fraud ::

The _____ refers to the requirement that certain kinds of contracts be memorialized in writing, signed by the party to be charged, with sufficient content to evidence the contract.

Exam Probability: **Medium**

6. *Answer choices:*
(see index for correct answer)

- a. Lip sync
- b. Voice phishing
- c. Employment fraud
- d. Essay mill

*Guidance:* level 1

---

:: United States securities law ::

_____ is a legal term for intent or knowledge of wrongdoing. An offending party then has knowledge of the "wrongness" of an act or event prior to committing it.

Exam Probability: **High**

7. *Answer choices:*
(see index for correct answer)

- a. Scienter
- b. Series 7 Exam
- c. United States person
- d. Uniform Securities Agent State Law Exam

*Guidance:* level 1

---

:: ::

The _____ is the highest court within the hierarchy of courts in many legal jurisdictions. Other descriptions for such courts include court of last resort, apex court, and high court of appeal. Broadly speaking, the decisions of a _____ are not subject to further review by any other court. _____ s typically function primarily as appellate courts, hearing appeals from decisions of lower trial courts, or from intermediate-level appellate courts.

Exam Probability: **Low**

8. *Answer choices:*

(see index for correct answer)

- a. Sarbanes-Oxley act of 2002
- b. imperative
- c. surface-level diversity
- d. Supreme Court

*Guidance:* level 1

:: Criminal procedure ::

In law, a verdict is the formal finding of fact made by a jury on matters or questions submitted to the jury by a judge. In a bench trial, the judge's decision near the end of the trial is simply referred to as a finding. In England and Wales, a coroner's findings are called verdicts.

Exam Probability: **Medium**

9. *Answer choices:*

(see index for correct answer)

- a. Directed verdict
- b. criminal procedure

*Guidance:* level 1

:: Monopoly (economics) ::

_____ is a category of property that includes intangible creations of the human intellect. _____ encompasses two types of rights: industrial property rights and copyright. It was not until the 19th century that the term " _____ " began to be used, and not until the late 20th century that it became commonplace in the majority of the world.

Exam Probability: **Low**

10. *Answer choices:*
(see index for correct answer)

- a. Concentration ratio
- b. Third-party access
- c. De facto monopoly
- d. Intellectual property

*Guidance:* level 1

:: Commercial item transport and distribution ::

_____ s may be negotiable or non-negotiable. Negotiable _____ s allow transfer of ownership of that commodity without having to deliver the physical commodity. See Delivery order.

Exam Probability: **Low**

11. *Answer choices:*
(see index for correct answer)

- a. SAP EWM
- b. Distribution deal
- c. Cabotage
- d. E2open

*Guidance:* level 1

:: Commerce ::

_____ relates to "the exchange of goods and services, especially on a large scale". It includes legal, economic, political, social, cultural and technological systems that operate in a country or in international trade.

Exam Probability: **Low**

12. *Answer choices:*

(see index for correct answer)

- a. Factory
- b. Drawback
- c. Trade credit
- d. Commerce

*Guidance:* level 1

:: ::

An _____ is a criminal accusation that a person has committed a crime. In jurisdictions that use the concept of felonies, the most serious criminal offence is a felony; jurisdictions that do not use the felonies concept often use that of an indictable offence, an offence that requires an _____.

Exam Probability: **Low**

13. *Answer choices:*

(see index for correct answer)

- a. process perspective
- b. interpersonal communication
- c. Indictment
- d. empathy

*Guidance:* level 1

:: ::

_____ Corporation was an American energy, commodities, and services company based in Houston, Texas. It was founded in 1985 as a merger between Houston Natural Gas and InterNorth, both relatively small regional companies. Before its bankruptcy on December 3, 2001, _____ employed approximately 29,000 staff and was a major electricity, natural gas, communications and pulp and paper company, with claimed revenues of nearly $101 billion during 2000. Fortune named _____ "America's Most Innovative Company" for six consecutive years.

Exam Probability: **Medium**

14. *Answer choices:*

(see index for correct answer)

- a. Character
- b. hierarchical perspective
- c. Enron
- d. similarity-attraction theory

*Guidance:* level 1

---

:: Contract law ::

In the law of contracts, the _____ , also referred to as an unequivocal and absolute acceptance requirement, states that an offer must be accepted exactly with no modifications. The offeror is the master of one's own offer. An attempt to accept the offer on different terms instead creates a counter-offer, and this constitutes a rejection of the original offer.

Exam Probability: **Medium**

15. *Answer choices:*

(see index for correct answer)

- a. Nudum pactum
- b. Meeting of the minds
- c. Mirror image rule
- d. Job order contracting

*Guidance:* level 1

---

:: Stock market ::

_____ is freedom from, or resilience against, potential harm caused by others. Beneficiaries of _____ may be of persons and social groups, objects and institutions, ecosystems or any other entity or phenomenon vulnerable to unwanted change by its environment.

Exam Probability: **Low**

16. *Answer choices:*

(see index for correct answer)

- a. Automated trading system
- b. Security
- c. Pattern day trader
- d. Depositary receipt

*Guidance:* level 1

:: Contract law ::

In common law jurisdictions, an _____ is a contract law term for certain assurances that are presumed to be made in the sale of products or real property, due to the circumstances of the sale. These assurances are characterized as warranties irrespective of whether the seller has expressly promised them orally or in writing. They include an _____ of fitness for a particular purpose, an _____ of merchantability for products, _____ of workmanlike quality for services, and an _____ of habitability for a home.

Exam Probability: **Medium**

17. *Answer choices:*

(see index for correct answer)

- a. Severability
- b. Warranty
- c. Transmutation agreement
- d. Domicilium citandi et executandi

*Guidance:* level 1

:: Finance ::

_____ is the investigation or exercise of care that a reasonable business or person is expected to take before entering into an agreement or contract with another party, or an act with a certain standard of care.

Exam Probability: **High**

18. *Answer choices:*

(see index for correct answer)

- a. Securities market
- b. Profit taking
- c. Yield
- d. Due diligence

*Guidance:* level 1

:: Contract law ::

_____ of Contract is a legal term. In contract law, it is the implied ability of an individual to make a legally binding contract on behalf of an organization, by way of uniform or interaction with the public on behalf of that organization. When a person is wearing a uniform or nametag bearing the logo or trademark of a business or organization; or if that person is functioning in an obviously authorized capacity on behalf of a business or organization, that person carries an _____ of Contract. _____ is authority that is not express or written into the contract, but which the agent is assumed to have in order to transact the business of insurance for the principal. _____ is incidental to express authority since not every single detail of an agent's authority can be spelled out in the written contract.

Exam Probability: **Medium**

19. *Answer choices:*
(see index for correct answer)

- a. Indian contract law
- b. Implied authority
- c. Service plan
- d. Oral contract

*Guidance:* level 1

:: Insurance law ::

_____ exists when an insured person derives a financial or other kind of benefit from the continuous existence, without repairment or damage, of the insured object. A person has an _____ in something when loss of or damage to that thing would cause the person to suffer a financial or other kind of loss. Normally, _____ is established by ownership, possession, or direct relationship. For example, people have _____ s in their own homes and vehicles, but not in their neighbors' homes and vehicles, and almost certainly not those of strangers.

Exam Probability: **High**

20. *Answer choices:*
(see index for correct answer)

- a. Marine Insurance Act 1906
- b. Insurance regulatory law

- c. Assigned risk
- d. Insurable interest

*Guidance:* level 1

:: ::

_____ is the collection of techniques, skills, methods, and processes used in the production of goods or services or in the accomplishment of objectives, such as scientific investigation. _____ can be the knowledge of techniques, processes, and the like, or it can be embedded in machines to allow for operation without detailed knowledge of their workings. Systems applying _____ by taking an input, changing it according to the system's use, and then producing an outcome are referred to as _____ systems or technological systems.

Exam Probability: **High**

21. *Answer choices:*
(see index for correct answer)

- a. Technology
- b. hierarchical
- c. open system
- d. information systems assessment

*Guidance:* level 1

:: Business law ::

An _____ is an agreement in which a producer agrees to sell his or her entire production to the buyer, who in turn agrees to purchase the entire output. Example: an almond grower enters into an _____ with an almond packer: thus the producer has a "home" for output of nuts, and the packer of nuts is happy to try the particular product. The converse of this situation is a requirements contract, under which a seller agrees to supply the buyer with as much of a good or service as the buyer wants, in exchange for the buyer's agreement not to buy that good or service elsewhere.

Exam Probability: **High**

22. *Answer choices:*
(see index for correct answer)

- a. Practicing without a license
- b. Relational contract
- c. Valuation using the Market Penetration Model
- d. Leave of absence

*Guidance:* level 1

:: ::

_____ is a type of government support for the citizens of that society. _____ may be provided to people of any income level, as with social security, but it is usually intended to ensure that the poor can meet their basic human needs such as food and shelter. _____ attempts to provide poor people with a minimal level of well-being, usually either a free- or a subsidized-supply of certain goods and social services, such as healthcare, education, and vocational training.

Exam Probability: **Low**

23. *Answer choices:*
(see index for correct answer)

- a. Welfare
- b. imperative
- c. personal values
- d. surface-level diversity

*Guidance:* level 1

:: ::

_____ is the assignment of any responsibility or authority to another person to carry out specific activities. It is one of the core concepts of management leadership. However, the person who delegated the work remains accountable for the outcome of the delegated work. _____ empowers a subordinate to make decisions, i.e. it is a shifting of decision-making authority from one organizational level to a lower one. _____ , if properly done, is not fabrication. The opposite of effective _____ is micromanagement, where a manager provides too much input, direction, and review of delegated work. In general, _____ is good and can save money and time, help in building skills, and motivate people. On the other hand, poor _____ might cause frustration and confusion to all the involved parties. Some agents, however, do not favour a _____ and consider the power of making a decision rather burdensome.

Exam Probability: **Medium**

24. *Answer choices:*

(see index for correct answer)

- a. levels of analysis
- b. interpersonal communication
- c. Delegation
- d. process perspective

*Guidance:* level 1

:: ::

_____ is that part of a civil law legal system which is part of the jus commune that involves relationships between individuals, such as the law of contracts or torts , and the law of obligations . It is to be distinguished from public law, which deals with relationships between both natural and artificial persons and the state, including regulatory statutes, penal law and other law that affects the public order. In general terms, _____ involves interactions between private citizens, whereas public law involves interrelations between the state and the general population.

Exam Probability: **Medium**

25. *Answer choices:*

(see index for correct answer)

- a. open system
- b. levels of analysis
- c. similarity-attraction theory
- d. process perspective

*Guidance:* level 1

:: ::

A contract is a legally-binding agreement which recognises and governs the rights and duties of the parties to the agreement. A contract is legally enforceable because it meets the requirements and approval of the law. An agreement typically involves the exchange of goods, services, money, or promises of any of those. In the event of breach of contract, the law awards the injured party access to legal remedies such as damages and cancellation.

Exam Probability: **High**

26. *Answer choices:*
(see index for correct answer)

- a. Contract law
- b. functional perspective
- c. corporate values
- d. hierarchical

*Guidance:* level 1

:: ::

An _____ is an area of the production, distribution, or trade, and consumption of goods and services by different agents. Understood in its broadest sense, 'The _____ is defined as a social domain that emphasize the practices, discourses, and material expressions associated with the production, use, and management of resources'. Economic agents can be individuals, businesses, organizations, or governments. Economic transactions occur when two parties agree to the value or price of the transacted good or service, commonly expressed in a certain currency. However, monetary transactions only account for a small part of the economic domain.

Exam Probability: **Medium**

27. *Answer choices:*

(see index for correct answer)

- a. similarity-attraction theory
- b. hierarchical
- c. Economy
- d. cultural

Guidance: level 1

:: ::

In common law legal systems, _____ is a principle or rule established in a previous legal case that is either binding on or persuasive for a court or other tribunal when deciding subsequent cases with similar issues or facts. Common-law legal systems place great value on deciding cases according to consistent principled rules, so that similar facts will yield similar and predictable outcomes, and observance of _____ is the mechanism by which that goal is attained. The principle by which judges are bound to _____ s is known as stare decisis. Common-law _____ is a third kind of law, on equal footing with statutory law and delegated legislation or regulatory law.

Exam Probability: **Low**

28. *Answer choices:*
(see index for correct answer)

- a. process perspective
- b. Precedent
- c. Character
- d. interpersonal communication

Guidance: level 1

:: International relations ::

_____ is double mindedness or double heartedness in duplicity, fraud, or deception. It may involve intentional deceit of others, or self-deception.

Exam Probability: **Medium**

29. *Answer choices:*
(see index for correct answer)

- a. Periphery countries

- b. Diplomatic protection
- c. International community
- d. Bad faith

*Guidance:* level 1

:: ::

_____ is the collection of mechanisms, processes and relations by which corporations are controlled and operated. Governance structures and principles identify the distribution of rights and responsibilities among different participants in the corporation and include the rules and procedures for making decisions in corporate affairs. _____ is necessary because of the possibility of conflicts of interests between stakeholders, primarily between shareholders and upper management or among shareholders.

Exam Probability: **Medium**

30. *Answer choices:*
(see index for correct answer)

- a. interpersonal communication
- b. hierarchical perspective
- c. co-culture
- d. Corporate governance

*Guidance:* level 1

:: Contract law ::

In the United States, the _____ rule refers to the legal right for a buyer of goods to insist upon "_____" by the seller. In a contract for the sale of goods, if the goods fail to conform exactly to the description in the contract the buyer may nonetheless accept the goods, or reject the goods, or reject the nonconforming part of the tender and accept the conforming part. The buyer does not have an unfettered ability to reject tender.

Exam Probability: **Medium**

31. *Answer choices:*
(see index for correct answer)

- a. Capacity
- b. Extinguishment

- c. Perfect tender
- d. Quasi-contract

*Guidance:* level 1

:: ::

_____ is a means of protection from financial loss. It is a form of risk management, primarily used to hedge against the risk of a contingent or uncertain loss

Exam Probability: **High**

32. *Answer choices:*
(see index for correct answer)

- a. functional perspective
- b. Insurance
- c. personal values
- d. surface-level diversity

*Guidance:* level 1

:: ::

A _____ is a formal presentation of a matter such as a complaint, indictment or bill of exchange. In early-medieval England, juries of _____ would hear inquests in order to establish whether someone should be presented for a crime.

Exam Probability: **Low**

33. *Answer choices:*
(see index for correct answer)

- a. Presentment
- b. cultural
- c. personal values
- d. deep-level diversity

*Guidance:* level 1

:: Forgery ::

_____ is a white-collar crime that generally refers to the false making or material alteration of a legal instrument with the specific intent to defraud anyone. Tampering with a certain legal instrument may be forbidden by law in some jurisdictions but such an offense is not related to _____ unless the tampered legal instrument was actually used in the course of the crime to defraud another person or entity. Copies, studio replicas, and reproductions are not considered forgeries, though they may later become forgeries through knowing and willful misrepresentations.

Exam Probability: **Low**

34. *Answer choices:*
(see index for correct answer)

- a. Forgery
- b. Archaeological forgery
- c. Void pantograph
- d. Counterfeit electronic components

*Guidance:* level 1

:: ::

In logic and philosophy, an _____ is a series of statements, called the premises or premisses, intended to determine the degree of truth of another statement, the conclusion. The logical form of an _____ in a natural language can be represented in a symbolic formal language, and independently of natural language formally defined " _____ s" can be made in math and computer science.

Exam Probability: **High**

35. *Answer choices:*
(see index for correct answer)

- a. similarity-attraction theory
- b. Character
- c. surface-level diversity
- d. levels of analysis

*Guidance:* level 1

:: Money market instruments ::

_____, in the global financial market, is an unsecured promissory note with a fixed maturity of not more than 270 days.

Exam Probability: **Medium**

36. *Answer choices:*

(see index for correct answer)

- a. Banker's acceptance
- b. Commercial Paper

*Guidance:* level 1

:: Financial regulatory authorities of the United States ::

The _____ is the revenue service of the United States federal government. The government agency is a bureau of the Department of the Treasury, and is under the immediate direction of the Commissioner of Internal Revenue, who is appointed to a five-year term by the President of the United States. The IRS is responsible for collecting taxes and administering the Internal Revenue Code, the main body of federal statutory tax law of the United States. The duties of the IRS include providing tax assistance to taxpayers and pursuing and resolving instances of erroneous or fraudulent tax filings. The IRS has also overseen various benefits programs, and enforces portions of the Affordable Care Act.

Exam Probability: **Medium**

37. *Answer choices:*

(see index for correct answer)

- a. Office of the Comptroller of the Currency
- b. National Futures Association
- c. Internal Revenue Service
- d. Office of Thrift Supervision

*Guidance:* level 1

:: ::

In general, _____ is a form of dishonesty or criminal activity undertaken by a person or organization entrusted with a position of authority, often to acquire illicit benefit. _____ may include many activities including bribery and embezzlement, though it may also involve practices that are legal in many countries. Political _____ occurs when an office-holder or other governmental employee acts in an official capacity for personal gain. _____ is most commonplace in kleptocracies, oligarchies, narco-states and mafia states.

Exam Probability: **Medium**

38. *Answer choices:*
(see index for correct answer)

- a. cultural
- b. co-culture
- c. Corruption
- d. hierarchical

*Guidance:* level 1

:: ::

An _____ , commonly called an appeals court, court of appeals , appeal court , court of second instance or second instance court, is any court of law that is empowered to hear an appeal of a trial court or other lower tribunal. In most jurisdictions, the court system is divided into at least three levels: the trial court, which initially hears cases and reviews evidence and testimony to determine the facts of the case; at least one intermediate _____ ; and a supreme court which primarily reviews the decisions of the intermediate courts. A jurisdiction's supreme court is that jurisdiction's highest _____ . _____ s nationwide can operate under varying rules.

Exam Probability: **Low**

39. *Answer choices:*
(see index for correct answer)

- a. Character
- b. hierarchical
- c. levels of analysis
- d. personal values

*Guidance:* level 1

:: Sexual harassment in the United States ::

In law, a _____ , reasonable man, or the man on the Clapham omnibus is a hypothetical person of legal fiction crafted by the courts and communicated through case law and jury instructions.

Exam Probability: **Low**

40. *Answer choices:*

(see index for correct answer)

- a. Reasonable person
- b. Alexander v. Yale
- c. Sandy Gallin
- d. Blakey v. Continental Airlines

*Guidance:* level 1

:: Monopoly (economics) ::

A _____ is a form of intellectual property that gives its owner the legal right to exclude others from making, using, selling, and importing an invention for a limited period of years, in exchange for publishing an enabling public disclosure of the invention. In most countries _____ rights fall under civil law and the _____ holder needs to sue someone infringing the _____ in order to enforce his or her rights. In some industries _____ s are an essential form of competitive advantage; in others they are irrelevant.

Exam Probability: **Medium**

41. *Answer choices:*

(see index for correct answer)

- a. Complementary monopoly
- b. Competition Commission
- c. Government-granted monopoly
- d. Patent

*Guidance:* level 1

:: ::

Industrial espionage, _____, corporate spying or corporate espionage is a form of espionage conducted for commercial purposes instead of purely national security. While _____ is conducted or orchestrated by governments and is international in scope, industrial or corporate espionage is more often national and occurs between companies or corporations.

Exam Probability: **Medium**

42. *Answer choices:*

(see index for correct answer)

- a. personal values
- b. Character
- c. deep-level diversity
- d. Economic espionage

*Guidance:* level 1

:: Commercial crimes ::

_____ is the act of withholding assets for the purpose of conversion of such assets, by one or more persons to whom the assets were entrusted, either to be held or to be used for specific purposes. _____ is a type of financial fraud. For example, a lawyer might embezzle funds from the trust accounts of their clients; a financial advisor might embezzle the funds of investors; and a husband or a wife might embezzle funds from a bank account jointly held with the spouse.

Exam Probability: **Low**

43. *Answer choices:*

(see index for correct answer)

- a. 2008 Liechtenstein tax affair
- b. National White Collar Crime Center
- c. Gold laundering
- d. Embezzlement

*Guidance:* level 1

:: Contract law ::

A _____ is a legally-binding agreement which recognises and governs the rights and duties of the parties to the agreement. A _____ is legally enforceable because it meets the requirements and approval of the law. An agreement typically involves the exchange of goods, services, money, or promises of any of those. In the event of breach of _____, the law awards the injured party access to legal remedies such as damages and cancellation.

Exam Probability: **Medium**

44. *Answer choices:*
(see index for correct answer)

- a. Contractual term
- b. Sweetheart deal
- c. Pirate code
- d. Contract

*Guidance:* level 1

:: ::

A lawsuit is a proceeding by a party or parties against another in the civil court of law. The archaic term "suit in law" is found in only a small number of laws still in effect today. The term "lawsuit" is used in reference to a civil action brought in a court of law in which a plaintiff, a party who claims to have incurred loss as a result of a defendant's actions, demands a legal or equitable remedy. The defendant is required to respond to the plaintiff's complaint. If the plaintiff is successful, judgment is in the plaintiff's favor, and a variety of court orders may be issued to enforce a right, award damages, or impose a temporary or permanent injunction to prevent an act or compel an act. A declaratory judgment may be issued to prevent future legal disputes.

Exam Probability: **High**

45. *Answer choices:*
(see index for correct answer)

- a. Sarbanes-Oxley act of 2002
- b. cultural
- c. co-culture
- d. Litigation

*Guidance:* level 1

:: ::

_____ is a concept of English common law and is a necessity for simple contracts but not for special contracts. The concept has been adopted by other common law jurisdictions, including the US.

Exam Probability: **High**

46. *Answer choices:*

(see index for correct answer)

- a. hierarchical
- b. information systems assessment
- c. corporate values
- d. Consideration

*Guidance:* level 1

:: Legal procedure ::

_____, adjective law, or rules of court comprises the rules by which a court hears and determines what happens in civil, lawsuit, criminal or administrative proceedings. The rules are designed to ensure a fair and consistent application of due process or fundamental justice to all cases that come before a court.

Exam Probability: **High**

47. *Answer choices:*

(see index for correct answer)

- a. appellate
- b. Closing argument
- c. civil procedure
- d. Opening statement

*Guidance:* level 1

:: Legal doctrines and principles ::

In the United States, the _____ is a legal rule, based on constitutional law, that prevents evidence collected or analyzed in violation of the defendant's constitutional rights from being used in a court of law. This may be considered an example of a prophylactic rule formulated by the judiciary in order to protect a constitutional right. The _____ may also, in some circumstances at least, be considered to follow directly from the constitutional language, such as the Fifth Amendment's command that no person "shall be compelled in any criminal case to be a witness against himself" and that no person "shall be deprived of life, liberty or property without due process of law".

Exam Probability: **Medium**

48. *Answer choices:*

(see index for correct answer)

- a. unconscionable contract
- b. Act of state doctrine
- c. Eminent domain
- d. Exclusionary rule

*Guidance:* level 1

---

:: Marketing ::

_____ or stock is the goods and materials that a business holds for the ultimate goal of resale.

Exam Probability: **Medium**

49. *Answer choices:*

(see index for correct answer)

- a. Hype cycle
- b. One Town One Product
- c. Pink money
- d. Contribution margin-based pricing

*Guidance:* level 1

---

:: Contract law ::

_____ is a doctrine in contract law that describes terms that are so extremely unjust, or overwhelmingly one-sided in favor of the party who has the superior bargaining power, that they are contrary to good conscience. Typically, an unconscionable contract is held to be unenforceable because no reasonable or informed person would otherwise agree to it. The perpetrator of the conduct is not allowed to benefit, because the consideration offered is lacking, or is so obviously inadequate, that to enforce the contract would be unfair to the party seeking to escape the contract.

Exam Probability: **High**

50. *Answer choices:*
(see index for correct answer)

- a. Job order contracting
- b. Mirror image rule
- c. Indian contract law
- d. Contingent contracts

*Guidance:* level 1

:: ::

The _____ of 1977 is a United States federal law known primarily for two of its main provisions: one that addresses accounting transparency requirements under the Securities Exchange Act of 1934 and another concerning bribery of foreign officials. The Act was amended in 1988 and in 1998, and has been subject to continued congressional concerns, namely whether its enforcement discourages U.S. companies from investing abroad.

Exam Probability: **Medium**

51. *Answer choices:*
(see index for correct answer)

- a. Foreign Corrupt Practices Act
- b. personal values
- c. open system
- d. Sarbanes-Oxley act of 2002

*Guidance:* level 1

:: Treaties ::

A _____ is an agreement under international law entered into by actors in international law, namely sovereign states and international organizations. A _____ may also be known as an agreement, protocol, covenant, convention, pact, or exchange of letters, among other terms. Regardless of terminology, all of these forms of agreements are, under international law, equally considered treaties and the rules are the same.

Exam Probability: **Medium**

52. *Answer choices:*
(see index for correct answer)

- a. Investor state dispute settlement
- b. Bilateral treaty
- c. Subsidiary alliance
- d. Treaty

*Guidance:* level 1

:: Criminal procedure ::

_____ is the adjudication process of the criminal law. While _____ differs dramatically by jurisdiction, the process generally begins with a formal criminal charge with the person on trial either being free on bail or incarcerated, and results in the conviction or acquittal of the defendant. _____ can be either in form of inquisitorial or adversarial _____.

Exam Probability: **Medium**

53. *Answer choices:*
(see index for correct answer)

- a. Exoneration
- b. directed verdict

*Guidance:* level 1

:: ::

_____ is a process whereby a person assumes the parenting of another, usually a child, from that person's biological or legal parent or parents. Legal _____ s permanently transfers all rights and responsibilities, along with filiation, from the biological parent or parents.

Exam Probability: **Low**

54. *Answer choices:*
(see index for correct answer)

- a. corporate values
- b. co-culture
- c. Adoption
- d. similarity-attraction theory

*Guidance:* level 1

---

:: ::

The _____ of 1933, also known as the 1933 Act, the _____ , the Truth in _____ , the Federal _____ , and the `33 Act, was enacted by the United States Congress on May 27, 1933, during the Great Depression, after the stock market crash of 1929. Legislated pursuant to the Interstate Commerce Clause of the Constitution, it requires every offer or sale of securities that uses the means and instrumentalities of interstate commerce to be registered with the SEC pursuant to the 1933 Act, unless an exemption from registration exists under the law. The term "means and instrumentalities of interstate commerce" is extremely broad and it is virtually impossible to avoid the operation of the statute by attempting to offer or sell a security without using an "instrumentality" of interstate commerce. Any use of a telephone, for example, or the mails would probably be enough to subject the transaction to the statute.

Exam Probability: **Medium**

55. *Answer choices:*
(see index for correct answer)

- a. imperative
- b. levels of analysis
- c. co-culture
- d. cultural

*Guidance:* level 1

:: Insolvency ::

_____ is a legal process through which people or other entities who cannot repay debts to creditors may seek relief from some or all of their debts. In most jurisdictions, _____ is imposed by a court order, often initiated by the debtor.

Exam Probability: **Medium**

56. *Answer choices:*

(see index for correct answer)

- a. Liquidator
- b. Financial distress
- c. Bankruptcy
- d. United Kingdom insolvency law

*Guidance:* level 1

:: Debt ::

A _____ is a party that has a claim on the services of a second party. It is a person or institution to whom money is owed. The first party, in general, has provided some property or service to the second party under the assumption that the second party will return an equivalent property and service. The second party is frequently called a debtor or borrower. The first party is called the _____, which is the lender of property, service, or money.

Exam Probability: **Medium**

57. *Answer choices:*

(see index for correct answer)

- a. Creditor
- b. Financial assistance
- c. External financing
- d. Vulture fund

*Guidance:* level 1

:: Decision theory ::

Within economics the concept of _____ is used to model worth or value, but its usage has evolved significantly over time. The term was introduced initially as a measure of pleasure or satisfaction within the theory of utilitarianism by moral philosophers such as Jeremy Bentham and John Stuart Mill. But the term has been adapted and reapplied within neoclassical economics, which dominates modern economic theory, as a _____ function that represents a consumer's preference ordering over a choice set. As such, it is devoid of its original interpretation as a measurement of the pleasure or satisfaction obtained by the consumer from that choice.

Exam Probability: **Low**

58. *Answer choices:*
(see index for correct answer)

- a. Utility
- b. Shared decision-making
- c. Ambiguity aversion
- d. Negotiation theory

*Guidance:* level 1

:: ::

In English law, a _____ or _____ absolute is an estate in land, a form of freehold ownership. It is a way that real estate and land may be owned in common law countries, and is the highest possible ownership interest that can be held in real property. Allodial title is reserved to governments under a civil law structure. The rights of the _____ owner are limited by government powers of taxation, compulsory purchase, police power, and escheat, and it could also be limited further by certain encumbrances or conditions in the deed, such as, for example, a condition that required the land to be used as a public park, with a reversion interest in the grantor if the condition fails; this is a _____ conditional.

Exam Probability: **High**

59. *Answer choices:*
(see index for correct answer)

- a. open system
- b. Fee simple
- c. empathy

- d. corporate values

*Guidance:* level 1

## Finance

Finance is a field that is concerned with the allocation (investment) of assets and liabilities over space and time, often under conditions of risk or uncertainty. Finance can also be defined as the science of money management. Participants in the market aim to price assets based on their risk level, fundamental value, and their expected rate of return. Finance can be split into three sub-categories: public finance, corporate finance and personal finance.

---

:: Legal terms ::

_____ s may be governments, corporations or investment trusts. _____ s are legally responsible for the obligations of the issue and for reporting financial conditions, material developments and any other operational activities as required by the regulations of their jurisdictions.

Exam Probability: **Low**

1. *Answer choices:*
(see index for correct answer)

- a. Issuer
- b. Allegation
- c. Police caution
- d. Docket

*Guidance:* level 1

---

:: ::

A _____ is an organization, usually a group of people or a company, authorized to act as a single entity and recognized as such in law. Early incorporated entities were established by charter. Most jurisdictions now allow the creation of new _____ s through registration.

Exam Probability: **High**

2. *Answer choices:*

(see index for correct answer)

- a. empathy
- b. similarity-attraction theory
- c. interpersonal communication
- d. Corporation

*Guidance:* level 1

---

:: Costs ::

In microeconomic theory, the _____ , or alternative cost, of making a particular choice is the value of the most valuable choice out of those that were not taken. In other words, opportunity that will require sacrifices.

Exam Probability: **Low**

3. *Answer choices:*

(see index for correct answer)

- a. Average cost
- b. labor cost
- c. Opportunity cost
- d. Khozraschyot

*Guidance:* level 1

---

:: ::

_____ focuses on ratios, equities and debts. It is useful for portfolio management, distribution of dividend, capital raising, hedging and looking after fluctuations in foreign currency and product cycles. Financial managers are the people who will do research and based on the research, decide what sort of capital to obtain in order to fund the company's assets as well as maximizing the value of the firm for all the stakeholders. It also refers to the efficient and effective management of money in such a manner as to accomplish the objectives of the organization. It is the specialized function directly associated with the top management. The significance of this function is not seen in the 'Line' but also in the capacity of the 'Staff' in overall of a company. It has been defined differently by different experts in the field.

Exam Probability: **Medium**

4. *Answer choices:*
(see index for correct answer)

- a. Character
- b. cultural
- c. Financial management
- d. hierarchical

*Guidance:* level 1

:: Elementary geometry ::

The _____ is the front of an animal's head that features three of the head's sense organs, the eyes, nose, and mouth, and through which animals express many of their emotions. The _____ is crucial for human identity, and damage such as scarring or developmental deformities affects the psyche adversely.

Exam Probability: **Low**

5. *Answer choices:*
(see index for correct answer)

- a. Shape
- b. 3-sphere
- c. Face
- d. Golden angle

*Guidance:* level 1

:: Asset ::

In accounting, a _____ is any asset which can reasonably be expected to be sold, consumed, or exhausted through the normal operations of a business within the current fiscal year or operating cycle. Typical _____ s include cash, cash equivalents, short-term investments, accounts receivable, stock inventory, supplies, and the portion of prepaid liabilities which will be paid within a year. In simple words, assets which are held for a short period are known as _____ s. Such assets are expected to be realised in cash or consumed during the normal operating cycle of the business.

Exam Probability: **Medium**

6. *Answer choices:*

(see index for correct answer)

- a. Asset
- b. Fixed asset

*Guidance:* level 1

:: Accounting terminology ::

_____ of something is, in finance, the adding together of interest or different investments over a period of time. It holds specific meanings in accounting, where it can refer to accounts on a balance sheet that represent liabilities and non-cash-based assets used in _____ -based accounting. These types of accounts include, among others, accounts payable, accounts receivable, goodwill, deferred tax liability and future interest expense.

Exam Probability: **High**

7. *Answer choices:*

(see index for correct answer)

- a. Basis of accounting
- b. Accrual
- c. Total absorption costing
- d. Capital expenditure

*Guidance:* level 1

:: Accounting ::

_____ is a process of providing relief to shared service organization's cost centers that provide a product or service. In turn, the associated expense is assigned to internal clients' cost centers that consume the products and services. For example, the CIO may provide all IT services within the company and assign the costs back to the business units that consume each offering.

Exam Probability: **High**

8. *Answer choices:*

(see index for correct answer)

- a. Accounting records
- b. CPA Site Solutions
- c. Teeming and lading

- d. Tax profit

*Guidance:* level 1

---

:: ::

_____ is a political and social philosophy promoting traditional social institutions in the context of culture and civilization. The central tenets of _____ include tradition, human imperfection, organic society, hierarchy, authority, and property rights. Conservatives seek to preserve a range of institutions such as religion, parliamentary government, and property rights, with the aim of emphasizing social stability and continuity. The more traditional elements—reactionaries—oppose modernism and seek a return to "the way things were".

Exam Probability: **Low**

9. *Answer choices:*

(see index for correct answer)

- a. interpersonal communication
- b. Sarbanes-Oxley act of 2002
- c. corporate values
- d. similarity-attraction theory

*Guidance:* level 1

---

:: ::

An _____ is an area of the production, distribution, or trade, and consumption of goods and services by different agents. Understood in its broadest sense, 'The _____ is defined as a social domain that emphasize the practices, discourses, and material expressions associated with the production, use, and management of resources'. Economic agents can be individuals, businesses, organizations, or governments. Economic transactions occur when two parties agree to the value or price of the transacted good or service, commonly expressed in a certain currency. However, monetary transactions only account for a small part of the economic domain.

Exam Probability: **Medium**

10. *Answer choices:*

(see index for correct answer)

- a. levels of analysis
- b. co-culture
- c. empathy
- d. Economy

*Guidance:* level 1

:: ::

MCI, Inc. was an American telecommunication corporation, currently a subsidiary of Verizon Communications, with its main office in Ashburn, Virginia. The corporation was formed originally as a result of the merger of _____ and MCI Communications corporations, and used the name MCI _____ , succeeded by _____ , before changing its name to the present version on April 12, 2003, as part of the corporation's ending of its bankruptcy status. The company traded on NASDAQ as WCOM and MCIP . The corporation was purchased by Verizon Communications with the deal finalizing on January 6, 2006, and is now identified as that company's Verizon Enterprise Solutions division with the local residential divisions being integrated slowly into local Verizon subsidiaries.

Exam Probability: **High**

11. *Answer choices:*
(see index for correct answer)

- a. WorldCom
- b. empathy
- c. imperative
- d. hierarchical perspective

*Guidance:* level 1

:: Investment ::

In finance, the benefit from an _____ is called a return. The return may consist of a gain realised from the sale of property or an _____ , unrealised capital appreciation , or _____ income such as dividends, interest, rental income etc., or a combination of capital gain and income. The return may also include currency gains or losses due to changes in foreign currency exchange rates.

Exam Probability: **Medium**

12. *Answer choices:*
(see index for correct answer)

- a. Investment
- b. Stabilization clause
- c. Buy to let
- d. Value premium

*Guidance:* level 1

---

:: Business law ::

The expression " _____ " is somewhat confusing as it has a different meaning based on the context that is under consideration. From a product characteristic stand point, this type of a lease, as distinguished from a finance lease, is one where the lessor takes residual risk. As such, the lease is non full payout. From an accounting stand point, this type of lease results in off balance sheet financing.

Exam Probability: **High**

13. *Answer choices:*
(see index for correct answer)

- a. Vehicle leasing
- b. Operating lease
- c. Consularization
- d. Lien

*Guidance:* level 1

---

:: ::

_____ is the production of products for use or sale using labour and machines, tools, chemical and biological processing, or formulation. The term may refer to a range of human activity, from handicraft to high tech, but is most commonly applied to industrial design, in which raw materials are transformed into finished goods on a large scale. Such finished goods may be sold to other manufacturers for the production of other, more complex products, such as aircraft, household appliances, furniture, sports equipment or automobiles, or sold to wholesalers, who in turn sell them to retailers, who then sell them to end users and consumers.

Exam Probability: **High**

14. *Answer choices:*
(see index for correct answer)

- a. hierarchical perspective
- b. co-culture
- c. cultural
- d. Manufacturing

*Guidance:* level 1

---

:: Actuarial science ::

The _____ is the greater benefit of receiving money now rather than an identical sum later. It is founded on time preference.

Exam Probability: **Low**

15. *Answer choices:*
(see index for correct answer)

- a. Time value of money
- b. Ogden tables
- c. Medical underwriting
- d. Age stratification

*Guidance:* level 1

---

:: Market research ::

_____, an acronym for Information through Disguised Experimentation is an annual market research fair conducted by the students of IIM-Lucknow. Students create games and use various other simulated environments to capture consumers' subconscious thoughts. This innovative method of market research removes the sensitization effect that might bias peoples answers to questions. This ensures that the most truthful answers are captured to research questions. The games are designed in such a way that the observers can elicit all the required information just by observing and noting down the behaviour and the responses of the participants.

Exam Probability: **Low**

16. *Answer choices:*
(see index for correct answer)

- a. INDEX
- b. Qualitative marketing research
- c. Shanghai Metals Market
- d. Automated Measurement of Lineups

*Guidance:* level 1

---

:: ::

An _____, for United States federal income tax, is a closely held corporation that makes a valid election to be taxed under Subchapter S of Chapter 1 of the Internal Revenue Code. In general, _____ s do not pay any income taxes. Instead, the corporation's income or losses are divided among and passed through to its shareholders. The shareholders must then report the income or loss on their own individual income tax returns.

Exam Probability: **Medium**

17. *Answer choices:*
(see index for correct answer)

- a. levels of analysis
- b. S corporation
- c. similarity-attraction theory
- d. corporate values

*Guidance:* level 1

---

:: Accounting journals and ledgers ::

A _____, in accounting, is the logging of a transaction in an accounting journal that shows a company's debit and credit balances. The _____ can consist of several recordings, each of which is either a debit or a credit. The total of the debits must equal the total of the credits or the _____ is considered unbalanced. Journal entries can record unique items or recurring items such as depreciation or bond amortization. In accounting software, journal entries are usually entered using a separate module from accounts payable, which typically has its own subledger, that indirectly affects the general ledger. As a result, journal entries directly change the account balances on the general ledger. A properly documented _____ consists of the correct date, amount that will be debited, amount that will be credited, description of transaction, and unique reference number .

Exam Probability: **High**

18. *Answer choices:*

(see index for correct answer)

- a. Subledger
- b. Cash receipts journal
- c. Journal entry
- d. Subsidiary ledger

*Guidance:* level 1

:: United States Generally Accepted Accounting Principles ::

In a companies' financial reporting, _____ "includes all changes in equity during a period except those resulting from investments by owners and distributions to owners". Because that use excludes the effects of changing ownership interest, an economic measure of _____ is necessary for financial analysis from the shareholders' point of view

Exam Probability: **High**

19. *Answer choices:*

(see index for correct answer)

- a. Working Group on Financial Markets
- b. FIN 46
- c. Comprehensive income
- d. GASB 34

*Guidance:* level 1

:: ::

_____ or accountancy is the measurement, processing, and communication of financial information about economic entities such as businesses and corporations. The modern field was established by the Italian mathematician Luca Pacioli in 1494. _____ , which has been called the "language of business", measures the results of an organization's economic activities and conveys this information to a variety of users, including investors, creditors, management, and regulators. Practitioners of _____ are known as accountants. The terms " _____ " and "financial reporting" are often used as synonyms.

Exam Probability: **Low**

20. *Answer choices:*
(see index for correct answer)

- a. information systems assessment
- b. hierarchical
- c. Accounting
- d. surface-level diversity

*Guidance:* level 1

:: Financial risk ::

_____ is any of various types of risk associated with financing, including financial transactions that include company loans in risk of default. Often it is understood to include only downside risk, meaning the potential for financial loss and uncertainty about its extent.

Exam Probability: **High**

21. *Answer choices:*
(see index for correct answer)

- a. Financial risk
- b. Financial risk management
- c. Equity risk
- d. Trading room

*Guidance:* level 1

:: Management accounting ::

_____ , or dollar contribution per unit, is the selling price per unit minus the variable cost per unit. "Contribution" represents the portion of sales revenue that is not consumed by variable costs and so contributes to the coverage of fixed costs. This concept is one of the key building blocks of break-even analysis.

Exam Probability: **High**

22. *Answer choices:*
(see index for correct answer)

- a. Customer profitability
- b. Fixed assets management

- c. Contribution margin
- d. Investment center

*Guidance:* level 1

---

:: Personal finance ::

_____ is income not spent, or deferred consumption. Methods of _____ include putting money aside in, for example, a deposit account, a pension account, an investment fund, or as cash. _____ also involves reducing expenditures, such as recurring costs. In terms of personal finance, _____ generally specifies low-risk preservation of money, as in a deposit account, versus investment, wherein risk is a lot higher; in economics more broadly, it refers to any income not used for immediate consumption.

Exam Probability: **Low**

23. *Answer choices:*

(see index for correct answer)

- a. HousePriceCrash
- b. Courtesy signing
- c. Saving
- d. Dissaving

*Guidance:* level 1

---

:: Stock market ::

A share price is the price of a single share of a number of saleable stocks of a company, derivative or other financial asset.In layman's terms, the _____ is the highest amount someone is willing to pay for the stock, or the lowest amount that it can be bought for.

Exam Probability: **Medium**

24. *Answer choices:*

(see index for correct answer)

- a. Reverse stock split
- b. Relative valuation
- c. Stock price
- d. Slippage

*Guidance:* level 1

:: Mathematical finance ::

_____ is the value of an asset at a specific date. It measures the nominal future sum of money that a given sum of money is "worth" at a specified time in the future assuming a certain interest rate, or more generally, rate of return; it is the present value multiplied by the accumulation function. The value does not include corrections for inflation or other factors that affect the true value of money in the future. This is used in time value of money calculations.

Exam Probability: **Medium**

25. *Answer choices:*

(see index for correct answer)

- a. No-arbitrage bounds
- b. Realized variance
- c. QuantLib
- d. Future value

*Guidance:* level 1

:: ::

A tax is a compulsory financial charge or some other type of levy imposed upon a taxpayer by a governmental organization in order to fund various public expenditures. A failure to pay, along with evasion of or resistance to _____, is punishable by law. Taxes consist of direct or indirect taxes and may be paid in money or as its labour equivalent.

Exam Probability: **Low**

26. *Answer choices:*

(see index for correct answer)

- a. Sarbanes-Oxley act of 2002
- b. Taxation
- c. hierarchical perspective
- d. open system

*Guidance:* level 1

:: Stock market ::

_____ is freedom from, or resilience against, potential harm caused by others. Beneficiaries of _____ may be of persons and social groups, objects and institutions, ecosystems or any other entity or phenomenon vulnerable to unwanted change by its environment.

Exam Probability: **High**

27. *Answer choices:*

(see index for correct answer)

- a. American Depositary Share
- b. Security
- c. Short-term trading
- d. Secondary market offering

*Guidance:* level 1

:: Investment ::

_____ , and investment appraisal, is the planning process used to determine whether an organization's long term investments such as new machinery, replacement of machinery, new plants, new products, and research development projects are worth the funding of cash through the firm's capitalization structure . It is the process of allocating resources for major capital, or investment, expenditures. One of the primary goals of _____ investments is to increase the value of the firm to the shareholders.

Exam Probability: **Medium**

28. *Answer choices:*

(see index for correct answer)

- a. Diamonds as an investment
- b. Share Incentive Plan
- c. Foreign portfolio investment
- d. Capital budgeting

*Guidance:* level 1

:: Inventory ::

_____ is a system of inventory in which updates are made on a periodic basis. This differs from perpetual inventory systems, where updates are made as seen fit.

Exam Probability: **Low**

29. *Answer choices:*

(see index for correct answer)

- a. Cost of goods sold
- b. Periodic inventory
- c. Cost of goods available for sale
- d. Order fulfillment

*Guidance:* level 1

:: Accounting terminology ::

_____ or capital expense is the money a company spends to buy, maintain, or improve its fixed assets, such as buildings, vehicles, equipment, or land. It is considered a _____ when the asset is newly purchased or when money is used towards extending the useful life of an existing asset, such as repairing the roof.

Exam Probability: **Medium**

30. *Answer choices:*

(see index for correct answer)

- a. Fair value accounting
- b. Capital expenditure
- c. Record to report
- d. Enterprise liquidity

*Guidance:* level 1

:: Debt ::

_____ is when something, usually money, is owed by one party, the borrower or _____ or, to a second party, the lender or creditor. _____ is a deferred payment, or series of payments, that is owed in the future, which is what differentiates it from an immediate purchase. The _____ may be owed by sovereign state or country, local government, company, or an individual. Commercial _____ is generally subject to contractual terms regarding the amount and timing of repayments of principal and interest. Loans, bonds, notes, and mortgages are all types of _____ . The term can also be used metaphorically to cover moral obligations and other interactions not based on economic value. For example, in Western cultures, a person who has been helped by a second person is sometimes said to owe a " _____ of gratitude" to the second person.

Exam Probability: **Low**

31. *Answer choices:*

(see index for correct answer)

- a. Debt
- b. Odious debt
- c. Peak debt
- d. Recourse debt

*Guidance:* level 1

:: Basic financial concepts ::

In finance, maturity or _____ refers to the final payment date of a loan or other financial instrument, at which point the principal is due to be paid.

Exam Probability: **Low**

32. *Answer choices:*

(see index for correct answer)

- a. Leverage cycle
- b. Future-oriented
- c. Deflation
- d. Inflation

*Guidance:* level 1

:: Stock market ::

_____ or stock market launch is a type of public offering in which shares of a company are sold to institutional investors and usually also retail investors; an IPO is underwritten by one or more investment banks, who also arrange for the shares to be listed on one or more stock exchanges. Through this process, colloquially known as floating, or going public, a privately held company is transformed into a public company. _____ s can be used: to raise new equity capital for the company concerned; to monetize the investments of private shareholders such as company founders or private equity investors; and to enable easy trading of existing holdings or future capital raising by becoming publicly traded enterprises.

Exam Probability: **High**

33. *Answer choices:*
(see index for correct answer)

- a. CEE Stock Exchange Group
- b. Chip
- c. Initial public offering
- d. Burgundy

*Guidance:* level 1

:: Financial accounting ::

_____ is a financial metric which represents operating liquidity available to a business, organisation or other entity, including governmental entities. Along with fixed assets such as plant and equipment, _____ is considered a part of operating capital. Gross _____ is equal to current assets. _____ is calculated as current assets minus current liabilities. If current assets are less than current liabilities, an entity has a _____ deficiency, also called a _____ deficit.

Exam Probability: **Medium**

34. *Answer choices:*
(see index for correct answer)

- a. Convenience translation
- b. Working capital
- c. Authorised capital
- d. Hidden asset

*Guidance:* level 1

:: Financial ratios ::

The _____ or dividend-price ratio of a share is the dividend per share, divided by the price per share. It is also a company's total annual dividend payments divided by its market capitalization, assuming the number of shares is constant. It is often expressed as a percentage.

Exam Probability: **Medium**

35. *Answer choices:*
(see index for correct answer)

- a. Current ratio
- b. Dividend yield
- c. Greeks
- d. Return on assets

*Guidance:* level 1

:: Management ::

_____ is the identification, evaluation, and prioritization of risks followed by coordinated and economical application of resources to minimize, monitor, and control the probability or impact of unfortunate events or to maximize the realization of opportunities.

Exam Probability: **Low**

36. *Answer choices:*
(see index for correct answer)

- a. Decentralized decision-making
- b. Quality, cost, delivery
- c. Risk management
- d. Intelligent customer

*Guidance:* level 1

:: Marketing ::

A _____ is an overall experience of a customer that distinguishes an organization or product from its rivals in the eyes of the customer. _____ s are used in business, marketing, and advertising. Name _____ s are sometimes distinguished from generic or store _____ s.

Exam Probability: **Medium**

37. *Answer choices:*
(see index for correct answer)

- a. Brand
- b. Market orientation
- c. Marchitecture
- d. Corporate identity

*Guidance:* level 1

:: Investment ::

The _____ is a measure of an investment's rate of return. The term internal refers to the fact that the calculation excludes external factors, such as the risk-free rate, inflation, the cost of capital, or various financial risks.

Exam Probability: **Medium**

38. *Answer choices:*
(see index for correct answer)

- a. Internal rate of return
- b. Investment function
- c. SharePlanner
- d. Value Research

*Guidance:* level 1

:: Accounting terminology ::

Accounts are typically defined by an identifier and a caption or header and are coded by account type. In computerized accounting systems with computable quantity accounting, the accounts can have a quantity measure definition.

Exam Probability: **High**

39. *Answer choices:*

(see index for correct answer)

- a. Chart of accounts
- b. Share premium
- c. Internal auditing
- d. Mark-to-market

Guidance: level 1

---

:: Fixed income market ::

In finance, the _____ is a curve showing several yields or interest rates across different contract lengths for a similar debt contract. The curve shows the relation between the interest rate and the time to maturity, known as the "term", of the debt for a given borrower in a given currency. For example, the U.S. dollar interest rates paid on U.S. Treasury securities for various maturities are closely watched by many traders, and are commonly plotted on a graph such as the one on the right which is informally called "the _____". More formal mathematical descriptions of this relation are often called the term structure of interest rates.

Exam Probability: **Medium**

40. *Answer choices:*

(see index for correct answer)

- a. Yield curve
- b. Fixed income
- c. Fixed-income attribution
- d. credit market

Guidance: level 1

---

:: ::

_____ is an eight-block-long street running roughly northwest to southeast from Broadway to South Street, at the East River, in the Financial District of Lower Manhattan in New York City. Over time, the term has become a metonym for the financial markets of the United States as a whole, the American financial services industry , or New York–based financial interests.

Exam Probability: **Low**

41. *Answer choices:*

(see index for correct answer)

- a. Character
- b. Wall Street
- c. similarity-attraction theory
- d. interpersonal communication

*Guidance:* level 1

---

:: Generally Accepted Accounting Principles ::

_____, or non-current liabilities, are liabilities that are due beyond a year or the normal operation period of the company. The normal operation period is the amount of time it takes for a company to turn inventory into cash. On a classified balance sheet, liabilities are separated between current and _____ to help users assess the company's financial standing in short-term and long-term periods. _____ give users more information about the long-term prosperity of the company, while current liabilities inform the user of debt that the company owes in the current period. On a balance sheet, accounts are listed in order of liquidity, so _____ come after current liabilities. In addition, the specific long-term liability accounts are listed on the balance sheet in order of liquidity. Therefore, an account due within eighteen months would be listed before an account due within twenty-four months. Examples of _____ are bonds payable, long-term loans, capital leases, pension liabilities, post-retirement healthcare liabilities, deferred compensation, deferred revenues, deferred income taxes, and derivative liabilities.

Exam Probability: **Medium**

42. *Answer choices:*

(see index for correct answer)

- a. Engagement letter
- b. Earnings before interest, taxes and depreciation
- c. deferred revenue
- d. Long-term liabilities

*Guidance:* level 1

---

:: Banking ::

A _____ is a financial institution that accepts deposits from the public and creates credit. Lending activities can be performed either directly or indirectly through capital markets. Due to their importance in the financial stability of a country, _____ s are highly regulated in most countries. Most nations have institutionalized a system known as fractional reserve _____ ing under which _____ s hold liquid assets equal to only a portion of their current liabilities. In addition to other regulations intended to ensure liquidity, _____ s are generally subject to minimum capital requirements based on an international set of capital standards, known as the Basel Accords.

Exam Probability: **High**

43. *Answer choices:*
(see index for correct answer)

- a. Bank
- b. Christmas club
- c. Banking agent
- d. Coin roll hunting

*Guidance:* level 1

:: Budgets ::

A _____ is a financial plan for a defined period, often one year. It may also include planned sales volumes and revenues, resource quantities, costs and expenses, assets, liabilities and cash flows. Companies, governments, families and other organizations use it to express strategic plans of activities or events in measurable terms.

Exam Probability: **Low**

44. *Answer choices:*
(see index for correct answer)

- a. Envelope system
- b. Budget
- c. Black budget
- d. Railway Budget

*Guidance:* level 1

:: Inventory ::

_____ is the amount of inventory a company has in stock at the end of its fiscal year. It is closely related with _____ cost, which is the amount of money spent to get these goods in stock. It should be calculated at the lower of cost or market.

Exam Probability: **Medium**

45. *Answer choices:*
(see index for correct answer)

- a. Phantom inventory
- b. GMROII
- c. Average cost method
- d. Stock control

*Guidance:* level 1

:: Corporate finance ::

_____ in corporate finance is the way a corporation finances its assets through some combination of equity, debt, or hybrid securities.

Exam Probability: **High**

46. *Answer choices:*
(see index for correct answer)

- a. Capital structure
- b. Small business financing
- c. Capitalization table
- d. Thin capitalisation rules

*Guidance:* level 1

:: Financial markets ::

For an individual, a _____ is the minimum amount of money by which the expected return on a risky asset must exceed the known return on a risk-free asset in order to induce an individual to hold the risky asset rather than the risk-free asset. It is positive if the person is risk averse. Thus it is the minimum willingness to accept compensation for the risk.

Exam Probability: **Medium**

47. *Answer choices:*

(see index for correct answer)

- a. Risk premium
- b. Convenience yield
- c. Private equity fund
- d. Clearing

*Guidance:* level 1

:: Scheduling (computing) ::

Ageing or _____ is the process of becoming older. The term refers especially to human beings, many animals, and fungi, whereas for example bacteria, perennial plants and some simple animals are potentially biologically immortal. In the broader sense, ageing can refer to single cells within an organism which have ceased dividing or to the population of a species.

Exam Probability: **Medium**

48. *Answer choices:*

(see index for correct answer)

- a. Run queue
- b. Light-weight process
- c. Affinity mask
- d. Server hog

*Guidance:* level 1

:: ::

In the field of analysis of algorithms in computer science, the _____ is a method of amortized analysis based on accounting. The _____ often gives a more intuitive account of the amortized cost of an operation than either aggregate analysis or the potential method. Note, however, that this does not guarantee such analysis will be immediately obvious; often, choosing the correct parameters for the _____ requires as much knowledge of the problem and the complexity bounds one is attempting to prove as the other two methods.

Exam Probability: **Low**

49. *Answer choices:*

(see index for correct answer)

- a. hierarchical
- b. Accounting method
- c. open system
- d. process perspective

*Guidance:* level 1

---

:: Accounting in the United States ::

The _____ is a private-sector, nonprofit corporation created by the Sarbanes–Oxley Act of 2002 to oversee the audits of public companies and other issuers in order to protect the interests of investors and further the public interest in the preparation of informative, accurate and independent audit reports. The PCAOB also oversees the audits of broker-dealers, including compliance reports filed pursuant to federal securities laws, to promote investor protection. All PCAOB rules and standards must be approved by the U.S. Securities and Exchange Commission .

Exam Probability: **Low**

50. *Answer choices:*

(see index for correct answer)

- a. Plug
- b. Public Company Accounting Oversight Board
- c. Financial Accounting Foundation
- d. Norwalk Agreement

*Guidance:* level 1

---

:: ::

A _____ is the process of presenting a topic to an audience. It is typically a demonstration, introduction, lecture, or speech meant to inform, persuade, inspire, motivate, or to build good will or to present a new idea or product. The term can also be used for a formal or ritualized introduction or offering, as with the _____ of a debutante. _____ s in certain formats are also known as keynote address.

Exam Probability: **High**

51. *Answer choices:*

(see index for correct answer)

- a. process perspective
- b. Presentation
- c. Character
- d. deep-level diversity

*Guidance:* level 1

:: Financial regulatory authorities of the United States ::

The _____ is the revenue service of the United States federal government. The government agency is a bureau of the Department of the Treasury, and is under the immediate direction of the Commissioner of Internal Revenue, who is appointed to a five-year term by the President of the United States. The IRS is responsible for collecting taxes and administering the Internal Revenue Code, the main body of federal statutory tax law of the United States. The duties of the IRS include providing tax assistance to taxpayers and pursuing and resolving instances of erroneous or fraudulent tax filings. The IRS has also overseen various benefits programs, and enforces portions of the Affordable Care Act.

Exam Probability: **Medium**

52. *Answer choices:*

(see index for correct answer)

- a. Consumer Financial Protection Bureau
- b. Securities Investor Protection Corporation
- c. Office of the Comptroller of the Currency
- d. Federal Reserve Board

*Guidance:* level 1

:: Financial accounting ::

In accounting, _____ is the value of an asset according to its balance sheet account balance. For assets, the value is based on the original cost of the asset less any depreciation, amortization or impairment costs made against the asset. Traditionally, a company's _____ is its total assets minus intangible assets and liabilities. However, in practice, depending on the source of the calculation, _____ may variably include goodwill, intangible assets, or both. The value inherent in its workforce, part of the intellectual capital of a company, is always ignored. When intangible assets and goodwill are explicitly excluded, the metric is often specified to be "tangible _____ ".

Exam Probability: **Medium**

53. *Answer choices:*

(see index for correct answer)

- a. Book value
- b. Convenience translation
- c. Carry
- d. Authorised capital

*Guidance:* level 1

---

:: Taxation ::

In a tax system, the _____ is the ratio at which a business or person is taxed. There are several methods used to present a _____ : statutory, average, marginal, and effective. These rates can also be presented using different definitions applied to a tax base: inclusive and exclusive.

Exam Probability: **Low**

54. *Answer choices:*

(see index for correct answer)

- a. Language tax
- b. Tax rate
- c. Fiscal memory devices
- d. Benefit principle

*Guidance:* level 1

---

:: ::

_____ , often abbreviated as B/E in finance, is the point of balance making neither a profit nor a loss. The term originates in finance but the concept has been applied in other fields.

Exam Probability: **Low**

55. *Answer choices:*

(see index for correct answer)

- a. Break-even
- b. surface-level diversity
- c. Sarbanes-Oxley act of 2002
- d. cultural

*Guidance:* level 1

:: Business law ::

_____ is where a person's financial liability is limited to a fixed sum, most commonly the value of a person's investment in a company or partnership. If a company with _____ is sued, then the claimants are suing the company, not its owners or investors. A shareholder in a limited company is not personally liable for any of the debts of the company, other than for the amount already invested in the company and for any unpaid amount on the shares in the company, if any. The same is true for the members of a _____ partnership and the limited partners in a limited partnership. By contrast, sole proprietors and partners in general partnerships are each liable for all the debts of the business.

Exam Probability: **Low**

56. *Answer choices:*

(see index for correct answer)

- a. Consumer privacy
- b. Limited liability
- c. Negotiable instrument
- d. Business method patent

*Guidance:* level 1

:: Accounting systems ::

In bookkeeping, a _____ statement is a process that explains the difference on a specified date between the bank balance shown in an organization's bank statement, as supplied by the bank and the corresponding amount shown in the organization's own accounting records.

Exam Probability: **Low**

57. *Answer choices:*
(see index for correct answer)

- a. Debits and credits
- b. Convention of consistency
- c. Confidence accounting
- d. Bank reconciliation

*Guidance:* level 1

---

:: Financial ratios ::

In finance, the _____ , also known as the acid-test ratio is a type of liquidity ratio which measures the ability of a company to use its near cash or quick assets to extinguish or retire its current liabilities immediately. Quick assets include those current assets that presumably can be quickly converted to cash at close to their book values. It is the ratio between quickly available or liquid assets and current liabilities.

Exam Probability: **Medium**

58. *Answer choices:*
(see index for correct answer)

- a. Debt ratio
- b. Market-to-book
- c. Quick ratio
- d. Average accounting return

*Guidance:* level 1

---

:: Leasing ::

A finance lease is a type of lease in which a finance company is typically the legal owner of the asset for the duration of the lease, while the lessee not only has operating control over the asset, but also has a some share of the economic risks and returns from the change in the valuation of the underlying asset.

Exam Probability: **Medium**

59. *Answer choices:*

(see index for correct answer)

- a. Capital lease
- b. Farmout agreement

*Guidance:* level 1

## Human resource management

Human resource (HR) management is the strategic approach to the effective management of organization workers so that they help the business gain a competitive advantage. It is designed to maximize employee performance in service of an employer's strategic objectives. HR is primarily concerned with the management of people within organizations, focusing on policies and on systems. HR departments are responsible for overseeing employee-benefits design, employee recruitment, training and development, performance appraisal, and rewarding (e.g., managing pay and benefit systems). HR also concerns itself with organizational change and industrial relations, that is, the balancing of organizational practices with requirements arising from collective bargaining and from governmental laws.

---

:: Business law ::

In professional sports, a _____ is a player who is eligible to freely sign with any club or franchise; i.e., not under contract to any specific team. The term is also used in reference to a player who is under contract at present but who is allowed to solicit offers from other teams. In some circumstances, the _____'s options are limited by league rules.

Exam Probability: **Low**

1. *Answer choices:*
(see index for correct answer)

- a. Output contract
- b. Voidable floating charge
- c. Business method patent
- d. Retained interest

*Guidance:* level 1

---

:: Occupational safety and health law ::

The _____ of 1970 is a US labor law governing the federal law of occupational health and safety in the private sector and federal government in the United States. It was enacted by Congress in 1970 and was signed by President Richard Nixon on December 29, 1970. Its main goal is to ensure that employers provide employees with an environment free from recognized hazards, such as exposure to toxic chemicals, excessive noise levels, mechanical dangers, heat or cold stress, or unsanitary conditions. The Act created the Occupational Safety and Health Administration and the National Institute for Occupational Safety and Health .

Exam Probability: **High**

2. *Answer choices:*
(see index for correct answer)

- a. Occupational Safety and Health Act 1994
- b. Mines and Collieries Act 1842
- c. Factory and Workshop Act 1895
- d. Labor Standards Act

*Guidance:* level 1

---

:: Packaging ::

In work place, _____ or job _____ means good ranking with the hypothesized conception of requirements of a role. There are two types of job _____ s: contextual and task. Task _____ is related to cognitive ability while contextual _____ is dependent upon personality. Task _____ are behavioral roles that are recognized in job descriptions and by remuneration systems, they are directly related to organizational _____ , whereas, contextual _____ are value based and additional behavioral roles that are not recognized in job descriptions and covered by compensation; they are extra roles that are indirectly related to organizational _____ . Citizenship _____ like contextual _____ means a set of individual activity/contribution that supports the organizational culture.

Exam Probability: **Low**

3. *Answer choices:*
(see index for correct answer)

- a. Album cover
- b. Tamper-evident

- c. Intermediate bulk container
- d. Performance

*Guidance:* level 1

:: ::

From an accounting perspective, _____ is crucial because _____ and _____ taxes considerably affect the net income of most companies and because they are subject to laws and regulations .

Exam Probability: **Low**

4. *Answer choices:*
(see index for correct answer)

- a. Sarbanes-Oxley act of 2002
- b. Payroll
- c. levels of analysis
- d. imperative

*Guidance:* level 1

:: United States federal labor legislation ::

The _____ of 1967 is a US labor law that forbids employment discrimination against anyone at least 40 years of age in the United States . In 1967, the bill was signed into law by President Lyndon B. Johnson. The ADEA prevents age discrimination and provides equal employment opportunity under conditions that were not explicitly covered in Title VII of the Civil Rights Act of 1964. It also applies to the standards for pensions and benefits provided by employers, and requires that information concerning the needs of older workers be provided to the general public.

Exam Probability: **Medium**

5. *Answer choices:*
(see index for correct answer)

- a. National Industrial Recovery Act
- b. Hiring Incentives to Restore Employment Act
- c. Age Discrimination in Employment Act
- d. Workforce Investment Act of 1998

*Guidance:* level 1

:: Employment compensation ::

A _____ is an agreement between a company and an employee specifying that the employee will receive certain significant benefits if employment is terminated. Most definitions specify the employment termination is as a result of a merger or takeover, also known as "Change-in-control benefits", but more recently the term has been used to describe perceived excessive CEO severance packages unrelated to change in ownership. The benefits may include severance pay, cash bonuses, stock options, or other benefits.

Exam Probability: **Low**

6. *Answer choices:*
(see index for correct answer)

- a. Labour code
- b. Golden parachute
- c. Wages for housework
- d. Spiff

*Guidance:* level 1

:: Human resource management ::

_____ is athletic training in sports other than the athlete's usual sport. The goal is improving overall performance. It takes advantage of the particular effectiveness of one training method to negate the shortcomings of another.

Exam Probability: **Low**

7. *Answer choices:*
(see index for correct answer)

- a. Cross-training
- b. Human relations movement
- c. Job sharing
- d. SLT Human Capital Solutions

*Guidance:* level 1

:: Human resource management ::

An _____ is a software application that enables the electronic handling of recruitment needs. An ATS can be implemented or accessed online on an enterprise or small business level, depending on the needs of the company and there is also free and open source ATS software available. An ATS is very similar to customer relationship management systems, but are designed for recruitment tracking purposes. In many cases they filter applications automatically based on given criteria such as keywords, skills, former employers, years of experience and schools attended. This has caused many to adapt resume optimization techniques similar to those used in search engine optimization when creating and formatting their résumé.

Exam Probability: **Low**

8. *Answer choices:*

(see index for correct answer)

- a. SLT Human Capital Solutions
- b. Talent management system
- c. Applicant tracking system
- d. Organizational culture

*Guidance:* level 1

:: Business terms ::

A _____ is a short statement of why an organization exists, what its overall goal is, identifying the goal of its operations: what kind of product or service it provides, its primary customers or market, and its geographical region of operation. It may include a short statement of such fundamental matters as the organization's values or philosophies, a business's main competitive advantages, or a desired future state—the "vision".

Exam Probability: **Low**

9. *Answer choices:*

(see index for correct answer)

- a. Mission statement
- b. organizational capital
- c. Owner Controlled Insurance Program
- d. year-to-date

*Guidance:* level 1

:: Human resource management ::

The _____ is a free online database that contains hundreds of occupational definitions to help students, job seekers, businesses and workforce development professionals to understand today's world of work in the United States. It was developed under the sponsorship of the US Department of Labor/Employment and Training Administration through a grant to the North Carolina Employment Security Commission during the 1990s. John L. Holland's vocational model, often referred to as the Holland Codes, is used in the "Interests" section of the O*NET.

Exam Probability: **High**

10. *Answer choices:*
(see index for correct answer)

- a. Occupational Information Network
- b. Flextime
- c. Open-book management
- d. Skills management

*Guidance:* level 1

:: Employment discrimination ::

A _____ is a metaphor used to represent an invisible barrier that keeps a given demographic from rising beyond a certain level in a hierarchy.

Exam Probability: **Medium**

11. *Answer choices:*
(see index for correct answer)

- a. Glass cliff
- b. LGBT employment discrimination in the United States
- c. Employment discrimination
- d. Glass ceiling

*Guidance:* level 1

:: ::

_____ is defined by sociologist John R. Schermerhorn as the "...degree to which the people affected by decision are treated by dignity and respect. The theory focuses on the interpersonal treatment people receive when procedures are implemented.

Exam Probability: **Low**

12. *Answer choices:*

(see index for correct answer)

- a. co-culture
- b. Interactional justice
- c. deep-level diversity
- d. imperative

*Guidance:* level 1

:: Belief ::

_____ is an umbrella term of influence. _____ can attempt to influence a person's beliefs, attitudes, intentions, motivations, or behaviors. In business, _____ is a process aimed at changing a person's attitude or behavior toward some event, idea, object, or other person, by using written, spoken words or visual tools to convey information, feelings, or reasoning, or a combination thereof. _____ is also an often used tool in the pursuit of personal gain, such as election campaigning, giving a sales pitch, or in trial advocacy. _____ can also be interpreted as using one's personal or positional resources to change people's behaviors or attitudes.Systematic _____ is the process through which attitudes or beliefs are leveraged by appeals to logic and reason. Heuristic _____ on the other hand is the process through which attitudes or beliefs are leveraged by appeals to habit or emotion.

Exam Probability: **Medium**

13. *Answer choices:*

(see index for correct answer)

- a. Persuasion
- b. Ideological assumption
- c. Availability cascade
- d. Opinio tolerata

*Guidance:* level 1

:: Trade unions in the United States ::

_____ is a labor union in the United States and Canada with roughly 300,000 active members. The union's members work predominantly in the hotel, food service, laundry, warehouse, and casino gaming industries. The union was formed in 2004 by the merger of Union of Needletrades, Industrial, and Textile Employees and Hotel Employees and Restaurant Employees Union.

Exam Probability: **High**

14. *Answer choices:*
(see index for correct answer)

- a. California Nurses Association/National Nurses Organizing Committee
- b. Workers United
- c. UNITE HERE
- d. Amalgamated Lithographers of America

*Guidance:* level 1

:: Employment ::

_____ is a relationship between two parties, usually based on a contract where work is paid for, where one party, which may be a corporation, for profit, not-for-profit organization, co-operative or other entity is the employer and the other is the employee. Employees work in return for payment, which may be in the form of an hourly wage, by piecework or an annual salary, depending on the type of work an employee does or which sector she or he is working in. Employees in some fields or sectors may receive gratuities, bonus payment or stock options. In some types of _____ , employees may receive benefits in addition to payment. Benefits can include health insurance, housing, disability insurance or use of a gym. _____ is typically governed by _____ laws, regulations or legal contracts.

Exam Probability: **Low**

15. *Answer choices:*
(see index for correct answer)

- a. Employment
- b. Work product
- c. Executive Order 10925
- d. Virtual Student Foreign Service

*Guidance:* level 1

---

:: Employment compensation ::

_____ s and benefits in kind include various types of non-wage compensation provided to employees in addition to their normal wages or salaries. Instances where an employee exchanges wages for some other form of benefit is generally referred to as a "salary packaging" or "salary exchange" arrangement. In most countries, most kinds of _____ s are taxable to at least some degree.Examples of these benefits include: housing furnished or not, with or without free utilities; group insurance ; disability income protection; retirement benefits; daycare; tuition reimbursement; sick leave; vacation ; social security; profit sharing; employer student loan contributions; conveyancing; domestic help ; and other specialized benefits.

Exam Probability: **Low**

16. *Answer choices:*
(see index for correct answer)

- a. New York Disability Benefits Law
- b. Commission
- c. Employee benefit
- d. Prevailing wage

*Guidance:* level 1

---

:: Leadership ::

_____ is a theory of leadership where a leader works with teams to identify needed change, creating a vision to guide the change through inspiration, and executing the change in tandem with committed members of a group; it is an integral part of the Full Range Leadership Model. _____ serves to enhance the motivation, morale, and job performance of followers through a variety of mechanisms; these include connecting the follower's sense of identity and self to a project and to the collective identity of the organization; being a role model for followers in order to inspire them and to raise their interest in the project; challenging followers to take greater ownership for their work, and understanding the strengths and weaknesses of followers, allowing the leader to align followers with tasks that enhance their performance.

Exam Probability: **Medium**

17. *Answer choices:*

(see index for correct answer)

- a. Jewish leadership
- b. Transformational leadership
- c. BTS Group
- d. Coro

*Guidance:* level 1

---

:: Workplace ::

A _____ is a process through which feedback from an employee's subordinates, colleagues, and supervisor, as well as a self-evaluation by the employee themselves is gathered. Such feedback can also include, when relevant, feedback from external sources who interact with the employee, such as customers and suppliers or other interested stakeholders. _____ is so named because it solicits feedback regarding an employee's behavior from a variety of points of view . It therefore may be contrasted with "downward feedback" , or "upward feedback" delivered to supervisory or management employees by subordinates only.

Exam Probability: **High**

18. *Answer choices:*

(see index for correct answer)

- a. Workplace violence
- b. 360-degree feedback
- c. Workplace phobia
- d. Staff turnover

*Guidance:* level 1

---

:: Human resource management ::

_____ is the application of information technology for both networking and supporting at least two individual or collective actors in their shared performing of HR activities.

Exam Probability: **High**

19. *Answer choices:*

(see index for correct answer)

- a. Progress, plans, problems
- b. Work activity management
- c. Management by observation
- d. SLT Human Capital Solutions

*Guidance:* level 1

:: ::

_____ is the moral stance, political philosophy, ideology, or social outlook that emphasizes the moral worth of the individual. Individualists promote the exercise of one's goals and desires and so value independence and self-reliance and advocate that interests of the individual should achieve precedence over the state or a social group, while opposing external interference upon one's own interests by society or institutions such as the government. _____ is often defined in contrast to totalitarianism, collectivism, and more corporate social forms.

Exam Probability: **Medium**

20. *Answer choices:*

(see index for correct answer)

- a. Individualism
- b. interpersonal communication
- c. functional perspective
- d. Sarbanes-Oxley act of 2002

*Guidance:* level 1

:: Majority–minority relations ::

_____, also known as reservation in India and Nepal, positive discrimination / action in the United Kingdom, and employment equity in Canada and South Africa, is the policy of promoting the education and employment of members of groups that are known to have previously suffered from discrimination. Historically and internationally, support for _____ has sought to achieve goals such as bridging inequalities in employment and pay, increasing access to education, promoting diversity, and redressing apparent past wrongs, harms, or hindrances.

Exam Probability: **Medium**

21. *Answer choices:*

(see index for correct answer)

- a. Affirmative action
- b. positive discrimination
- c. cultural dissonance

*Guidance:* level 1

:: Human resource management ::

A _____ is a group of people with different functional expertise working toward a common goal. It may include people from finance, marketing, operations, and human resources departments. Typically, it includes employees from all levels of an organization. Members may also come from outside an organization.

Exam Probability: **Low**

22. *Answer choices:*

(see index for correct answer)

- a. Talent management
- b. Cross-functional team
- c. Chief human resources officer
- d. Skills management

*Guidance:* level 1

:: ::

_____ is an important topic of Human Resource Management. It helps develop the career of the individual and the prosperous growth of the organization. On the job training is a form of training provided at the workplace. During the training, employees are familiarized with the working environment they will become part of. Employees also get a hands-on experience using machinery, equipment, tools, materials, etc. Part of is to face the challenges that occur during the performance of the job. An experienced employee or a manager are executing the role of the mentor who through written, or verbal instructions and demonstrations are passing on his/her knowledge and company-specific skills to the new employee. Executing the training on at the job location, rather than the classroom, creates a stress-free environment for the employees. _____ is the most popular method of training not only in the United States but in most of the developed countries, such as the United Kingdom, China, Russia, etc. Its effectiveness is based on the use of existing workplace tools, machines, documents and equipment, and the knowledge of specialists who are working in this field. _____ is easy to arrange and manage and it simplifies the process of adapting to the new workplace. OJT is highly used for practical tasks. It is inexpensive, and it doesn't require special equipment that is normally used for a specific job. Upon satisfaction of completion of the training, the employer is expected to retain participants as regular employees.

Exam Probability: **High**

23. *Answer choices:*

(see index for correct answer)

- a. On-the-job training
- b. hierarchical perspective
- c. imperative
- d. information systems assessment

*Guidance:* level 1

:: ::

_____ is the combination of structured planning and the active management choice of one's own professional career. _____ was first defined in a social work doctoral thesis by Mary Valentich as the implementation of a career strategy through application of career tactics in relation to chosen career orientation. Career orientation referred to the overall design or pattern of one's career, shaped by particular goals and interests and identifiable by particular positions that embody these goals and interests. Career strategy pertains to the individual's general approach to the realization of career goals, and to the specificity of the goals themselves. Two general strategy approaches are adaptive and planned. Career tactics are actions to maintain oneself in a satisfactory employment situation. Tactics may be more or less assertive, with assertiveness in the work situation referring to actions taken to advance one's career interests or to exercise one's legitimate rights while respecting the rights of others.

Exam Probability: **Low**

24. *Answer choices:*

(see index for correct answer)

- a. Career management
- b. levels of analysis
- c. hierarchical
- d. Character

*Guidance:* level 1

:: Social psychology ::

_____ is a type of nonverbal communication in which physical behaviors, as opposed to words, are used to express or convey information. Such behavior includes facial expressions, body posture, gestures, eye movement, touch and the use of space. _____ exists in both animals and humans, but this article focuses on interpretations of human _____. It is also known as kinesics.

Exam Probability: **Medium**

25. *Answer choices:*

(see index for correct answer)

- a. coercive persuasion
- b. brainwriting

- c. objectification
- d. Psychographic

*Guidance:* level 1

---

:: Problem solving ::

A _____ is a unit or formation established to work on a single defined task or activity. Originally introduced by the United States Navy, the term has now caught on for general usage and is a standard part of NATO terminology. Many non-military organizations now create "_____s" or task groups for temporary activities that might have once been performed by ad hoc committees.

Exam Probability: **Medium**

26. *Answer choices:*
(see index for correct answer)

- a. Working memory training
- b. Cognitive acceleration
- c. 5 Whys
- d. Task force

*Guidance:* level 1

---

:: Power (social and political) ::

_____ is a form of reverence gained by a leader who has strong interpersonal relationship skills. _____, as an aspect of personal power, becomes particularly important as organizational leadership becomes increasingly about collaboration and influence, rather than command and control.

Exam Probability: **Medium**

27. *Answer choices:*
(see index for correct answer)

- a. need for power
- b. Expert power
- c. Hard power

*Guidance:* level 1

A _____ is a fund into which a sum of money is added during an employee's employment years, and from which payments are drawn to support the person's retirement from work in the form of periodic payments. A _____ may be a "defined benefit plan" where a fixed sum is paid regularly to a person, or a "defined contribution plan" under which a fixed sum is invested and then becomes available at retirement age. _____ s should not be confused with severance pay; the former is usually paid in regular installments for life after retirement, while the latter is typically paid as a fixed amount after involuntary termination of employment prior to retirement.

Exam Probability: **High**

28. *Answer choices:*
(see index for correct answer)

- a. Pension
- b. similarity-attraction theory
- c. functional perspective
- d. process perspective

*Guidance:* level 1

:: Human resource management ::

_____ is an institutional process that maximizes performance levels and competency for an organization. The process includes all the activities needed to maintain a productive workforce, such as field service management, human resource management, performance and training management, data collection, recruiting, budgeting, forecasting, scheduling and analytics.

Exam Probability: **Low**

29. *Answer choices:*
(see index for correct answer)

- a. Workplace mentoring
- b. Perceived organizational support
- c. Experticity
- d. Workforce management

*Guidance:* level 1

:: United States federal labor legislation ::

The _____ of 1988 is a United States federal law that generally prevents employers from using polygraph tests, either for pre-employment screening or during the course of employment, with certain exemptions.

Exam Probability: **High**

30. *Answer choices:*

(see index for correct answer)

- a. Federal Employers Liability Act
- b. Employee Polygraph Protection Act
- c. Water Resources Development Act of 2007
- d. National Industrial Recovery Act

*Guidance:* level 1

:: Survey methodology ::

An _____ is a conversation where questions are asked and answers are given. In common parlance, the word "_____" refers to a one-on-one conversation between an _____ er and an _____ ee. The _____ er asks questions to which the _____ ee responds, usually so information may be transferred from _____ ee to _____ er. Sometimes, information can be transferred in both directions. It is a communication, unlike a speech, which produces a one-way flow of information.

Exam Probability: **Low**

31. *Answer choices:*

(see index for correct answer)

- a. Enterprise feedback management
- b. Interview
- c. Sampling
- d. World Association for Public Opinion Research

*Guidance:* level 1

:: Teams ::

A _____ usually refers to a group of individuals who work together from different geographic locations and rely on communication technology such as email, FAX, and video or voice conferencing services in order to collaborate. The term can also refer to groups or teams that work together asynchronously or across organizational levels. Powell, Piccoli and Ives define _____ s as "groups of geographically, organizationally and/or time dispersed workers brought together by information and telecommunication technologies to accomplish one or more organizational tasks." According to Ale Ebrahim et. al., _____ s can also be defined as "small temporary groups of geographically, organizationally and/or time dispersed knowledge workers who coordinate their work predominantly with electronic information and communication technologies in order to accomplish one or more organization tasks."

Exam Probability: **High**

32. *Answer choices:*

(see index for correct answer)

- a. team composition
- b. Team-building

*Guidance:* level 1

---

:: Business theory ::

_____ or cultural quotient is a term used in business, education, government and academic research. _____ can be understood as the capability to relate and work effectively across cultures. Originally, the term _____ and the abbreviation "CQ" was developed by the research done by Soon Ang and Linn Van Dyne as a researched-based way of measuring and predicting intercultural performance.

Exam Probability: **Medium**

33. *Answer choices:*

(see index for correct answer)

- a. Six forces model
- b. Communication quotient
- c. Cultural intelligence
- d. Pecking order theory

*Guidance:* level 1

:: Management ::

The term _____ refers to measures designed to increase the degree of autonomy and self-determination in people and in communities in order to enable them to represent their interests in a responsible and self-determined way, acting on their own authority. It is the process of becoming stronger and more confident, especially in controlling one's life and claiming one's rights.
_____ as action refers both to the process of self-_____ and to professional support of people, which enables them to overcome their sense of powerlessness and lack of influence, and to recognize and use their resources. To do work with power.

Exam Probability: **Low**

34. *Answer choices:*
(see index for correct answer)

- a. Omnex
- b. Local management board
- c. Empowerment
- d. Sensemaking

*Guidance:* level 1

:: ::

In organizational behavior and industrial/organizational psychology, proactivity or _____ behavior by individuals refers to anticipatory, change-oriented and self-initiated behavior in situations. _____ behavior involves acting in advance of a future situation, rather than just reacting. It means taking control and making things happen rather than just adjusting to a situation or waiting for something to happen. _____ employees generally do not need to be asked to act, nor do they require detailed instructions.

Exam Probability: **High**

35. *Answer choices:*
(see index for correct answer)

- a. hierarchical perspective
- b. surface-level diversity

- c. Character
- d. Proactive

*Guidance:* level 1

---

:: Labor rights ::

The _____ is the concept that people have a human _____, or engage in productive employment, and may not be prevented from doing so. The _____ is enshrined in the Universal Declaration of Human Rights and recognized in international human rights law through its inclusion in the International Covenant on Economic, Social and Cultural Rights, where the _____ emphasizes economic, social and cultural development.

Exam Probability: **Low**

36. *Answer choices:*

(see index for correct answer)

- a. Right to work
- b. Kate Mullany House
- c. Labor rights
- d. China Labour Bulletin

*Guidance:* level 1

---

:: Trade union legislation ::

The _____ of 1935 is a foundational statute of United States labor law which guarantees the right of private sector employees to organize into trade unions, engage in collective bargaining, and take collective action such as strikes. The act was written by Senator Robert F. Wagner, passed by the 74th United States Congress, and signed into law by President Franklin D. Roosevelt.

Exam Probability: **Medium**

37. *Answer choices:*

(see index for correct answer)

- a. National Labor Relations Act
- b. Employment Act 1980
- c. Employee Free Choice Act
- d. Trade Disputes and Trade Unions Act 1927

*Guidance:* level 1

:: Labor rights ::

A _____ is a wrong or hardship suffered, real or supposed, which forms legitimate grounds of complaint. In the past, the word meant the infliction or cause of hardship.

Exam Probability: **High**

38. *Answer choices:*

(see index for correct answer)

- a. Labor rights
- b. Kim Bobo
- c. Grievance
- d. The Hyatt 100

*Guidance:* level 1

:: Trade unions ::

An _____ is a form of union security agreement where the employer may hire union or non-union workers, and employees need not join the union in order to remain employed. However, the non-union worker must pay a fee to cover collective bargaining costs. The fee paid by non-union members under the _____ is known as the "agency fee".

Exam Probability: **Low**

39. *Answer choices:*

(see index for correct answer)

- a. LabourStart
- b. Agency shop
- c. Givebacks
- d. Independent union

*Guidance:* level 1

:: Unemployment ::

The _____ is the negative relationship between the levels of unemployment and wages that arises when these variables are expressed in local terms. According to David Blanchflower and Andrew Oswald, the _____ summarizes the fact that "A worker who is employed in an area of high unemployment earns less than an identical individual who works in a region with low joblessness."

Exam Probability: **High**

40. *Answer choices:*
(see index for correct answer)

- a. Wage curve
- b. Waithood
- c. Employment protection legislation
- d. Outplacement

*Guidance:* level 1

:: Employee relations ::

_____ ownership, or employee share ownership, is an ownership interest in a company held by the company's workforce. The ownership interest may be facilitated by the company as part of employees' remuneration or incentive compensation for work performed, or the company itself may be employee owned.

Exam Probability: **Low**

41. *Answer choices:*
(see index for correct answer)

- a. Industry Federation of the State of Rio de Janeiro
- b. employee stock ownership
- c. Employee handbook
- d. Employee motivation

*Guidance:* level 1

:: Occupational safety and health ::

A safety data sheet , _____ , or product safety data sheet is a
document that lists information relating to occupational safety and health for
the use of various substances and products. SDSs are a widely used system for
cataloging information on chemicals, chemical compounds, and chemical mixtures.
SDS information may include instructions for the safe use and potential hazards
associated with a particular material or product, along with spill-handling
procedures. SDS formats can vary from source to source within a country
depending on national requirements.

Exam Probability: **Low**

42. *Answer choices:*
(see index for correct answer)

- a. Asbestos-related diseases
- b. Kissing the shuttle
- c. Occupational rehabilitation
- d. Material safety data sheet

*Guidance:* level 1

:: Business law ::

_____ or employment relations is the multidisciplinary academic field
that studies the employment relationship; that is, the complex interrelations
between employers and employees, labor/trade unions, employer organizations and
the state.

Exam Probability: **Low**

43. *Answer choices:*
(see index for correct answer)

- a. Arbitration clause
- b. Chattel mortgage
- c. Industrial relations
- d. Ordinary resolution

*Guidance:* level 1

:: Human resource management ::

_____ refers to the ability of an organization to retain its employees. _____ can be represented by a simple statistic. However, many consider _____ as relating to the efforts by which employers attempt to retain the employees in their workforce. In this sense, retention becomes the strategies rather than the outcome.

Exam Probability: **Medium**

44. *Answer choices:*

(see index for correct answer)

- a. Job analysis
- b. E-HRM
- c. Broadbanding
- d. ROWE

*Guidance:* level 1

:: Unemployment benefits ::

_____ are payments made by back authorized bodies to unemployed people. In the United States, benefits are funded by a compulsory governmental insurance system, not taxes on individual citizens. Depending on the jurisdiction and the status of the person, those sums may be small, covering only basic needs, or may compensate the lost time proportionally to the previous earned salary.

Exam Probability: **High**

45. *Answer choices:*

(see index for correct answer)

- a. Unemployment benefits in Sweden
- b. National Insurance Act 1911
- c. Unemployment benefits in Spain
- d. Kela

*Guidance:* level 1

:: Recruitment ::

Recruitment refers to the overall process of attracting, shortlisting, selecting and appointing suitable candidates for jobs within an organization. Recruitment can also refer to processes involved in choosing individuals for unpaid roles. Managers, human resource generalists and recruitment specialists may be tasked with carrying out recruitment, but in some cases public-sector employment agencies, commercial recruitment agencies, or specialist search consultancies are used to undertake parts of the process. Internet-based technologies which support all aspects of recruitment have become widespread.

Exam Probability: **High**

46. *Answer choices:*

(see index for correct answer)

- a. Blind audition
- b. Social recruiting
- c. Employee referral
- d. Witwatersrand Native Labour Association

*Guidance:* level 1

:: Job interview ::

A _____ is a job interview in which the applicant is presented with a challenging business scenario that he/she must investigate and propose a solution to. _____ s are designed to test the candidate's analytical skills and "soft" skills within a realistic business context. The case is often a business situation or a business case that the interviewer has worked on in real life.

Exam Probability: **Medium**

47. *Answer choices:*

(see index for correct answer)

- a. SOARA
- b. Case interview
- c. Situation, Task, Action, Result
- d. Mock interview

*Guidance:* level 1

:: Business ethics ::

_____ is a pejorative term for a workplace that has very poor, socially unacceptable working conditions. The work may be difficult, dangerous, climatically challenged or underpaid. Workers in _____ s may work long hours with low pay, regardless of laws mandating overtime pay or a minimum wage; child labor laws may also be violated. The Fair Labor Association's "2006 Annual Public Report" inspected factories for FLA compliance in 18 countries including Bangladesh, El Salvador, Colombia, Guatemala, Malaysia, Thailand, Tunisia, Turkey, China, India, Vietnam, Honduras, Indonesia, Brazil, Mexico, and the US. The U.S. Department of Labor's "2015 Findings on the Worst Forms of Child Labor" found that "18 countries did not meet the International Labour Organization's recommendation for an adequate number of inspectors."

Exam Probability: **High**

48. *Answer choices:*
(see index for correct answer)

- a. Workplace bullying
- b. Perfect Relations
- c. Sweatshop
- d. Corporate behaviour

*Guidance:* level 1

:: Industrial agreements ::

_____ is a process in labour relations, where a trade union gains a new and superior entitlement from one employer and then uses that agreement as a precedent to demand the same entitlement or a superior one from other employers.

Exam Probability: **Low**

49. *Answer choices:*
(see index for correct answer)

- a. McCrone Agreement
- b. Court of Arbitration
- c. Conciliation and Arbitration Act 1904
- d. Pattern bargaining

*Guidance:* level 1

:: Workplace ::

A _____ , also referred to as a performance review, performance evaluation, development discussion, or employee appraisal is a method by which the job performance of an employee is documented and evaluated. _____ s are a part of career development and consist of regular reviews of employee performance within organizations.

Exam Probability: **Medium**

50. *Answer choices:*
(see index for correct answer)

- a. Performance appraisal
- b. Control freak
- c. Discrimination based on hair texture
- d. Evaluation

*Guidance:* level 1

---

:: Psychometrics ::

A _____ is a set of categories designed to elicit information about a quantitative or a qualitative attribute. In the social sciences, particularly psychology, common examples are the Likert response scale and 1-10 _____ s in which a person selects the number which is considered to reflect the perceived quality of a product.

Exam Probability: **Low**

51. *Answer choices:*
(see index for correct answer)

- a. Torrance Tests of Creative Thinking
- b. Congruence coefficient
- c. Multidimensional scaling
- d. Prometric

*Guidance:* level 1

---

:: Lean manufacturing ::

_____ is the Sino-Japanese word for "improvement". In business, _____ refers to activities that continuously improve all functions and involve all employees from the CEO to the assembly line workers. It also applies to processes, such as purchasing and logistics, that cross organizational boundaries into the supply chain. It has been applied in healthcare, psychotherapy, life-coaching, government, and banking.

Exam Probability: **High**

52. *Answer choices:*

(see index for correct answer)

- a. Setsuban Kanri
- b. Kaizen
- c. No value added
- d. Overall equipment effectiveness

*Guidance:* level 1

:: ::

The _____ or labour force is the labour pool in employment. It is generally used to describe those working for a single company or industry, but can also apply to a geographic region like a city, state, or country. Within a company, its value can be labelled as its "_____ in Place". The _____ of a country includes both the employed and the unemployed. The labour force participation rate, LFPR, is the ratio between the labour force and the overall size of their cohort. The term generally excludes the employers or management, and can imply those involved in manual labour. It may also mean all those who are available for work.

Exam Probability: **High**

53. *Answer choices:*

(see index for correct answer)

- a. levels of analysis
- b. deep-level diversity
- c. open system
- d. information systems assessment

*Guidance:* level 1

:: Industrial engineering ::

_____ is the formal process that sits alongside Requirements analysis and focuses on the human elements of the requirements.

Exam Probability: **Low**

54. *Answer choices:*
(see index for correct answer)

- a. Needs analysis
- b. PFD allowance
- c. Work sampling
- d. Bayesian experimental design

*Guidance:* level 1

---

:: Behavior ::

_____ refers to behavior-change procedures that were employed during the 1970s and early 1980s. Based on methodological behaviorism, overt behavior was modified with presumed consequences, including artificial positive and negative reinforcement contingencies to increase desirable behavior, or administering positive and negative punishment and/or extinction to reduce problematic behavior. For the treatment of phobias, habituation and punishment were the basic principles used in flooding, a subcategory of desensitization.

Exam Probability: **High**

55. *Answer choices:*
(see index for correct answer)

- a. Behavior modification
- b. theory of reasoned action

*Guidance:* level 1

---

:: Human resource management ::

_____ is the strategic approach to the effective management of people in an organization so that they help the business to gain a competitive advantage. It is designed to maximize employee performance in service of an employer's strategic objectives. HR is primarily concerned with the management of people within organizations, focusing on policies and on systems. HR departments are responsible for overseeing employee-benefits design, employee recruitment, training and development, performance appraisal, and Reward management. HR also concerns itself with organizational change and industrial relations, that is, the balancing of organizational practices with requirements arising from collective bargaining and from governmental laws.

Exam Probability: **Medium**

56. *Answer choices:*
(see index for correct answer)

- a. Employee exit management
- b. Incentive program
- c. Workforce sciences
- d. Management by objectives

*Guidance:* level 1

---

:: Recruitment ::

The _____ is an American nonprofit professional association established in 1956 in Bethlehem, Pennsylvania, for college career services, recruiting practitioners, and others who wish to hire the college educated.

Exam Probability: **Medium**

57. *Answer choices:*
(see index for correct answer)

- a. National Association of Colleges and Employers
- b. Background check
- c. Graduate recruitment
- d. Golden hello

*Guidance:* level 1

---

:: ::

The causes of _____ are heavily debated. Classical economics, new classical economics, and the Austrian School of economics argued that market mechanisms are reliable means of resolving _____ . These theories argue against interventions imposed on the labor market from the outside, such as unionization, bureaucratic work rules, minimum wage laws, taxes, and other regulations that they claim discourage the hiring of workers. Keynesian economics emphasizes the cyclical nature of _____ and recommends government interventions in the economy that it claims will reduce _____ during recessions. This theory focuses on recurrent shocks that suddenly reduce aggregate demand for goods and services and thus reduce demand for workers. Keynesian models recommend government interventions designed to increase demand for workers; these can include financial stimuli, publicly funded job creation, and expansionist monetary policies. Its namesake economist, John Maynard Keynes, believed that the root cause of _____ is the desire of investors to receive more money rather than produce more products, which is not possible without public bodies producing new money. A third group of theories emphasize the need for a stable supply of capital and investment to maintain full employment. On this view, government should guarantee full employment through fiscal policy, monetary policy and trade policy as stated, for example, in the US Employment Act of 1946, by counteracting private sector or trade investment volatility, and reducing inequality.

Exam Probability: **Low**

58. *Answer choices:*
(see index for correct answer)

- a. functional perspective
- b. similarity-attraction theory
- c. Unemployment
- d. personal values

*Guidance:* level 1

:: Learning methods ::

_____ is an approach to problem solving. It involves taking action and reflecting upon the results. This helps improve the problem-solving process as well as simplify the solutions developed by the team.

Exam Probability: **High**

59. *Answer choices:*
(see index for correct answer)

- a. Action learning
- b. Collaborative learning
- c. double loop learning
- d. Double-loop learning

*Guidance:* level 1

### Information systems

Information systems (IS) are formal, sociotechnical, organizational systems designed to collect, process, store, and distribute information. In a sociotechnical perspective Information Systems are composed by four components: technology, process, people and organizational structure.

---

:: Marketing ::

_____ is a business model in which consumers create value and businesses consume that value. For example, when a consumer writes reviews or when a consumer gives a useful idea for new product development then that consumer is creating value for the business if the business adopts the input.
In the C2B model, a reverse auction or demand collection model, enables buyers to name or demand their own price, which is often binding, for a specific good or service. Inside of a consumer to business market the roles involved in the transaction must be established and the consumer must offer something of value to the business.

Exam Probability: **Medium**

1. *Answer choices:*
(see index for correct answer)

- a. Consumer-to-business
- b. Ameritest
- c. Corporate identity
- d. Pick and pack

*Guidance:* level 1

---

:: Data security ::

_____ , sometimes shortened to InfoSec, is the practice of preventing unauthorized access, use, disclosure, disruption, modification, inspection, recording or destruction of information. The information or data may take any form, e.g. electronic or physical. _____ 's primary focus is the balanced protection of the confidentiality, integrity and availability of data while maintaining a focus on efficient policy implementation, all without hampering organization productivity. This is largely achieved through a multi-step risk management process that identifies assets, threat sources, vulnerabilities, potential impacts, and possible controls, followed by assessment of the effectiveness of the risk management plan.

Exam Probability: **Low**

2. *Answer choices:*
(see index for correct answer)

- a. National Industrial Security Program
- b. Relocatable user backup
- c. Transient-key cryptography
- d. Information security

*Guidance:* level 1

---

:: Data management ::

A _____ is a place where you can store data. Commonly used to refer to a column in a database or a field in a data entry form or web form.

Exam Probability: **High**

3. *Answer choices:*
(see index for correct answer)

- a. Content management
- b. British Oceanographic Data Centre
- c. Data field
- d. Uniform data access

*Guidance:* level 1

---

:: Information technology management ::

_____ is the use of software to control machine tools and related ones in the manufacturing of workpieces. This is not the only definition for CAM, but it is the most common; CAM may also refer to the use of a computer to assist in all operations of a manufacturing plant, including planning, management, transportation and storage. Its primary purpose is to create a faster production process and components and tooling with more precise dimensions and material consistency, which in some cases, uses only the required amount of raw material, while simultaneously reducing energy consumption. CAM is now a system used in schools and lower educational purposes. CAM is a subsequent computer-aided process after computer-aided design and sometimes computer-aided engineering, as the model generated in CAD and verified in CAE can be input into CAM software, which then controls the machine tool. CAM is used in many schools alongside Computer-Aided Design to create objects.

Exam Probability: **Low**

4. *Answer choices:*

(see index for correct answer)

- a. Runbook
- b. Computer-aided manufacturing
- c. HP Open Extensibility Platform
- d. Cable management

*Guidance:* level 1

:: ::

_____ is a set of documents provided on paper, or online, or on digital or analog media, such as audio tape or CDs. Examples are user guides, white papers, on-line help, quick-reference guides. It is becoming less common to see paper _____. _____ is distributed via websites, software products, and other on-line applications.

Exam Probability: **Medium**

5. *Answer choices:*

(see index for correct answer)

- a. Documentation
- b. personal values
- c. corporate values

- d. surface-level diversity

*Guidance:* level 1

---

:: Cloud storage ::

_____ was an online backup service for both Windows and macOS users. Linux support was made available in Q3, 2014. In 2007 _____ was acquired by EMC, and in 2013 _____ was included in the EMC Backup Recovery Systems division's product list.On September 7, 2016, Dell Inc. acquired EMC Corporation to form Dell Technologies, restructuring the original Dell Inc. as a subsidiary of Dell Technologies.. On March 19, 2018 Carbonite acquired _____ from Dell for $148.5 million in cash and in 2019 shut down the service, incorporating _____ 's clients into its own online backup service programs.

Exam Probability: **Low**

6. *Answer choices:*

(see index for correct answer)

- a. GreenQloud
- b. DocumentCloud
- c. Cooperative storage cloud
- d. SlideRocket

*Guidance:* level 1

---

:: Knowledge engineering ::

The _____ is an extension of the World Wide Web through standards by the World Wide Web Consortium . The standards promote common data formats and exchange protocols on the Web, most fundamentally the Resource Description Framework . According to the W3C, "The _____ provides a common framework that allows data to be shared and reused across application, enterprise, and community boundaries". The _____ is therefore regarded as an integrator across different content, information applications and systems.

Exam Probability: **Medium**

7. *Answer choices:*

(see index for correct answer)

- a. DTRules
- b. Knowledge level modeling
- c. International Journal of Software Engineering and Knowledge Engineering
- d. Semantic Web

*Guidance:* level 1

:: ::

_____ is software designed to provide a platform for other software. Examples of _____ include operating systems like macOS, Ubuntu and Microsoft Windows, computational science software, game engines, industrial automation, and software as a service applications.

Exam Probability: **Medium**

8. *Answer choices:*

(see index for correct answer)

- a. hierarchical
- b. Sarbanes-Oxley act of 2002
- c. personal values
- d. System software

*Guidance:* level 1

:: Industrial design ::

Across the many fields concerned with _____ , including information science, computer science, human-computer interaction, communication, and industrial design, there is little agreement over the meaning of the term " _____ ", although all are related to interaction with computers and other machines with a user interface.

Exam Probability: **High**

9. *Answer choices:*

(see index for correct answer)

- a. Dimension
- b. Deutscher Werkbund
- c. Interactivity
- d. Constructal law

*Guidance:* level 1

:: ::

A _____ or data centre is a building, dedicated space within a building, or a group of buildings used to house computer systems and associated components, such as telecommunications and storage systems.

Exam Probability: **Medium**

10. *Answer choices:*

(see index for correct answer)

- a. Data center
- b. process perspective
- c. hierarchical
- d. functional perspective

*Guidance:* level 1

:: Business ::

_____ is a sourcing model in which individuals or organizations obtain goods and services, including ideas and finances, from a large, relatively open and often rapidly-evolving group of internet users; it divides work between participants to achieve a cumulative result. The word _____ itself is a portmanteau of crowd and outsourcing, and was coined in 2005. As a mode of sourcing, _____ existed prior to the digital age.

Exam Probability: **Medium**

11. *Answer choices:*

(see index for correct answer)

- a. Crowdsourcing
- b. Street marketing
- c. Legal governance, risk management, and compliance
- d. Intangible asset finance

*Guidance:* level 1

:: Intelligence (information gathering) ::

_____ comprises the strategies and technologies used by enterprises for the data analysis of business information. BI technologies provide historical, current and predictive views of business operations. Common functions of _____ technologies include reporting, online analytical processing, analytics, data mining, process mining, complex event processing, business performance management, benchmarking, text mining, predictive analytics and prescriptive analytics. BI technologies can handle large amounts of structured and sometimes unstructured data to help identify, develop and otherwise create new strategic business opportunities. They aim to allow for the easy interpretation of these big data. Identifying new opportunities and implementing an effective strategy based on insights can provide businesses with a competitive market advantage and long-term stability.

Exam Probability: **High**

12. *Answer choices:*
(see index for correct answer)

- a. Semantic Intelligence
- b. Advanced Technical Intelligence Center
- c. Central media
- d. Criminal intelligence

*Guidance:* level 1

---

:: Survey methodology ::

A _____ is the procedure of systematically acquiring and recording information about the members of a given population. The term is used mostly in connection with national population and housing _____ es; other common _____ es include agriculture, business, and traffic _____ es. The United Nations defines the essential features of population and housing _____ es as "individual enumeration, universality within a defined territory, simultaneity and defined periodicity", and recommends that population _____ es be taken at least every 10 years. United Nations recommendations also cover _____ topics to be collected, official definitions, classifications and other useful information to co-ordinate international practice.

Exam Probability: **Medium**

13. *Answer choices:*

(see index for correct answer)

- a. American Association for Public Opinion Research
- b. Enterprise feedback management
- c. Census
- d. Scale analysis

*Guidance:* level 1

:: Payment systems ::

An _____ is an electronic telecommunications device that enables customers of financial institutions to perform financial transactions, such as cash withdrawals, deposits, transfer funds, or obtaining account information, at any time and without the need for direct interaction with bank staff.

Exam Probability: **Medium**

14. *Answer choices:*

(see index for correct answer)

- a. BPAY
- b. SuperRewards
- c. 1LINK
- d. EDesk

*Guidance:* level 1

:: Management ::

_____ is the discipline of strategically planning for, and managing, all interactions with third party organizations that supply goods and/or services to an organization in order to maximize the value of those interactions. In practice, SRM entails creating closer, more collaborative relationships with key suppliers in order to uncover and realize new value and reduce risk of failure.

Exam Probability: **Medium**

15. *Answer choices:*

(see index for correct answer)

- a. Integrated master plan
- b. Double linking

- c. Supplier relationship management
- d. Reval

*Guidance:* level 1

---

:: Information technology management ::

_____ within quality management systems and information technology systems is a process—either formal or informal—used to ensure that changes to a product or system are introduced in a controlled and coordinated manner. It reduces the possibility that unnecessary changes will be introduced to a system without forethought, introducing faults into the system or undoing changes made by other users of software. The goals of a _____ procedure usually include minimal disruption to services, reduction in back-out activities, and cost-effective utilization of resources involved in implementing change.

Exam Probability: **Low**

16. *Answer choices:*
(see index for correct answer)

- a. Change control
- b. Enterprise IT Management
- c. Automic
- d. OpenACS

*Guidance:* level 1

---

:: Procurement practices ::

_____ or commercially available off-the-shelf products are packaged solutions which are then adapted to satisfy the needs of the purchasing organization, rather than the commissioning of custom-made, or bespoke, solutions. A related term, Mil-COTS, refers to COTS products for use by the U.S. military.

Exam Probability: **Low**

17. *Answer choices:*
(see index for correct answer)

- a. Construction by configuration
- b. Syndicated procurement

*Guidance:* level 1

:: E-commerce ::

_____ , cybersecurity or information technology security is the protection of computer systems from theft or damage to their hardware, software or electronic data, as well as from disruption or misdirection of the services they provide.

Exam Probability: **High**

18. *Answer choices:*

(see index for correct answer)

- a. Electronic commerce
- b. Computer security
- c. Cleaning card
- d. Ven

*Guidance:* level 1

:: Internet governance ::

A _____ is one of the domains at the highest level in the hierarchical Domain Name System of the Internet. The _____ names are installed in the root zone of the name space. For all domains in lower levels, it is the last part of the domain name, that is, the last label of a fully qualified domain name. For example, in the domain name www.example.com, the _____ is com. Responsibility for management of most _____ s is delegated to specific organizations by the Internet Corporation for Assigned Names and Numbers , which operates the Internet Assigned Numbers Authority , and is in charge of maintaining the DNS root zone.

Exam Probability: **Medium**

19. *Answer choices:*

(see index for correct answer)

- a. Internet organizations
- b. Top-level domain
- c. Adrian Kinderis
- d. Uniform Domain-Name Dispute-Resolution Policy

*Guidance:* level 1

:: Production and manufacturing ::

_____ is the manufacturing approach of using computers to control entire production process. This integration allows individual processes to exchange information with each other and initiate actions. Although manufacturing can be faster and less error-prone by the integration of computers, the main advantage is the ability to create automated manufacturing processes. Typically CIM relies of closed-loop control processes, based on real-time input from sensors. It is also known as flexible design and manufacturing.

Exam Probability: **Medium**

20. *Answer choices:*
(see index for correct answer)

- a. Virtual manufacturing network
- b. Order to cash
- c. PA512
- d. Computer-integrated manufacturing

*Guidance:* level 1

:: Sound recording ::

_____ is a medium for magnetic recording, made of a thin, magnetizable coating on a long, narrow strip of plastic film. It was developed in Germany in 1928, based on magnetic wire recording. Devices that record and play back audio and video using _____ are tape recorders and video tape recorders respectively. A device that stores computer data on _____ is known as a tape drive.

Exam Probability: **High**

21. *Answer choices:*
(see index for correct answer)

- a. Voice banking
- b. Tape recorder
- c. School of Sound Recording
- d. Pitch shift

*Guidance:* level 1

:: Data ::

_____ is viewed by many disciplines as a modern equivalent of visual communication. It involves the creation and study of the visual representation of data.

Exam Probability: **Low**

22. *Answer choices:*
(see index for correct answer)

- a. Biological data
- b. Empress Embedded Database
- c. Statistics
- d. Data visualization

*Guidance:* level 1

:: Google services ::

_____ is a time-management and scheduling calendar service developed by Google. It became available in beta release April 13, 2006, and in general release in July 2009, on the web and as mobile apps for the Android and iOS platforms.

Exam Probability: **Medium**

23. *Answer choices:*
(see index for correct answer)

- a. Google Books Library Project
- b. AdWords
- c. Picasa
- d. Google Sites

*Guidance:* level 1

:: Telecommunication theory ::

In reliability theory and reliability engineering, the term _____ has the following meanings.

Exam Probability: **Low**

24. *Answer choices:*

(see index for correct answer)

- a. Root-raised-cosine filter
- b. Round-trip delay time
- c. Availability
- d. Electrical length

*Guidance:* level 1

:: Payment systems ::

A _____ is any system used to settle financial transactions through the transfer of monetary value. This includes the institutions, instruments, people, rules, procedures, standards, and technologies that make it exchange possible. A common type of _____ is called an operational network that links bank accounts and provides for monetary exchange using bank deposits. Some _____ s also include credit mechanisms, which are essentially a different aspect of payment.

Exam Probability: **Medium**

25. *Answer choices:*

(see index for correct answer)

- a. Money transmitter
- b. Argentum album
- c. Transit check
- d. Payment system

*Guidance:* level 1

:: Data privacy ::

_____ is the relationship between the collection and dissemination of data, technology, the public expectation of privacy, legal and political issues surrounding them. It is also known as data privacy or data protection.

Exam Probability: **Low**

26. *Answer choices:*

(see index for correct answer)

- a. Information privacy
- b. ChoicePoint

- c. Personal Data Privacy and Security Act of 2009
- d. Client confidentiality

*Guidance:* level 1

---

:: Data management ::

_____ is a data management concept concerning the capability that enables an organization to ensure that high data quality exists throughout the complete lifecycle of the data. The key focus areas of _____ include availability, usability, consistency, data integrity and data security and includes establishing processes to ensure effective data management throughout the enterprise such as accountability for the adverse effects of poor data quality and ensuring that the data which an enterprise has can be used by the entire organization.

Exam Probability: **Low**

27. *Answer choices:*
(see index for correct answer)

- a. Data classification
- b. Data governance
- c. PL/Perl
- d. ROOT

*Guidance:* level 1

---

:: ::

In linguistics, a _____ is the smallest element that can be uttered in isolation with objective or practical meaning.

Exam Probability: **Medium**

28. *Answer choices:*
(see index for correct answer)

- a. hierarchical
- b. Character
- c. levels of analysis
- d. personal values

*Guidance:* level 1

:: Transaction processing ::

In _____ , information systems typically facilitate and manage transaction-oriented applications.

Exam Probability: **Medium**

29. *Answer choices:*
(see index for correct answer)

- a. Online transaction processing
- b. Transaction Processing Facility
- c. Oracle Coherence
- d. Tuxedo

*Guidance:* level 1

:: Information technology management ::

B2B is often contrasted with business-to-consumer . In B2B commerce, it is often the case that the parties to the relationship have comparable negotiating power, and even when they do not, each party typically involves professional staff and legal counsel in the negotiation of terms, whereas B2C is shaped to a far greater degree by economic implications of information asymmetry. However, within a B2B context, large companies may have many commercial, resource and information advantages over smaller businesses. The United Kingdom government, for example, created the post of Small Business Commissioner under the Enterprise Act 2016 to "enable small businesses to resolve disputes" and "consider complaints by small business suppliers about payment issues with larger businesses that they supply."

Exam Probability: **High**

30. *Answer choices:*
(see index for correct answer)

- a. Imaging for Windows
- b. Prolifics
- c. CatDV
- d. Business-to-business

*Guidance:* level 1

:: Virtual economies ::

_____ Inc. is an American social game developer running social video game services founded in April 2007 and headquartered in San Francisco, California, United States. The company primarily focuses on mobile and social networking platforms. _____ states its mission as "connecting the world through games."

Exam Probability: **Low**

31. *Answer choices:*

(see index for correct answer)

- a. Massively multiplayer online real-time strategy game
- b. Star Wars Galaxies
- c. Zynga
- d. There

*Guidance:* level 1

:: Financial markets ::

The _____ business model is a business model in which a customer must pay a recurring price at regular intervals for access to a product or service. The model was pioneered by publishers of books and periodicals in the 17th century, and is now used by many businesses and websites.

Exam Probability: **High**

32. *Answer choices:*

(see index for correct answer)

- a. Price-weighted index
- b. Subscription
- c. Capital market
- d. Limits to arbitrage

*Guidance:* level 1

:: Data transmission ::

In telecommunication a _____ is the means of connecting one location to another for the purpose of transmitting and receiving digital information. It can also refer to a set of electronics assemblies, consisting of a transmitter and a receiver and the interconnecting data telecommunication circuit. These are governed by a link protocol enabling digital data to be transferred from a data source to a data sink.

Exam Probability: **Medium**

33. *Answer choices:*
(see index for correct answer)

- a. Data link
- b. Bit-count integrity
- c. Syncword
- d. Reliable byte stream

*Guidance:* level 1

:: ::

_____ Holdings, Inc. is an American company operating a worldwide online payments system that supports online money transfers and serves as an electronic alternative to traditional paper methods like checks and money orders. The company operates as a payment processor for online vendors, auction sites, and many other commercial users, for which it charges a fee in exchange for benefits such as one-click transactions and password memory. _____'s payment system, also called _____, is considered a type of payment rail.

Exam Probability: **High**

34. *Answer choices:*
(see index for correct answer)

- a. functional perspective
- b. deep-level diversity
- c. imperative
- d. hierarchical

*Guidance:* level 1

:: Data analysis ::

_____ is a process of inspecting, cleansing, transforming, and modeling data with the goal of discovering useful information, informing conclusions, and supporting decision-making. _____ has multiple facets and approaches, encompassing diverse techniques under a variety of names, and is used in different business, science, and social science domains. In today's business world, _____ plays a role in making decisions more scientific and helping businesses operate more effectively.

Exam Probability: **Low**

35. *Answer choices:*
(see index for correct answer)

- a. Photoanalysis
- b. Subgroup analysis
- c. Visual comparison
- d. Data analysis

*Guidance:* level 1

:: ::

The _____, commonly known as the Web, is an information system where documents and other web resources are identified by Uniform Resource Locators, which may be interlinked by hypertext, and are accessible over the Internet. The resources of the WWW may be accessed by users by a software application called a web browser.

Exam Probability: **Medium**

36. *Answer choices:*
(see index for correct answer)

- a. similarity-attraction theory
- b. cultural
- c. levels of analysis
- d. World Wide Web

*Guidance:* level 1

:: Web security exploits ::

A _____ is a baked or cooked food that is small, flat and sweet. It usually contains flour, sugar and some type of oil or fat. It may include other ingredients such as raisins, oats, chocolate chips, nuts, etc.

Exam Probability: **High**

37. *Answer choices:*

(see index for correct answer)

- a. Web threat
- b. Reflected DOM Injection
- c. Cross-site request forgery
- d. Cookie

*Guidance:* level 1

:: Critical thinking ::

In psychology, _____ is regarded as the cognitive process resulting in the selection of a belief or a course of action among several alternative possibilities. Every _____ process produces a final choice, which may or may not prompt action.

Exam Probability: **Medium**

38. *Answer choices:*

(see index for correct answer)

- a. Explanation
- b. Explanatory power
- c. Scientific temper
- d. Decision-making

*Guidance:* level 1

:: Identity management ::

_____ is the ability of an individual or group to seclude themselves, or information about themselves, and thereby express themselves selectively. The boundaries and content of what is considered private differ among cultures and individuals, but share common themes. When something is private to a person, it usually means that something is inherently special or sensitive to them. The domain of _____ partially overlaps with security, which can include the concepts of appropriate use, as well as protection of information. _____ may also take the form of bodily integrity.

Exam Probability: **Low**

39. *Answer choices:*
(see index for correct answer)

- a. Privacy
- b. Identity change
- c. Identity assurance
- d. EduGAIN

*Guidance:* level 1

:: Information systems ::

_____ is the process of creating, sharing, using and managing the knowledge and information of an organisation. It refers to a multidisciplinary approach to achieving organisational objectives by making the best use of knowledge.

Exam Probability: **High**

40. *Answer choices:*
(see index for correct answer)

- a. Knowledge management
- b. Xcon
- c. Information Systems Security Association
- d. Process development execution system

*Guidance:* level 1

:: Tag editors ::

_____ is a media player, media library, Internet radio broadcaster, and mobile device management application developed by Apple Inc. It was announced on January 9, 2001. It is used to play, download, and organize digital multimedia files, including music and video, on personal computers running the macOS and Windows operating systems. Content must be purchased through the _____ Store, whereas _____ is the software letting users manage their purchases.

Exam Probability: **High**

41. *Answer choices:*

(see index for correct answer)

- a. Ex Falso
- b. Quod Libet
- c. Mp3tag
- d. QuuxPlayer

*Guidance:* level 1

:: ::

_____ is software designed to perform a group of coordinated functions, tasks, or activities for the benefit of the user. Examples of an application include a word processor, a spreadsheet, an accounting application, a web browser, an email client, a media player, a file viewer, an aeronautical flight simulator, a console game or a photo editor. The collective noun _____ refers to all applications collectively. This contrasts with system software, which is mainly involved with running the computer.

Exam Probability: **Low**

42. *Answer choices:*

(see index for correct answer)

- a. process perspective
- b. deep-level diversity
- c. corporate values
- d. Character

*Guidance:* level 1

:: Data ::

_____ is a branch of mathematics working with data collection, organization, analysis, interpretation and presentation. In applying _____ to, for example, a scientific, industrial, or social problem, it is conventional to begin with a statistical population or a statistical model process to be studied. Populations can be diverse topics such as "all people living in a country" or "every atom composing a crystal". _____ deals with every aspect of data, including the planning of data collection in terms of the design of surveys and experiments. See glossary of probability and _____ .

Exam Probability: **Medium**

43. *Answer choices:*
(see index for correct answer)

- a. Dummy data
- b. Serial concatenated convolutional codes
- c. primary data
- d. Data citation

*Guidance:* level 1

:: Google services ::

_____ is a web mapping service developed by Google. It offers satellite imagery, aerial photography, street maps, 360° panoramic views of streets, real-time traffic conditions, and route planning for traveling by foot, car, bicycle and air , or public transportation.

Exam Probability: **Low**

44. *Answer choices:*
(see index for correct answer)

- a. Google Developers
- b. Google Custom Search
- c. A Google A Day
- d. Blogger

*Guidance:* level 1

:: Data management ::

_____ , or OLAP , is an approach to answer multi-dimensional analytical queries swiftly in computing. OLAP is part of the broader category of business intelligence, which also encompasses relational databases, report writing and data mining. Typical applications of OLAP include business reporting for sales, marketing, management reporting, business process management , budgeting and forecasting, financial reporting and similar areas, with new applications emerging, such as agriculture. The term OLAP was created as a slight modification of the traditional database term online transaction processing .

Exam Probability: **High**

45. *Answer choices:*

(see index for correct answer)

- a. Online analytical processing
- b. Asset Description Metadata Schema
- c. ROOT
- d. Database server

*Guidance:* level 1

:: Management ::

The _____ is a strategy performance management tool – a semi-standard structured report, that can be used by managers to keep track of the execution of activities by the staff within their control and to monitor the consequences arising from these actions.

Exam Probability: **High**

46. *Answer choices:*

(see index for correct answer)

- a. Balanced scorecard
- b. Telescopic observations strategic framework
- c. Dominant design
- d. Management buyout

*Guidance:* level 1

:: ::

_____ is a kind of action that occur as two or more objects have an effect upon one another. The idea of a two-way effect is essential in the concept of _____, as opposed to a one-way causal effect. A closely related term is interconnectivity, which deals with the _____ s of _____ s within systems: combinations of many simple _____ s can lead to surprising emergent phenomena. _____ has different tailored meanings in various sciences. Changes can also involve _____.

Exam Probability: **Low**

47. *Answer choices:*
(see index for correct answer)

- a. similarity-attraction theory
- b. information systems assessment
- c. cultural
- d. Sarbanes-Oxley act of 2002

*Guidance:* level 1

:: Internet marketing ::

_____ is the process of increasing the quality and quantity of website traffic, increasing visibility of a website or a web page to users of a web search engine.SEO refers to the improvement of unpaid results , and excludes the purchase of paid placement.

Exam Probability: **Low**

48. *Answer choices:*
(see index for correct answer)

- a. Search engine optimization
- b. Organization of Search Engine Optimization Professionals
- c. Social media optimization
- d. SocialFlow

*Guidance:* level 1

:: Information technology ::

_____ is the use of computers to store, retrieve, transmit, and manipulate data, or information, often in the context of a business or other enterprise. IT is considered to be a subset of information and communications technology. An _____ system is generally an information system, a communications system or, more specifically speaking, a computer system – including all hardware, software and peripheral equipment – operated by a limited group of users.

Exam Probability: **High**

49. *Answer choices:*

(see index for correct answer)

- a. Information technology
- b. Design for All
- c. SPAN Infotech
- d. Antlabs

*Guidance:* level 1

:: Data quality ::

_____ is the maintenance of, and the assurance of the accuracy and consistency of, data over its entire life-cycle, and is a critical aspect to the design, implementation and usage of any system which stores, processes, or retrieves data. The term is broad in scope and may have widely different meanings depending on the specific context even under the same general umbrella of computing. It is at times used as a proxy term for data quality, while data validation is a pre-requisite for _____ . _____ is the opposite of data corruption. The overall intent of any _____ technique is the same: ensure data is recorded exactly as intended and upon later retrieval, ensure the data is the same as it was when it was originally recorded. In short, _____ aims to prevent unintentional changes to information. _____ is not to be confused with data security, the discipline of protecting data from unauthorized parties.

Exam Probability: **High**

50. *Answer choices:*

(see index for correct answer)

- a. Data integrity
- b. Data degradation

- c. Link rot
- d. Data quality assessment

*Guidance:* level 1

---

:: Distribution, retailing, and wholesaling ::

_____ measures the performance of a system. Certain goals are defined and the _____ gives the percentage to which those goals should be achieved. Fill rate is different from _____ .

Exam Probability: **Low**

51. *Answer choices:*

(see index for correct answer)

- a. Service level
- b. Teleflorist
- c. Diamond Comic Distributors
- d. Fast Fiction

*Guidance:* level 1

---

:: Digital rights management ::

_____ tools or technological protection measures are a set of access control technologies for restricting the use of proprietary hardware and copyrighted works. DRM technologies try to control the use, modification, and distribution of copyrighted works , as well as systems within devices that enforce these policies.

Exam Probability: **Medium**

52. *Answer choices:*

(see index for correct answer)

- a. Content Scramble System
- b. The Pig and the Box
- c. Digital rights management
- d. Rightscorp, Inc.

*Guidance:* level 1

---

:: Strategic management ::

_____ is a management term for an element that is necessary for an organization or project to achieve its mission. Alternative terms are key result area and key success factor.

Exam Probability: **Medium**

53. *Answer choices:*
(see index for correct answer)

- a. Strategic delegation
- b. Functional Strategy
- c. Critical success factor
- d. VRIO

*Guidance:* level 1

:: Global Positioning System ::

The _____, originally Navstar GPS, is a satellite-based radionavigation system owned by the United States government and operated by the United States Air Force. It is a global navigation satellite system that provides geolocation and time information to a GPS receiver anywhere on or near the Earth where there is an unobstructed line of sight to four or more GPS satellites. Obstacles such as mountains and buildings block the relatively weak GPS signals.

Exam Probability: **Medium**

54. *Answer choices:*
(see index for correct answer)

- a. Dash Express
- b. Earthscope
- c. RailRider
- d. Global Positioning System

*Guidance:* level 1

:: Data management ::

An _____ is any kind of information system which improves the functions of enterprise business processes by integration. This means typically offering high quality of service, dealing with large volumes of data and capable of supporting some large and possibly complex organization or enterprise. An EIS must be able to be used by all parts and all levels of an enterprise.

Exam Probability: **Low**

55. *Answer choices:*

(see index for correct answer)

- a. Electronically stored information
- b. Data dictionary
- c. Enterprise information system
- d. Content repository

*Guidance:* level 1

---

:: Advertising techniques ::

The _____ is a story from the Trojan War about the subterfuge that the Greeks used to enter the independent city of Troy and win the war. In the canonical version, after a fruitless 10-year siege, the Greeks constructed a huge wooden horse, and hid a select force of men inside including Odysseus. The Greeks pretended to sail away, and the Trojans pulled the horse into their city as a victory trophy. That night the Greek force crept out of the horse and opened the gates for the rest of the Greek army, which had sailed back under cover of night. The Greeks entered and destroyed the city of Troy, ending the war.

Exam Probability: **Medium**

56. *Answer choices:*

(see index for correct answer)

- a. Trojan horse
- b. Debranding
- c. FAST marketing
- d. Roll-in

*Guidance:* level 1

:: ::

A _____ is a discussion or informational website published on the World Wide Web consisting of discrete, often informal diary-style text entries. Posts are typically displayed in reverse chronological order, so that the most recent post appears first, at the top of the web page. Until 2009, _____ s were usually the work of a single individual, occasionally of a small group, and often covered a single subject or topic. In the 2010s, "multi-author _____ s" emerged, featuring the writing of multiple authors and sometimes professionally edited. MABs from newspapers, other media outlets, universities, think tanks, advocacy groups, and similar institutions account for an increasing quantity of _____ traffic. The rise of Twitter and other "micro _____ ging" systems helps integrate MABs and single-author _____ s into the news media. _____ can also be used as a verb, meaning to maintain or add content to a _____ .

Exam Probability: **Medium**

57. *Answer choices:*

(see index for correct answer)

- a. similarity-attraction theory
- b. functional perspective
- c. Blog
- d. open system

*Guidance:* level 1

:: E-commerce ::

_____ generally refer to payment services operated under financial regulation and performed from or via a mobile device. Instead of paying with cash, cheque, or credit cards, a consumer can use a mobile to pay for a wide range of services and digital or hard goods. Although the concept of using non-coin-based currency systems has a long history, it is only recently that the technology to support such systems has become widely available.

Exam Probability: **Low**

58. *Answer choices:*

(see index for correct answer)

- a. Mobile payment

- b. MusicPass
- c. Inventory Information Approval System
- d. Sears Israel

Guidance: level 1

:: Customer relationship management software ::

_____ Software Corporation is a Global Business Software company based in Austin, TX and was founded in 1972. Its products are aimed at the manufacturing, distribution, retail and services industries.

Exam Probability: **High**

59. *Answer choices:*
(see index for correct answer)

- a. Epicor
- b. Tessitura
- c. SmartFocus
- d. NetSuite OneWorld

Guidance: level 1

## Marketing

Marketing is the study and management of exchange relationships. Marketing is the business process of creating relationships with and satisfying customers. With its focus on the customer, marketing is one of the premier components of business management.

Marketing is defined by the American Marketing Association as "the activity, set of institutions, and processes for creating, communicating, delivering, and exchanging offerings that have value for customers, clients, partners, and society at large."

---

:: ::

In marketing, a _____ is a ticket or document that can be redeemed for a financial discount or rebate when purchasing a product.

Exam Probability: **Medium**

1. *Answer choices:*

(see index for correct answer)

- a. levels of analysis
- b. Coupon
- c. open system
- d. co-culture

*Guidance:* level 1

---

:: Goods ::

In most contexts, the concept of _____ denotes the conduct that should be preferred when posed with a choice between possible actions. _____ is generally considered to be the opposite of evil, and is of interest in the study of morality, ethics, religion and philosophy. The specific meaning and etymology of the term and its associated translations among ancient and contemporary languages show substantial variation in its inflection and meaning depending on circumstances of place, history, religious, or philosophical context.

Exam Probability: **Medium**

2. *Answer choices:*
(see index for correct answer)

- a. Good
- b. Superior good
- c. Anti-rival good
- d. Bad

*Guidance:* level 1

:: Advertising ::

_____ is the behavioral and cognitive process of selectively concentrating on a discrete aspect of information, whether deemed subjective or objective, while ignoring other perceivable information. It is a state of arousal. It is the taking possession by the mind in clear and vivid form of one out of what seem several simultaneous objects or trains of thought. Focalization, the concentration of consciousness, is of its essence. _____ has also been described as the allocation of limited cognitive processing resources.

Exam Probability: **High**

3. *Answer choices:*
(see index for correct answer)

- a. Advertising management
- b. Attention
- c. Gender advertisement
- d. Legal advertising

*Guidance:* level 1

:: Consumer theory ::

_____ is the quantity of a good that consumers are willing and able to purchase at various prices during a given period of time.

Exam Probability: **Medium**

4. *Answer choices:*
(see index for correct answer)

- a. Engel curve
- b. Induced consumption
- c. Demand
- d. Demand vacuum

*Guidance:* level 1

:: Consumer behaviour ::

_____ refers to the ability of a company or product to retain its customers over some specified period. High _____ means customers of the product or business tend to return to, continue to buy or in some other way not defect to another product or business, or to non-use entirely. Selling organizations generally attempt to reduce customer defections. _____ starts with the first contact an organization has with a customer and continues throughout the entire lifetime of a relationship and successful retention efforts take this entire lifecycle into account. A company's ability to attract and retain new customers is related not only to its product or services, but also to the way it services its existing customers, the value the customers actually generate as a result of utilizing the solutions, and the reputation it creates within and across the marketplace.

Exam Probability: **Medium**

5. *Answer choices:*
(see index for correct answer)

- a. Blissful ignorance effect
- b. Mobile anthropology
- c. Customer retention
- d. Denomination effect

*Guidance:* level 1

:: Direct marketing ::

_____ is a method of direct marketing in which a salesperson solicits prospective customers to buy products or services, either over the phone or through a subsequent face to face or Web conferencing appointment scheduled during the call. _____ can also include recorded sales pitches programmed to be played over the phone via automatic dialing.

Exam Probability: **Medium**

6. *Answer choices:*

(see index for correct answer)

- a. Robinson list
- b. The Cobra Group
- c. Telemarketing
- d. Cold calling

*Guidance:* level 1

---

:: Marketing ::

_____ is multi-channel online marketing technique focused at reaching a specific audience on their smartphones, tablets, or any other related devices through websites, E-mail, SMS and MMS, social media, or mobile applications. _____ can provide customers with time and location sensitive, personalized information that promotes goods, services and ideas. In a more theoretical manner, academic Andreas Kaplan defines _____ as "any marketing activity conducted through a ubiquitous network to which consumers are constantly connected using a personal mobile device".

Exam Probability: **Low**

7. *Answer choices:*

(see index for correct answer)

- a. Email production
- b. Mobile marketing
- c. Pick and pack
- d. Ben Franklin effect

*Guidance:* level 1

---

:: ::

A _____ is the process of presenting a topic to an audience. It is typically a demonstration, introduction, lecture, or speech meant to inform, persuade, inspire, motivate, or to build good will or to present a new idea or product. The term can also be used for a formal or ritualized introduction or offering, as with the _____ of a debutante. _____ s in certain formats are also known as keynote address.

Exam Probability: **High**

8. *Answer choices:*

(see index for correct answer)

- a. cultural
- b. similarity-attraction theory
- c. empathy
- d. surface-level diversity

*Guidance:* level 1

:: ::

_____ , known in Europe as research and technological development , refers to innovative activities undertaken by corporations or governments in developing new services or products, or improving existing services or products. _____ constitutes the first stage of development of a potential new service or the production process.

Exam Probability: **Low**

9. *Answer choices:*

(see index for correct answer)

- a. Research and development
- b. Sarbanes-Oxley act of 2002
- c. imperative
- d. corporate values

*Guidance:* level 1

:: Organizational structure ::

An _____ defines how activities such as task allocation, coordination, and supervision are directed toward the achievement of organizational aims.

Exam Probability: **High**

10. *Answer choices:*

(see index for correct answer)

- a. Organization of the New York City Police Department
- b. Followership
- c. Automated Bureaucracy
- d. Organizational structure

*Guidance:* level 1

:: Business ethics ::

_____ is a microeconomic pricing strategy where identical or largely similar goods or services are transacted at different prices by the same provider in different markets. _____ is distinguished from product differentiation by the more substantial difference in production cost for the differently priced products involved in the latter strategy. Price differentiation essentially relies on the variation in the customers' willingness to pay and in the elasticity of their demand.

Exam Probability: **Medium**

11. *Answer choices:*

(see index for correct answer)

- a. Price discrimination
- b. Corporate Knights
- c. Black Company
- d. Bribery Act 2010

*Guidance:* level 1

:: Debt ::

_____, in finance and economics, is payment from a borrower or deposit-taking financial institution to a lender or depositor of an amount above repayment of the principal sum, at a particular rate. It is distinct from a fee which the borrower may pay the lender or some third party. It is also distinct from dividend which is paid by a company to its shareholders from its profit or reserve, but not at a particular rate decided beforehand, rather on a pro rata basis as a share in the reward gained by risk taking entrepreneurs when the revenue earned exceeds the total costs.

Exam Probability: **Medium**

12. *Answer choices:*
(see index for correct answer)

- a. Interest
- b. Vulture fund
- c. Debt crisis
- d. Recourse debt

*Guidance:* level 1

---

:: Asset ::

In financial accounting, an _____ is any resource owned by the business. Anything tangible or intangible that can be owned or controlled to produce value and that is held by a company to produce positive economic value is an _____. Simply stated, _____ s represent value of ownership that can be converted into cash. The balance sheet of a firm records the monetary value of the _____ s owned by that firm. It covers money and other valuables belonging to an individual or to a business.

Exam Probability: **High**

13. *Answer choices:*
(see index for correct answer)

- a. Fixed asset
- b. Asset

*Guidance:* level 1

---

:: ::

_____ is the study and management of exchange relationships. _____ is the business process of creating relationships with and satisfying customers. With its focus on the customer, _____ is one of the premier components of business management.

Exam Probability: **High**

14. *Answer choices:*

(see index for correct answer)

- a. cultural
- b. corporate values
- c. Sarbanes-Oxley act of 2002
- d. Marketing

*Guidance:* level 1

:: ::

An _____ is a contingent motivator. Traditional _____ s are extrinsic motivators which reward actions to yield a desired outcome. The effectiveness of traditional _____ s has changed as the needs of Western society have evolved. While the traditional _____ model is effective when there is a defined procedure and goal for a task, Western society started to require a higher volume of critical thinkers, so the traditional model became less effective. Institutions are now following a trend in implementing strategies that rely on intrinsic motivations rather than the extrinsic motivations that the traditional _____ s foster.

Exam Probability: **Medium**

15. *Answer choices:*

(see index for correct answer)

- a. Incentive
- b. similarity-attraction theory
- c. levels of analysis
- d. imperative

*Guidance:* level 1

:: Product management ::

A _____, trade mark, or trade-mark is a recognizable sign, design, or expression which identifies products or services of a particular source from those of others, although _____ s used to identify services are usually called service marks. The _____ owner can be an individual, business organization, or any legal entity. A _____ may be located on a package, a label, a voucher, or on the product itself. For the sake of corporate identity, _____ s are often displayed on company buildings. It is legally recognized as a type of intellectual property.

Exam Probability: **High**

16. *Answer choices:*

(see index for correct answer)

- a. Electronic registration mark
- b. Requirement prioritization
- c. Product cost management
- d. Diffusion of innovations

*Guidance:* level 1

---

:: Brokered programming ::

An _____ is a form of television commercial, which generally includes a toll-free telephone number or website. Most often used as a form of direct response television, long-form _____ s are typically 28:30 or 58:30 minutes in length. _____ s are also known as paid programming. This phenomenon started in the United States, where _____ s were typically shown overnight, outside peak prime time hours for commercial broadcasters. Some television stations chose to air _____ s as an alternative to the former practice of signing off. Some channels air _____ s 24 hours. Some stations also choose to air _____ s during the daytime hours mostly on weekends to fill in for unscheduled network or syndicated programming. By 2009, most _____ spending in the U.S. occurred during the early morning, daytime and evening hours, or in the afternoon. Stations in most countries around the world have instituted similar media structures. The _____ industry is worth over $200 billion.

Exam Probability: **High**

17. *Answer choices:*

(see index for correct answer)

- a. Toonzai
- b. Brokered programming
- c. Leased access
- d. One Magnificent Morning

*Guidance:* level 1

---

:: Marketing ::

A _____ is the people, organizations, and activities necessary to transfer the ownership of goods from the point of production to the point of consumption. It is the way products get to the end-user, the consumer; and is also known as a distribution channel. A _____ is a useful tool for management, and is crucial to creating an effective and well-planned marketing strategy.

Exam Probability: **High**

18. *Answer choices:*
(see index for correct answer)

- a. Buy one, get one free
- b. Inventory
- c. Marketing channel
- d. Customer acquisition management

*Guidance:* level 1

---

:: ::

Advertising is a marketing communication that employs an openly sponsored, non-personal message to promote or sell a product, service or idea. Sponsors of advertising are typically businesses wishing to promote their products or services. Advertising is differentiated from public relations in that an advertiser pays for and has control over the message. It differs from personal selling in that the message is non-personal, i.e., not directed to a particular individual.Advertising is communicated through various mass media, including traditional media such as newspapers, magazines, television, radio, outdoor advertising or direct mail; and new media such as search results, blogs, social media, websites or text messages. The actual presentation of the message in a medium is referred to as an _____ , or "ad" or advert for short.

Exam Probability: **High**

19. *Answer choices:*

(see index for correct answer)

- a. information systems assessment
- b. levels of analysis
- c. Advertisement
- d. imperative

*Guidance:* level 1

:: ::

_____ is a means of protection from financial loss. It is a form of risk management, primarily used to hedge against the risk of a contingent or uncertain loss

Exam Probability: **Low**

20. *Answer choices:*

(see index for correct answer)

- a. deep-level diversity
- b. cultural
- c. hierarchical perspective
- d. Insurance

*Guidance:* level 1

:: Project management ::

_____ is the right to exercise power, which can be formalized by a state and exercised by way of judges, appointed executives of government, or the ecclesiastical or priestly appointed representatives of a God or other deities.

Exam Probability: **Low**

21. *Answer choices:*

(see index for correct answer)

- a. Organizational project management
- b. Authority
- c. Vertical slice
- d. Disciplined Agile Delivery

*Guidance:* level 1

:: Direct selling ::

_____ consists of two main business models: single-level marketing, in which a direct seller makes money by buying products from a parent organization and selling them directly to customers, and multi-level marketing, in which the direct seller may earn money from both direct sales to customers and by sponsoring new direct sellers and potentially earning a commission from their efforts.

Exam Probability: **Low**

22. *Answer choices:*
(see index for correct answer)

- a. The Longaberger Company
- b. Direct Selling Association
- c. Direct Selling News
- d. Direct selling

*Guidance:* level 1

:: ::

_____ , also referred to as orthostasis, is a human position in which the body is held in an upright position and supported only by the feet.

Exam Probability: **Medium**

23. *Answer choices:*
(see index for correct answer)

- a. hierarchical
- b. imperative
- c. hierarchical perspective
- d. Standing

*Guidance:* level 1

:: Business ::

The seller, or the provider of the goods or services, completes a sale in response to an acquisition, appropriation, requisition or a direct interaction with the buyer at the point of sale. There is a passing of title of the item, and the settlement of a price, in which agreement is reached on a price for which transfer of ownership of the item will occur. The seller, not the purchaser typically executes the sale and it may be completed prior to the obligation of payment. In the case of indirect interaction, a person who sells goods or service on behalf of the owner is known as a _____ man or _____ woman or _____ person, but this often refers to someone selling goods in a store/shop, in which case other terms are also common, including _____ clerk, shop assistant, and retail clerk.

Exam Probability: **High**

24. *Answer choices:*
(see index for correct answer)

- a. Price adjustment
- b. Sales
- c. Business service management
- d. Business directory

*Guidance:* level 1

:: Survey methodology ::

A _____ is the procedure of systematically acquiring and recording information about the members of a given population. The term is used mostly in connection with national population and housing _____ es; other common _____ es include agriculture, business, and traffic _____ es. The United Nations defines the essential features of population and housing _____ es as "individual enumeration, universality within a defined territory, simultaneity and defined periodicity", and recommends that population _____ es be taken at least every 10 years. United Nations recommendations also cover _____ topics to be collected, official definitions, classifications and other useful information to co-ordinate international practice.

Exam Probability: **High**

25. *Answer choices:*
(see index for correct answer)

- a. Self-report
- b. Census
- c. National Health Interview Survey
- d. Sampling

*Guidance:* level 1

:: ::

_____ or accountancy is the measurement, processing, and communication of financial information about economic entities such as businesses and corporations. The modern field was established by the Italian mathematician Luca Pacioli in 1494. _____, which has been called the "language of business", measures the results of an organization's economic activities and conveys this information to a variety of users, including investors, creditors, management, and regulators. Practitioners of _____ are known as accountants. The terms "_____" and "financial reporting" are often used as synonyms.

Exam Probability: **Medium**

26. *Answer choices:*
(see index for correct answer)

- a. imperative
- b. hierarchical perspective
- c. co-culture
- d. Accounting

*Guidance:* level 1

:: Types of marketing ::

_____ is "marketing on a worldwide scale reconciling or taking commercial advantage of global operational differences, similarities and opportunities in order to meet global objectives".

Exam Probability: **Medium**

27. *Answer choices:*
(see index for correct answer)

- a. Global marketing
- b. Secret brand
- c. Project SCUM

- d. Account planning

*Guidance: level 1*

---

:: Commerce ::

_____ relates to "the exchange of goods and services, especially on a large scale". It includes legal, economic, political, social, cultural and technological systems that operate in a country or in international trade.

Exam Probability: **Medium**

28. *Answer choices:*
(see index for correct answer)

- a. Group buying
- b. DataCash
- c. International Marketmakers Combination
- d. Staple right

*Guidance: level 1*

---

:: Marketing ::

A _____ is a group of customers within a business's serviceable available market at which a business aims its marketing efforts and resources. A _____ is a subset of the total market for a product or service. The _____ typically consists of consumers who exhibit similar characteristics and are considered most likely to buy a business's market offerings or are likely to be the most profitable segments for the business to service.

Exam Probability: **Low**

29. *Answer choices:*
(see index for correct answer)

- a. Health marketing
- b. Bayesian inference in marketing
- c. Target market
- d. Product literature

*Guidance: level 1*

---

:: Commodities ::

In economics, a _____ is an economic good or service that has full or substantial fungibility: that is, the market treats instances of the good as equivalent or nearly so with no regard to who produced them. Most commodities are raw materials, basic resources, agricultural, or mining products, such as iron ore, sugar, or grains like rice and wheat. Commodities can also be mass-produced unspecialized products such as chemicals and computer memory.

Exam Probability: **Low**

30. *Answer choices:*

(see index for correct answer)

- a. Sample grade
- b. IRely
- c. Commodity money
- d. Commoditization

*Guidance:* level 1

:: Marketing analytics ::

_____ is a long-term, forward-looking approach to planning with the fundamental goal of achieving a sustainable competitive advantage. Strategic planning involves an analysis of the company's strategic initial situation prior to the formulation, evaluation and selection of market-oriented competitive position that contributes to the company's goals and marketing objectives.

Exam Probability: **High**

31. *Answer choices:*

(see index for correct answer)

- a. Marketing accountability
- b. Marketing performance measurement and management
- c. Market share analysis
- d. Marketing strategy

*Guidance:* level 1

:: ::

_____s uses different marketing channels and tools in combination: _____ channels focus on any way a business communicates a message to its desired market, or the market in general. A _____ tool can be anything from: advertising, personal selling, direct marketing, sponsorship, communication, and promotion to public relations.

Exam Probability: **Medium**

32. *Answer choices:*

(see index for correct answer)

- a. imperative
- b. Marketing communication
- c. interpersonal communication
- d. process perspective

*Guidance:* level 1

:: Marketing ::

A business can use a variety of _____ when selling a product or service. The price can be set to maximize profitability for each unit sold or from the market overall. It can be used to defend an existing market from new entrants, to increase market share within a market or to enter a new market.

Exam Probability: **Low**

33. *Answer choices:*

(see index for correct answer)

- a. Pricing strategies
- b. Customer acquisition management
- c. Branding national myths and symbols
- d. Blind taste test

*Guidance:* level 1

:: ::

_____ consists of using generic or ad hoc methods in an orderly manner to find solutions to problems. Some of the problem-solving techniques developed and used in philosophy, artificial intelligence, computer science, engineering, mathematics, or medicine are related to mental problem-solving techniques studied in psychology.

Exam Probability: **Low**

34. *Answer choices:*
(see index for correct answer)

- a. Problem Solving
- b. open system
- c. imperative
- d. corporate values

*Guidance:* level 1

:: Brand management ::

_____ is defined as positive feelings towards a brand and dedication to purchase the same product or service repeatedly now and in the future from the same brand, regardless of a competitor's actions or changes in the environment. It can also be demonstrated with other behaviors such as positive word-of-mouth advocacy. _____ is where an individual buys products from the same manufacturer repeatedly rather than from other suppliers. Businesses whose financial and ethical values, for example ESG responsibilities, rest in large part on their _____ are said to use the loyalty business model.

Exam Probability: **Low**

35. *Answer choices:*
(see index for correct answer)

- a. Giant Step
- b. Brand loyalty
- c. Solution brand
- d. Brand preference

*Guidance:* level 1

:: ::

_____ is the practice of deliberately managing the spread of information between an individual or an organization and the public. _____ may include an organization or individual gaining exposure to their audiences using topics of public interest and news items that do not require direct payment. This differentiates it from advertising as a form of marketing communications. _____ is the idea of creating coverage for clients for free, rather than marketing or advertising. But now, advertising is also a part of greater PR Activities. An example of good _____ would be generating an article featuring a client, rather than paying for the client to be advertised next to the article. The aim of _____ is to inform the public, prospective customers, investors, partners, employees, and other stakeholders and ultimately persuade them to maintain a positive or favorable view about the organization, its leadership, products, or political decisions. _____ professionals typically work for PR and marketing firms, businesses and companies, government, and public officials as PIOs and nongovernmental organizations, and nonprofit organizations. Jobs central to _____ include account coordinator, account executive, account supervisor, and media relations manager.

Exam Probability: **Medium**

36. *Answer choices:*
(see index for correct answer)

- a. personal values
- b. Public relations
- c. similarity-attraction theory
- d. co-culture

*Guidance:* level 1

---

:: ::

_____ is a concept of English common law and is a necessity for simple contracts but not for special contracts. The concept has been adopted by other common law jurisdictions, including the US.

Exam Probability: **High**

37. *Answer choices:*
(see index for correct answer)

- a. deep-level diversity
- b. empathy
- c. Consideration
- d. hierarchical perspective

*Guidance:* level 1

---

:: Business terms ::

_____ occurs when a sales representative meets with a potential client for the purpose of transacting a sale. Many sales representatives rely on a sequential sales process that typically includes nine steps. Some sales representatives develop scripts for all or part of the sales process. The sales process can be used in face-to-face encounters and in telemarketing.

Exam Probability: **High**

38. *Answer choices:*
(see index for correct answer)

- a. operating cost
- b. churn rate
- c. organizational capital
- d. Personal selling

*Guidance:* level 1

---

:: Planning ::

_____ is a high level plan to achieve one or more goals under conditions of uncertainty. In the sense of the "art of the general," which included several subsets of skills including tactics, siegecraft, logistics etc., the term came into use in the 6th century C.E. in East Roman terminology, and was translated into Western vernacular languages only in the 18th century. From then until the 20th century, the word "_____" came to denote "a comprehensive way to try to pursue political ends, including the threat or actual use of force, in a dialectic of wills" in a military conflict, in which both adversaries interact.

Exam Probability: **Medium**

39. *Answer choices:*
(see index for correct answer)

- a. Strategy
- b. Interactive planning
- c. Plano Trienal
- d. Default effect

*Guidance:* level 1

:: Advertising techniques ::

In promotion and of advertising, a _____ or show consists of a person's written or spoken statement extolling the virtue of a product. The term "_____" most commonly applies to the sales-pitches attributed to ordinary citizens, whereas the word "endorsement" usually applies to pitches by celebrities. _____ s can be part of communal marketing. Sometimes, the cartoon character can be a _____ in a commercial.

Exam Probability: **High**

40. *Answer choices:*
(see index for correct answer)

- a. Roll-in
- b. Transfer
- c. Soft sell
- d. Testimonial

*Guidance:* level 1

:: International trade ::

In finance, an _____ is the rate at which one currency will be exchanged for another. It is also regarded as the value of one country's currency in relation to another currency. For example, an interbank _____ of 114 Japanese yen to the United States dollar means that ¥114 will be exchanged for each US$1 or that US$1 will be exchanged for each ¥114. In this case it is said that the price of a dollar in relation to yen is ¥114, or equivalently that the price of a yen in relation to dollars is $1/114.

Exam Probability: **Medium**

41. *Answer choices:*
(see index for correct answer)

- a. Exchange rate

- b. Export function
- c. Invisible balance
- d. Portuguese India Armadas

*Guidance:* level 1

---

:: Stochastic processes ::

_____ in its modern meaning is a "new idea, creative thoughts, new imaginations in form of device or method". _____ is often also viewed as the application of better solutions that meet new requirements, unarticulated needs, or existing market needs. Such _____ takes place through the provision of more-effective products, processes, services, technologies, or business models that are made available to markets, governments and society. An _____ is something original and more effective and, as a consequence, new, that "breaks into" the market or society. _____ is related to, but not the same as, invention, as _____ is more apt to involve the practical implementation of an invention to make a meaningful impact in the market or society, and not all _____ s require an invention. _____ often manifests itself via the engineering process, when the problem being solved is of a technical or scientific nature. The opposite of _____ is exnovation.

Exam Probability: **Medium**

42. *Answer choices:*

(see index for correct answer)

- a. Additive Markov chain
- b. Innovation
- c. Product-form solution
- d. Disorder problem

*Guidance:* level 1

---

:: Marketing ::

_____ is the process of using surveys to evaluate consumer acceptance of a new product idea prior to the introduction of a product to the market. It is important not to confuse _____ with advertising testing, brand testing and packaging testing; as is sometimes done. _____ focuses on the basic product idea, without the embellishments and puffery inherent in advertising.

Exam Probability: **Low**

43. *Answer choices:*
(see index for correct answer)

- a. Existing visitor optimisation
- b. Concept testing
- c. DeusM
- d. Azerbaijan Marketing Society

*Guidance:* level 1

:: Library science ::

_____ refers to data which is collected by someone who is someone other than the user. Common sources of _____ for social science include censuses, information collected by government departments, organizational records and data that was originally collected for other research purposes. Primary data, by contrast, are collected by the investigator conducting the research.

Exam Probability: **High**

44. *Answer choices:*
(see index for correct answer)

- a. Arthur Curley
- b. Secondary data
- c. Collection of German Prints
- d. Scholarly communication

*Guidance:* level 1

:: ::

Management is the administration of an organization, whether it is a business, a not-for-profit organization, or government body. Management includes the activities of setting the strategy of an organization and coordinating the efforts of its employees to accomplish its objectives through the application of available resources, such as financial, natural, technological, and human resources. The term "management" may also refer to those people who manage an organization.

Exam Probability: **Low**

45. *Answer choices:*

(see index for correct answer)

- a. Character
- b. Manager
- c. functional perspective
- d. hierarchical

*Guidance:* level 1

:: Advertising by type ::

_____ or advertising war is an advertisement in which a particular product, or service, specifically mentions a competitor by name for the express purpose of showing why the competitor is inferior to the product naming it. Also referred to as "knocking copy", it is loosely defined as advertising where "the advertised brand is explicitly compared with one or more competing brands and the comparison is obvious to the audience."

Exam Probability: **High**

46. *Answer choices:*

(see index for correct answer)

- a. Virtual advertising
- b. Informative advertising
- c. Out-of-home advertising
- d. Comparative advertising

*Guidance:* level 1

:: ::

A brand is an overall experience of a customer that distinguishes an organization or product from its rivals in the eyes of the customer. Brands are used in business, marketing, and advertising. Name brands are sometimes distinguished from generic or store brands.

Exam Probability: **High**

47. *Answer choices:*

(see index for correct answer)

- a. Sarbanes-Oxley act of 2002
- b. surface-level diversity

- c. information systems assessment
- d. Brand image

*Guidance:* level 1

---

:: Information technology ::

_____ is the use of computers to store, retrieve, transmit, and manipulate data, or information, often in the context of a business or other enterprise. IT is considered to be a subset of information and communications technology. An _____ system is generally an information system, a communications system or, more specifically speaking, a computer system – including all hardware, software and peripheral equipment – operated by a limited group of users.

Exam Probability: **Medium**

48. *Answer choices:*

(see index for correct answer)

- a. Information technology
- b. Collabera
- c. Normalized Systems
- d. Micro-innovation

*Guidance:* level 1

---

:: Behaviorism ::

In behavioral psychology, _____ is a consequence applied that will strengthen an organism's future behavior whenever that behavior is preceded by a specific antecedent stimulus. This strengthening effect may be measured as a higher frequency of behavior, longer duration, greater magnitude, or shorter latency. There are two types of _____, known as positive _____ and negative _____; positive is where by a reward is offered on expression of the wanted behaviour and negative is taking away an undesirable element in the persons environment whenever the desired behaviour is achieved.

Exam Probability: **Low**

49. *Answer choices:*

(see index for correct answer)

- a. Programmed instruction

- b. social facilitation
- c. contingency management
- d. chaining

*Guidance:* level 1

:: Promotion and marketing communications ::

A _____ is the intended audience or readership of a publication, advertisement, or other message. In marketing and advertising, it is a particular group of consumers within the predetermined target market, identified as the targets or recipients for a particular advertisement or message. Businesses that have a wide target market will focus on a specific _____ for certain messages to send, such as The Body Shops Mother's Day advertisements, which were aimed at the children and spouses of women, rather than the whole market which would have included the women themselves.

Exam Probability: **Medium**

50. *Answer choices:*
(see index for correct answer)

- a. Target audience
- b. Underwriting spot
- c. News propaganda
- d. The One Club

*Guidance:* level 1

:: ::

_____ is the production of products for use or sale using labour and machines, tools, chemical and biological processing, or formulation. The term may refer to a range of human activity, from handicraft to high tech, but is most commonly applied to industrial design, in which raw materials are transformed into finished goods on a large scale. Such finished goods may be sold to other manufacturers for the production of other, more complex products, such as aircraft, household appliances, furniture, sports equipment or automobiles, or sold to wholesalers, who in turn sell them to retailers, who then sell them to end users and consumers.

Exam Probability: **Low**

51. *Answer choices:*

(see index for correct answer)

- a. interpersonal communication
- b. imperative
- c. co-culture
- d. open system

*Guidance:* level 1

---

:: Progressive Era in the United States ::

The Clayton Antitrust Act of 1914 , was a part of United States antitrust law with the goal of adding further substance to the U.S. antitrust law regime; the _____ sought to prevent anticompetitive practices in their incipiency. That regime started with the Sherman Antitrust Act of 1890, the first Federal law outlawing practices considered harmful to consumers . The _____ specified particular prohibited conduct, the three-level enforcement scheme, the exemptions, and the remedial measures.

Exam Probability: **Medium**

52. *Answer choices:*

(see index for correct answer)

- a. pragmatism
- b. Clayton Antitrust Act
- c. Mann Act

*Guidance:* level 1

---

:: Business law ::

A _____ is an arrangement where parties, known as partners, agree to cooperate to advance their mutual interests. The partners in a _____ may be individuals, businesses, interest-based organizations, schools, governments or combinations. Organizations may partner to increase the likelihood of each achieving their mission and to amplify their reach. A _____ may result in issuing and holding equity or may be only governed by a contract.

Exam Probability: **High**

53. *Answer choices:*

(see index for correct answer)

- a. Financial Security Law of France
- b. Installment sale
- c. Certificate of incorporation
- d. Lex mercatoria

*Guidance:* level 1

---

:: Industry ::

_____ describes various measures of the efficiency of production. Often , a _____ measure is expressed as the ratio of an aggregate output to a single input or an aggregate input used in a production process, i.e. output per unit of input. Most common example is the labour _____ measure, e.g., such as GDP per worker. There are many different definitions of _____ and the choice among them depends on the purpose of the _____ measurement and/or data availability. The key source of difference between various _____ measures is also usually related to how the outputs and the inputs are aggregated into scalars to obtain such a ratio-type measure of _____ .

Exam Probability: **Medium**

54. *Answer choices:*
(see index for correct answer)

- a. Light industry
- b. Productivity
- c. Sunrise industry
- d. Industrial control system

*Guidance:* level 1

---

:: ::

A _____ is a person who trades in commodities produced by other people. Historically, a _____ is anyone who is involved in business or trade. _____ s have operated for as long as industry, commerce, and trade have existed. During the 16th-century, in Europe, two different terms for _____ s emerged: One term, meerseniers, described local traders such as bakers, grocers, etc.; while a new term, koopman (Dutch: koopman, described _____ s who operated on a global stage, importing and exporting goods over vast distances, and offering added-value services such as credit and finance.

Exam Probability: **Low**

55. *Answer choices:*
(see index for correct answer)

- a. hierarchical perspective
- b. personal values
- c. levels of analysis
- d. Merchant

*Guidance:* level 1

:: Economic globalization ::

_____ is an agreement in which one company hires another company to be responsible for a planned or existing activity that is or could be done internally, and sometimes involves transferring employees and assets from one firm to another.

Exam Probability: **Low**

56. *Answer choices:*
(see index for correct answer)

- a. Outsourcing
- b. reshoring

*Guidance:* level 1

:: Project management ::

Contemporary business and science treat as a _____ any undertaking, carried out individually or collaboratively and possibly involving research or design, that is carefully planned to achieve a particular aim.

Exam Probability: **Low**

57. *Answer choices:*
(see index for correct answer)

- a. Confluence Project Management
- b. Project plan
- c. Project
- d. Project management office

*Guidance:* level 1

:: ::

_____ is change in the heritable characteristics of biological populations over successive generations. These characteristics are the expressions of genes that are passed on from parent to offspring during reproduction. Different characteristics tend to exist within any given population as a result of mutation, genetic recombination and other sources of genetic variation. _____ occurs when _____ ary processes such as natural selection and genetic drift act on this variation, resulting in certain characteristics becoming more common or rare within a population. It is this process of _____ that has given rise to biodiversity at every level of biological organisation, including the levels of species, individual organisms and molecules.

Exam Probability: **Low**

58. *Answer choices:*
(see index for correct answer)

- a. process perspective
- b. Sarbanes-Oxley act of 2002
- c. Evolution
- d. corporate values

*Guidance:* level 1

:: International trade ::

_____ or globalisation is the process of interaction and integration among people, companies, and governments worldwide. As a complex and multifaceted phenomenon, _____ is considered by some as a form of capitalist expansion which entails the integration of local and national economies into a global, unregulated market economy. _____ has grown due to advances in transportation and communication technology. With the increased global interactions comes the growth of international trade, ideas, and culture. _____ is primarily an economic process of interaction and integration that's associated with social and cultural aspects. However, conflicts and diplomacy are also large parts of the history of _____ , and modern _____ .

Exam Probability: **High**

59. *Answer choices:*
(see index for correct answer)

- a. Pauper labor argument
- b. Single-window system
- c. Strong dollar policy
- d. Globalization

*Guidance:* level 1

## Manufacturing

Manufacturing is the production of merchandise for use or sale using labor and machines, tools, chemical and biological processing, or formulation. The term may refer to a range of human activity, from handicraft to high tech, but is most commonly applied to industrial design, in which raw materials are transformed into finished goods on a large scale. Such finished goods may be sold to other manufacturers for the production of other, more complex products, such as aircraft, household appliances, furniture, sports equipment or automobiles, or sold to wholesalers, who in turn sell them to retailers, who then sell them to end users and consumers.

---

:: Manufacturing ::

A _____ is an object used to extend the ability of an individual to modify features of the surrounding environment. Although many animals use simple _____ s, only human beings, whose use of stone _____ s dates back hundreds of millennia, use _____ s to make other _____ s. The set of _____ s needed to perform different tasks that are part of the same activity is called gear or equipment.

Exam Probability: **Medium**

1. *Answer choices:*
(see index for correct answer)

- a. Dimensional metrology
- b. Manufacturing overhead
- c. Point cloud
- d. Fixture

*Guidance:* level 1

---

:: Quality management ::

_____ ensures that an organization, product or service is consistent. It has four main components: quality planning, quality assurance, quality control and quality improvement. _____ is focused not only on product and service quality, but also on the means to achieve it. _____ , therefore, uses quality assurance and control of processes as well as products to achieve more consistent quality. What a customer wants and is willing to pay for it determines quality. It is written or unwritten commitment to a known or unknown consumer in the market . Thus, quality can be defined as fitness for intended use or, in other words, how well the product performs its intended function

Exam Probability: **Medium**

2. *Answer choices:*

(see index for correct answer)

- a. Quality management
- b. Product quality risk in supply chain
- c. European Quality in Social Services
- d. Germanischer Lloyd

*Guidance:* level 1

:: Management ::

_____ is a formal technique useful where many possible courses of action are competing for attention. In essence, the problem-solver estimates the benefit delivered by each action, then selects a number of the most effective actions that deliver a total benefit reasonably close to the maximal possible one.

Exam Probability: **High**

3. *Answer choices:*

(see index for correct answer)

- a. Pareto analysis
- b. Relational view
- c. Strategic management
- d. Systems analysis

*Guidance:* level 1

:: Project management ::

A _____ is a type of bar chart that illustrates a project schedule, named after its inventor, Henry Gantt , who designed such a chart around the years 1910–1915. Modern _____ s also show the dependency relationships between activities and current schedule status.

Exam Probability: **Medium**

4. *Answer choices:*

(see index for correct answer)

- a. Integrated product team
- b. Gantt chart
- c. Executive sponsor
- d. Logical framework approach

*Guidance:* level 1

---

:: Water ::

_____ is a transparent, tasteless, odorless, and nearly colorless chemical substance, which is the main constituent of Earth's streams, lakes, and oceans, and the fluids of most living organisms. It is vital for all known forms of life, even though it provides no calories or organic nutrients. Its chemical formula is H2O, meaning that each of its molecules contains one oxygen and two hydrogen atoms, connected by covalent bonds. _____ is the name of the liquid state of H2O at standard ambient temperature and pressure. It forms precipitation in the form of rain and aerosols in the form of fog. Clouds are formed from suspended droplets of _____ and ice, its solid state. When finely divided, crystalline ice may precipitate in the form of snow. The gaseous state of _____ is steam or _____ vapor. _____ moves continually through the _____ cycle of evaporation, transpiration , condensation, precipitation, and runoff, usually reaching the sea.

Exam Probability: **Low**

5. *Answer choices:*

(see index for correct answer)

- a. Water
- b. Superheated steam
- c. Limescale
- d. UN-Water

*Guidance:* level 1

:: Elementary mathematics ::

In mathematics, a _____ is an enumerated collection of objects in which repetitions are allowed. Like a set, it contains members. The number of elements is called the length of the _____ . Unlike a set, the same elements can appear multiple times at different positions in a _____ , and order matters. Formally, a _____ can be defined as a function whose domain is either the set of the natural numbers or the set of the first n natural numbers. The position of an element in a _____ is its rank or index; it is the natural number from which the element is the image. It depends on the context or a specific convention, if the first element has index 0 or 1.
When a symbol has been chosen for denoting a _____ , the nth element of the _____ is denoted by this symbol with n as subscript; for example, the nth element of the Fibonacci _____ is generally denoted Fn.

Exam Probability: **High**

6. *Answer choices:*

(see index for correct answer)

- a. Elementary proof
- b. Functional notation
- c. Cartesian coordinate system
- d. Elementary mathematics

*Guidance:* level 1

:: Business ::

The seller, or the provider of the goods or services, completes a sale in response to an acquisition, appropriation, requisition or a direct interaction with the buyer at the point of sale. There is a passing of title of the item, and the settlement of a price, in which agreement is reached on a price for which transfer of ownership of the item will occur. The seller, not the purchaser typically executes the sale and it may be completed prior to the obligation of payment. In the case of indirect interaction, a person who sells goods or service on behalf of the owner is known as a _____ man or _____ woman or _____ person, but this often refers to someone selling goods in a store/shop, in which case other terms are also common, including _____ clerk, shop assistant, and retail clerk.

Exam Probability: **High**

7. *Answer choices:*

(see index for correct answer)

- a. Architecture of Interoperable Information Systems
- b. Sales
- c. Absentee business owner
- d. Staff and line

*Guidance:* level 1

:: Production and manufacturing ::

_____ consists of organization-wide efforts to "install and make permanent climate where employees continuously improve their ability to provide on demand products and services that customers will find of particular value." "Total" emphasizes that departments in addition to production are obligated to improve their operations; "management" emphasizes that executives are obligated to actively manage quality through funding, training, staffing, and goal setting. While there is no widely agreed-upon approach, TQM efforts typically draw heavily on the previously developed tools and techniques of quality control. TQM enjoyed widespread attention during the late 1980s and early 1990s before being overshadowed by ISO 9000, Lean manufacturing, and Six Sigma.

Exam Probability: **Medium**

8. *Answer choices:*

(see index for correct answer)

- a. Predetermined motion time system
- b. Total quality management
- c. Object Process Methodology
- d. Enterprise control

*Guidance:* level 1

:: Management ::

_____ is a category of business activity made possible by software tools that aim to provide customers with both independence from vendors and better means for engaging with vendors. These same tools can also apply to individuals' relations with other institutions and organizations.

Exam Probability: **High**

9. *Answer choices:*
(see index for correct answer)

- a. Director
- b. Bed management
- c. Organizational conflict
- d. Vendor relationship management

*Guidance:* level 1

---

:: Product management ::

_____ s, also known as Shewhart charts or process-behavior charts, are a statistical process control tool used to determine if a manufacturing or business process is in a state of control.

Exam Probability: **Medium**

10. *Answer choices:*
(see index for correct answer)

- a. Product manager
- b. Mid-life update
- c. Product information
- d. Control chart

*Guidance:* level 1

---

:: Casting (manufacturing) ::

A _____ is a regularity in the world, man-made design, or abstract ideas. As such, the elements of a _____ repeat in a predictable manner. A geometric _____ is a kind of _____ formed of geometric shapes and typically repeated like a wallpaper design.

Exam Probability: **Low**

11. *Answer choices:*
(see index for correct answer)

- a. Investment casting
- b. Castability
- c. Controlled permeability formwork
- d. Lost-foam casting

*Guidance:* level 1

:: E-commerce ::

_____ is the activity of buying or selling of products on online services or over the Internet. Electronic commerce draws on technologies such as mobile commerce, electronic funds transfer, supply chain management, Internet marketing, online transaction processing, electronic data interchange , inventory management systems, and automated data collection systems.

Exam Probability: **High**

12. *Answer choices:*

(see index for correct answer)

- a. Online flower delivery
- b. E-commerce
- c. Online savings account
- d. Presumed security

*Guidance:* level 1

:: Production and manufacturing ::

_____ is a theory of management that analyzes and synthesizes workflows. Its main objective is improving economic efficiency, especially labor productivity. It was one of the earliest attempts to apply science to the engineering of processes and to management. _____ is sometimes known as Taylorism after its founder, Frederick Winslow Taylor.

Exam Probability: **Low**

13. *Answer choices:*

(see index for correct answer)

- a. Scientific management
- b. Copacker
- c. SynqNet
- d. Fieldbus

*Guidance:* level 1

:: Project management ::

A _____ is the approximation of the cost of a program, project, or operation. The _____ is the product of the cost estimating process. The _____ has a single total value and may have identifiable component values. A problem with a cost overrun can be avoided with a credible, reliable, and accurate _____. A cost estimator is the professional who prepares _____s. There are different types of cost estimators, whose title may be preceded by a modifier, such as building estimator, or electrical estimator, or chief estimator. Other professionals such as quantity surveyors and cost engineers may also prepare _____s or contribute to _____s. In the US, according to the Bureau of Labor Statistics, there were 185,400 cost estimators in 2010. There are around 75,000 professional quantity surveyors working in the UK.

Exam Probability: **Medium**

14. *Answer choices:*

(see index for correct answer)

- a. ISO 10006
- b. Cost estimate
- c. Project management process
- d. Theory X and Theory Y

*Guidance:* level 1

---

:: Production economics ::

_____ is the creation of a whole that is greater than the simple sum of its parts. The term _____ comes from the Attic Greek word sea synergia from synergos, , meaning "working together".

Exam Probability: **Medium**

15. *Answer choices:*

(see index for correct answer)

- a. Marginal product
- b. Productive capacity
- c. Marginal product of labor
- d. Post-Fordism

*Guidance:* level 1

---

:: Management ::

_____ is a process by which entities review the quality of all factors involved in production. ISO 9000 defines _____ as "A part of quality management focused on fulfilling quality requirements".

Exam Probability: **Medium**

16. *Answer choices:*
(see index for correct answer)

- a. Quality control
- b. Project stakeholder
- c. Line management
- d. Goals Breakdown Structure

*Guidance:* level 1

:: ::

_____ is the quantity of three-dimensional space enclosed by a closed surface, for example, the space that a substance or shape occupies or contains. _____ is often quantified numerically using the SI derived unit, the cubic metre. The _____ of a container is generally understood to be the capacity of the container; i. e., the amount of fluid that the container could hold, rather than the amount of space the container itself displaces. Three dimensional mathematical shapes are also assigned _____ s. _____ s of some simple shapes, such as regular, straight-edged, and circular shapes can be easily calculated using arithmetic formulas. _____ s of complicated shapes can be calculated with integral calculus if a formula exists for the shape's boundary. One-dimensional figures and two-dimensional shapes are assigned zero _____ in the three-dimensional space.

Exam Probability: **Medium**

17. *Answer choices:*
(see index for correct answer)

- a. Sarbanes-Oxley act of 2002
- b. hierarchical
- c. Volume
- d. interpersonal communication

*Guidance:* level 1

:: Production and manufacturing ::

_____ is a systematic method to improve the "value" of goods or products and services by using an examination of function. Value, as defined, is the ratio of function to cost. Value can therefore be manipulated by either improving the function or reducing the cost. It is a primary tenet of _____ that basic functions be preserved and not be reduced as a consequence of pursuing value improvements.

Exam Probability: **Low**

18. *Answer choices:*
(see index for correct answer)

- a. Beltweigher
- b. Virtual manufacturing network
- c. Low rate initial production
- d. Six Sigma

*Guidance:* level 1

---

:: Chemical processes ::

_____ is the understanding and application of the fundamental principles and laws of nature that allow us to transform raw material and energy into products that are useful to society, at an industrial level. By taking advantage of the driving forces of nature such as pressure, temperature and concentration gradients, as well as the law of conservation of mass, process engineers can develop methods to synthesize and purify large quantities of desired chemical products. _____ focuses on the design, operation, control, optimization and intensification of chemical, physical, and biological processes. _____ encompasses a vast range of industries, such as agriculture, automotive, biotechnical, chemical, food, material development, mining, nuclear, petrochemical, pharmaceutical, and software development. The application of systematic computer-based methods to _____ is "process systems engineering".

Exam Probability: **High**

19. *Answer choices:*
(see index for correct answer)

- a. Process engineering

- b. Decrepitation
- c. Flue-gas emissions from fossil-fuel combustion
- d. Petersen matrix

*Guidance:* level 1

---

:: Production and manufacturing ::

_____ is a production planning, scheduling, and inventory control system used to manage manufacturing processes. Most MRP systems are software-based, but it is possible to conduct MRP by hand as well.

Exam Probability: **Low**

20. *Answer choices:*
(see index for correct answer)

- a. STEP-NC
- b. Original design manufacturer
- c. Material requirements planning
- d. International Automotive Task Force

*Guidance:* level 1

---

:: Management ::

Business _____ is a discipline in operations management in which people use various methods to discover, model, analyze, measure, improve, optimize, and automate business processes. BPM focuses on improving corporate performance by managing business processes. Any combination of methods used to manage a company's business processes is BPM. Processes can be structured and repeatable or unstructured and variable. Though not required, enabling technologies are often used with BPM.

Exam Probability: **Low**

21. *Answer choices:*
(see index for correct answer)

- a. Planning
- b. Cross ownership
- c. Process management
- d. Demand chain management

*Guidance:* level 1

:: Business planning ::

_____ is an organization's process of defining its strategy, or direction, and making decisions on allocating its resources to pursue this strategy. It may also extend to control mechanisms for guiding the implementation of the strategy. _____ became prominent in corporations during the 1960s and remains an important aspect of strategic management. It is executed by strategic planners or strategists, who involve many parties and research sources in their analysis of the organization and its relationship to the environment in which it competes.

Exam Probability: **Low**

22. *Answer choices:*
(see index for correct answer)

- a. Strategic planning
- b. Community Futures
- c. Customer Demand Planning
- d. Stakeholder management

*Guidance:* level 1

:: Alchemical processes ::

In chemistry, a _____ is a special type of homogeneous mixture composed of two or more substances. In such a mixture, a solute is a substance dissolved in another substance, known as a solvent. The mixing process of a _____ happens at a scale where the effects of chemical polarity are involved, resulting in interactions that are specific to solvation. The _____ assumes the phase of the solvent when the solvent is the larger fraction of the mixture, as is commonly the case. The concentration of a solute in a _____ is the mass of that solute expressed as a percentage of the mass of the whole _____. The term aqueous _____ is when one of the solvents is water.

Exam Probability: **Medium**

23. *Answer choices:*
(see index for correct answer)

- a. Ceration
- b. Putrefying bacteria
- c. Fermentation

- d. Solution

*Guidance:* level 1

---

:: Quality assurance ::

The _____ is a United States-based nonprofit tax-exempt 501 organization that accredits more than 21,000 US health care organizations and programs. The international branch accredits medical services from around the world. A majority of US state governments recognize _____ accreditation as a condition of licensure for the receipt of Medicaid and Medicare reimbursements.

Exam Probability: **High**

24. *Answer choices:*

(see index for correct answer)

- a. Quality Assurance Agency for Higher Education
- b. Quality Assurance Authority for Education and Training
- c. Joint Commission
- d. Load testing

*Guidance:* level 1

---

:: Data management ::

_____ is an object-oriented program and library developed by CERN. It was originally designed for particle physics data analysis and contains several features specific to this field, but it is also used in other applications such as astronomy and data mining. The latest release is 6.16.00, as of 2018-11-14.

Exam Probability: **Medium**

25. *Answer choices:*

(see index for correct answer)

- a. Data proliferation
- b. Modular serializability
- c. Automated tiered storage
- d. Data migration

*Guidance:* level 1

:: Industrial processes ::

A _____ is a device used for high-temperature heating. The name derives from Latin word fornax, which means oven. The heat energy to fuel a _____ may be supplied directly by fuel combustion, by electricity such as the electric arc _____ , or through induction heating in induction _____ s.

Exam Probability: **High**

26. *Answer choices:*
(see index for correct answer)

- a. Furnace
- b. Electrosynthesis
- c. Photonic curing
- d. Perforation

*Guidance:* level 1

---

:: Information technology management ::

_____ is a collective term for all approaches to prepare, support and help individuals, teams, and organizations in making organizational change. The most common change drivers include: technological evolution, process reviews, crisis, and consumer habit changes; pressure from new business entrants, acquisitions, mergers, and organizational restructuring. It includes methods that redirect or redefine the use of resources, business process, budget allocations, or other modes of operation that significantly change a company or organization. Organizational _____ considers the full organization and what needs to change, while _____ may be used solely to refer to how people and teams are affected by such organizational transition. It deals with many different disciplines, from behavioral and social sciences to information technology and business solutions.

Exam Probability: **Medium**

27. *Answer choices:*
(see index for correct answer)

- a. Knowledge management software
- b. Cable management
- c. Process-driven application
- d. Speech analytics

*Guidance:* level 1

:: Insulators ::

A _____ is a piece of soft cloth large enough either to cover or to enfold a great portion of the user's body, usually when sleeping or otherwise at rest, thereby trapping radiant bodily heat that otherwise would be lost through convection, and so keeping the body warm.

Exam Probability: **High**

28. *Answer choices:*

(see index for correct answer)

- a. Dynamic insulation
- b. R-value
- c. Draught excluder
- d. Blanket

*Guidance:* level 1

:: Planning ::

_____ is a high level plan to achieve one or more goals under conditions of uncertainty. In the sense of the "art of the general," which included several subsets of skills including tactics, siegecraft, logistics etc., the term came into use in the 6th century C.E. in East Roman terminology, and was translated into Western vernacular languages only in the 18th century. From then until the 20th century, the word "_____" came to denote "a comprehensive way to try to pursue political ends, including the threat or actual use of force, in a dialectic of wills" in a military conflict, in which both adversaries interact.

Exam Probability: **High**

29. *Answer choices:*

(see index for correct answer)

- a. School timetable
- b. Default effect
- c. Strategy
- d. Disruption

*Guidance:* level 1

:: Metalworking ::

A _____ is a round object with various uses. It is used in _____ games, where the play of the game follows the state of the _____ as it is hit, kicked or thrown by players. _____ s can also be used for simpler activities, such as catch or juggling. _____ s made from hard-wearing materials are used in engineering applications to provide very low friction bearings, known as _____ bearings. Black-powder weapons use stone and metal _____ s as projectiles.

Exam Probability: **High**

30. *Answer choices:*
(see index for correct answer)

- a. Ironwork
- b. Cladding
- c. Slotted angle
- d. Ball

*Guidance:* level 1

:: Production and manufacturing ::

_____ is the process of determining the production capacity needed by an organization to meet changing demands for its products. In the context of _____ , design capacity is the maximum amount of work that an organization is capable of completing in a given period. Effective capacity is the maximum amount of work that an organization is capable of completing in a given period due to constraints such as quality problems, delays, material handling, etc.

Exam Probability: **Low**

31. *Answer choices:*
(see index for correct answer)

- a. Equipment service management and rental
- b. Master production schedule
- c. Highly accelerated life test
- d. Wireless DNC

*Guidance:* level 1

:: Business planning ::

_____ is a critical component to the successful delivery of any project, programme or activity. A stakeholder is any individual, group or organization that can affect, be affected by, or perceive itself to be affected by a programme.

Exam Probability: **Medium**

32. *Answer choices:*

(see index for correct answer)

- a. Business war games
- b. Customer Demand Planning
- c. Strategic planning
- d. Stakeholder management

*Guidance:* level 1

---

:: E-commerce ::

_____ is the business-to-business or business-to-consumer or business-to-government purchase and sale of supplies, work, and services through the Internet as well as other information and networking systems, such as electronic data interchange and enterprise resource planning.

Exam Probability: **Low**

33. *Answer choices:*

(see index for correct answer)

- a. E-procurement
- b. KonaKart
- c. Buyhatke
- d. Self-certifying key

*Guidance:* level 1

---

:: Natural resources ::

_____s are resources that exist without actions of humankind. This includes all valued characteristics such as magnetic, gravitational, electrical properties and forces etc. On Earth it includes sunlight, atmosphere, water, land along with all vegetation, crops and animal life that naturally subsists upon or within the heretofore identified characteristics and substances.

Exam Probability: **Medium**

34. *Answer choices:*

(see index for correct answer)

- a. Natural resource
- b. Dryland salinity
- c. QEMSCAN
- d. Consolidated Natural Resources Act of 2008

*Guidance:* level 1

---

:: Project management ::

A _____ is a professional in the field of project management. _____ s have the responsibility of the planning, procurement and execution of a project, in any undertaking that has a defined scope, defined start and a defined finish; regardless of industry. _____ s are first point of contact for any issues or discrepancies arising from within the heads of various departments in an organization before the problem escalates to higher authorities. Project management is the responsibility of a _____. This individual seldom participates directly in the activities that produce the end result, but rather strives to maintain the progress, mutual interaction and tasks of various parties in such a way that reduces the risk of overall failure, maximizes benefits, and minimizes costs.

Exam Probability: **Low**

35. *Answer choices:*

(see index for correct answer)

- a. Theory Z of Ouchi
- b. Schedule
- c. Libyan Project Management Association
- d. Project manager

*Guidance:* level 1

:: Natural materials ::

_____ is a finely-grained natural rock or soil material that combines one or more _____ minerals with possible traces of quartz, metal oxides and organic matter. Geologic _____ deposits are mostly composed of phyllosilicate minerals containing variable amounts of water trapped in the mineral structure. _____ s are plastic due to particle size and geometry as well as water content, and become hard, brittle and non–plastic upon drying or firing. Depending on the soil's content in which it is found, _____ can appear in various colours from white to dull grey or brown to deep orange-red.

Exam Probability: **High**

36. *Answer choices:*
(see index for correct answer)

- a. Decomposed granite
- b. Cobblestone
- c. Withy
- d. Levant bole

*Guidance:* level 1

:: ::

_____ is the process of making predictions of the future based on past and present data and most commonly by analysis of trends. A commonplace example might be estimation of some variable of interest at some specified future date. Prediction is a similar, but more general term. Both might refer to formal statistical methods employing time series, cross-sectional or longitudinal data, or alternatively to less formal judgmental methods. Usage can differ between areas of application: for example, in hydrology the terms "forecast" and "_____" are sometimes reserved for estimates of values at certain specific future times, while the term "prediction" is used for more general estimates, such as the number of times floods will occur over a long period.

Exam Probability: **High**

37. *Answer choices:*
(see index for correct answer)

- a. open system

- b. hierarchical
- c. Sarbanes-Oxley act of 2002
- d. co-culture

*Guidance:* level 1

:: Business process ::

_____ is the value to an enterprise which is derived from the techniques, procedures, and programs that implement and enhance the delivery of goods and services. _____ is one of the three components of structural capital, itself a component of intellectual capital. _____ can be seen as the value of processes to any entity, whether for profit or not-for profit, but is most commonly used in reference to for-profit entities.

Exam Probability: **High**

38. *Answer choices:*
(see index for correct answer)

- a. Extended Enterprise Modeling Language
- b. Real-time enterprise
- c. Social BPM
- d. Order processing

*Guidance:* level 1

:: Data management ::

_____ refers to a data-driven improvement cycle used for improving, optimizing and stabilizing business processes and designs. The _____ improvement cycle is the core tool used to drive Six Sigma projects. However, _____ is not exclusive to Six Sigma and can be used as the framework for other improvement applications.

Exam Probability: **Medium**

39. *Answer choices:*
(see index for correct answer)

- a. Core data integration
- b. Single customer view
- c. Tuple
- d. Automated tiered storage

Guidance: level 1

:: Project management ::

_____ is the right to exercise power, which can be formalized by a state and exercised by way of judges, appointed executives of government, or the ecclesiastical or priestly appointed representatives of a God or other deities.

Exam Probability: **High**

40. *Answer choices:*
(see index for correct answer)

- a. Research program
- b. Authority
- c. Budgeted cost of work performed
- d. Trenegy Incorporated

Guidance: level 1

:: Management ::

A process is a unique combination of tools, materials, methods, and people engaged in producing a measurable output; for example a manufacturing line for machine parts. All processes have inherent statistical variability which can be evaluated by statistical methods.

Exam Probability: **Low**

41. *Answer choices:*
(see index for correct answer)

- a. Goals Breakdown Structure
- b. Process capability
- c. Quality, cost, delivery
- d. Document automation

Guidance: level 1

:: Building materials ::

_____ is an alloy of iron and carbon, and sometimes other elements. Because of its high tensile strength and low cost, it is a major component used in buildings, infrastructure, tools, ships, automobiles, machines, appliances, and weapons.

Exam Probability: **Low**

42. *Answer choices:*
(see index for correct answer)

- a. Turbo seal
- b. Hydraulic lime
- c. Vinyl siding
- d. Engineered wood

*Guidance:* level 1

---

:: Management ::

_____ is a term used in business and Information Technology to describe the in-depth process of capturing customer's expectations, preferences and aversions. Specifically, the _____ is a market research technique that produces a detailed set of customer wants and needs, organized into a hierarchical structure, and then prioritized in terms of relative importance and satisfaction with current alternatives. _____ studies typically consist of both qualitative and quantitative research steps. They are generally conducted at the start of any new product, process, or service design initiative in order to better understand the customer's wants and needs, and as the key input for new product definition, Quality Function Deployment, and the setting of detailed design specifications.

Exam Probability: **Medium**

43. *Answer choices:*
(see index for correct answer)

- a. Voice of the customer
- b. Corporate recovery
- c. Behavioral risk management
- d. Community-based management

*Guidance:* level 1

:: Project management ::

Contemporary business and science treat as a _____ any undertaking, carried out individually or collaboratively and possibly involving research or design, that is carefully planned to achieve a particular aim.

Exam Probability: **Low**

44. *Answer choices:*
(see index for correct answer)

- a. Student syndrome
- b. TELOS
- c. Project
- d. Vertical slice

*Guidance:* level 1

:: Quality control tools ::

A _____ is a type of diagram that represents an algorithm, workflow or process. _____ can also be defined as a diagramatic representation of an algorithm.

Exam Probability: **Low**

45. *Answer choices:*
(see index for correct answer)

- a. Scatter diagram
- b. Flowchart
- c. X-bar chart
- d. P-chart

*Guidance:* level 1

:: Marketing techniques ::

A _____ is an award to be given to a person, a group of people like a sports team, or organization to recognise and reward actions or achievements. Official _____ s often involve monetary rewards as well as the fame that comes with them. Some _____ s are also associated with extravagant awarding ceremonies, such as the Academy Awards.

Exam Probability: **Medium**

46. *Answer choices:*

(see index for correct answer)

- a. Prize
- b. Wait marketing
- c. Virtual event
- d. Blackout dates

*Guidance:* level 1

:: Goods ::

In most contexts, the concept of _____ denotes the conduct that should be preferred when posed with a choice between possible actions. _____ is generally considered to be the opposite of evil, and is of interest in the study of morality, ethics, religion and philosophy. The specific meaning and etymology of the term and its associated translations among ancient and contemporary languages show substantial variation in its inflection and meaning depending on circumstances of place, history, religious, or philosophical context.

Exam Probability: **Low**

47. *Answer choices:*

(see index for correct answer)

- a. Case
- b. Positional good
- c. Good
- d. Rivalry

*Guidance:* level 1

:: Commercial item transport and distribution ::

In commerce, supply-chain management, the management of the flow of goods and services, involves the movement and storage of raw materials, of work-in-process inventory, and of finished goods from point of origin to point of consumption. Interconnected or interlinked networks, channels and node businesses combine in the provision of products and services required by end customers in a supply chain. Supply-chain management has been defined as the "design, planning, execution, control, and monitoring of supply-chain activities with the objective of creating net value, building a competitive infrastructure, leveraging worldwide logistics, synchronizing supply with demand and measuring performance globally."SCM practice draws heavily from the areas of industrial engineering, systems engineering, operations management, logistics, procurement, information technology, and marketing and strives for an integrated approach. Marketing channels play an important role in supply-chain management. Current research in supply-chain management is concerned with topics related to sustainability and risk management, among others. Some suggest that the "people dimension" of SCM, ethical issues, internal integration, transparency/visibility, and human capital/talent management are topics that have, so far, been underrepresented on the research agenda.

Exam Probability: **Medium**

48. *Answer choices:*
(see index for correct answer)

- a. Spoke-hub distribution paradigm
- b. Supply chain management
- c. Dock
- d. Oversize load

*Guidance:* level 1

---

:: Accounting source documents ::

A _____ is a commercial document and first official offer issued by a buyer to a seller indicating types, quantities, and agreed prices for products or services. It is used to control the purchasing of products and services from external suppliers. _____ s can be an essential part of enterprise resource planning system orders.

Exam Probability: **Medium**

49. *Answer choices:*

(see index for correct answer)

- a. Parcel audit
- b. Invoice
- c. Credit memo
- d. Bank statement

*Guidance:* level 1

:: Monopoly (economics) ::

_____ are "efficiencies formed by variety, not volume". For example, a gas station that sells gasoline can sell soda, milk, baked goods, etc through their customer service representatives and thus achieve gasoline companies _____ .

Exam Probability: **Low**

50. *Answer choices:*

(see index for correct answer)

- a. Economies of scope
- b. Monopsony
- c. Concentration ratio
- d. Price-cap regulation

*Guidance:* level 1

:: Commerce ::

A _____ is an employee within a company, business or other organization who is responsible at some level for buying or approving the acquisition of goods and services needed by the company. Responsible for buying the best quality products, goods and services for their company at the most competitive prices, _____ s work in a wide range of sectors for many different organizations. The position responsibilities may be the same as that of a buyer or purchasing agent, or may include wider supervisory or managerial responsibilities. A _____ may oversee the acquisition of materials needed for production, general supplies for offices and facilities, equipment, or construction contracts. A _____ often supervises purchasing agents and buyers, but in small companies the _____ may also be the purchasing agent or buyer. The _____ position may also carry the title "Procurement Manager" or in the public sector, "Procurement Officer". He or she can come from both an Engineering or Economics background.

Exam Probability: **Low**

51. *Answer choices:*

(see index for correct answer)

- a. Hong Kong Mercantile Exchange
- b. Haul video
- c. Issuing bank
- d. Purchasing manager

*Guidance:* level 1

---

:: Costs ::

In process improvement efforts, _____ or cost of quality is a means to quantify the total cost of quality-related efforts and deficiencies. It was first described by Armand V. Feigenbaum in a 1956 Harvard Business Review article.

Exam Probability: **Medium**

52. *Answer choices:*

(see index for correct answer)

- a. Customer Cost
- b. Quality costs
- c. Total cost of acquisition
- d. Cost per paper

*Guidance:* level 1

:: ::

Catalysis is the process of increasing the rate of a chemical reaction by adding a substance known as a _____ , which is not consumed in the catalyzed reaction and can continue to act repeatedly. Because of this, only very small amounts of _____ are required to alter the reaction rate in principle.

Exam Probability: **Medium**

53. *Answer choices:*
(see index for correct answer)

- a. Catalyst
- b. functional perspective
- c. interpersonal communication
- d. open system

*Guidance:* level 1

:: Project management ::

_____ is a marketing activity that does an aggregate plan for the production process, in advance of 6 to 18 months, to give an idea to management as to what quantity of materials and other resources are to be procured and when, so that the total cost of operations of the organization is kept to the minimum over that period.

Exam Probability: **Medium**

54. *Answer choices:*
(see index for correct answer)

- a. Project manager
- b. Outcome mapping
- c. Trenegy Incorporated
- d. Pre-mortem

*Guidance:* level 1

:: Project management ::

A _____ is a source or supply from which a benefit is produced and it has some utility. _____ s can broadly be classified upon their availability—they are classified into renewable and non-renewable _____ s. Examples of non renewable _____ s are coal ,crude oil natural gas nuclear energy etc. Examples of renewable _____ s are air,water,wind,solar energy etc. They can also be classified as actual and potential on the basis of level of development and use, on the basis of origin they can be classified as biotic and abiotic, and on the basis of their distribution, as ubiquitous and localized . An item becomes a _____ with time and developing technology. Typically, _____ s are materials, energy, services, staff, knowledge, or other assets that are transformed to produce benefit and in the process may be consumed or made unavailable. Benefits of _____ utilization may include increased wealth, proper functioning of a system, or enhanced well-being. From a human perspective a natural _____ is anything obtained from the environment to satisfy human needs and wants. From a broader biological or ecological perspective a _____ satisfies the needs of a living organism .

Exam Probability: **High**

55. *Answer choices:*

(see index for correct answer)

- a. Graphical Evaluation and Review Technique
- b. American Society of Professional Estimators
- c. Research program
- d. Theory Z of Ouchi

*Guidance:* level 1

:: Fault-tolerant computer systems ::

_____ decision-making is a group decision-making process in which group members develop, and agree to support a decision in the best interest of the whole group or common goal. _____ may be defined professionally as an acceptable resolution, one that can be supported, even if not the "favourite" of each individual. It has its origin in the Latin word consensus , which is from consentio meaning literally feel together. It is used to describe both the decision and the process of reaching a decision. _____ decision-making is thus concerned with the process of deliberating and finalizing a decision, and the social, economic, legal, environmental and political effects of applying this process.

Exam Probability: **Medium**

56. *Answer choices:*

(see index for correct answer)

- a. Raft
- b. RAID
- c. SpaceWire
- d. Consensus

*Guidance:* level 1

:: ::

_____ refers to the confirmation of certain characteristics of an object, person, or organization. This confirmation is often, but not always, provided by some form of external review, education, assessment, or audit. Accreditation is a specific organization's process of _____ . According to the National Council on Measurement in Education, a _____ test is a credentialing test used to determine whether individuals are knowledgeable enough in a given occupational area to be labeled "competent to practice" in that area.

Exam Probability: **Medium**

57. *Answer choices:*

(see index for correct answer)

- a. Certification
- b. information systems assessment
- c. Character
- d. levels of analysis

*Guidance:* level 1

:: Process management ::

_____ is a statistics package developed at the Pennsylvania State University by researchers Barbara F. Ryan, Thomas A. Ryan, Jr., and Brian L. Joiner in 1972. It began as a light version of OMNITAB 80, a statistical analysis program by NIST. Statistical analysis software such as _____ automates calculations and the creation of graphs, allowing the user to focus more on the analysis of data and the interpretation of results. It is compatible with other _____ , Inc. software.

Exam Probability: **Medium**

58. *Answer choices:*
(see index for correct answer)

- a. Process specification
- b. business process re-engineering
- c. YAWL
- d. Proactive contracting

*Guidance:* level 1

:: Sampling (statistics) ::

_____ uses statistical sampling to determine whether to accept or reject a production lot of material. It has been a common quality control technique used in industry. It is usually done as products leaves the factory, or in some cases even within the factory. Most often a producer supplies a consumer a number of items and a decision to accept or reject the items is made by determining the number of defective items in a sample from the lot. The lot is accepted if the number of defects falls below where the acceptance number or otherwise the lot is rejected.

Exam Probability: **High**

59. *Answer choices:*
(see index for correct answer)

- a. Non-sampling error
- b. Survey of Consumer Finances
- c. Acceptance sampling
- d. Inclusion probability

*Guidance*: level 1

## Commerce

Commerce relates to "the exchange of goods and services, especially on a large scale." It includes legal, economic, political, social, cultural and technological systems that operate in any country or internationally.

---

:: Minimum wage ::

A _____ is the lowest remuneration that employers can legally pay their workers—the price floor below which workers may not sell their labor. Most countries had introduced _____ legislation by the end of the 20th century.

Exam Probability: **High**

1. *Answer choices:*

(see index for correct answer)

- a. Minimum wage
- b. Minimum wage in Taiwan
- c. Minimum Wage Fairness Act
- d. Working poor

*Guidance:* level 1

---

:: ::

_____ Corporation is an American multinational technology company with headquarters in Redmond, Washington. It develops, manufactures, licenses, supports and sells computer software, consumer electronics, personal computers, and related services. Its best known software products are the _____ Windows line of operating systems, the _____ Office suite, and the Internet Explorer and Edge Web browsers. Its flagship hardware products are the Xbox video game consoles and the _____ Surface lineup of touchscreen personal computers. As of 2016, it is the world's largest software maker by revenue, and one of the world's most valuable companies. The word "_____" is a portmanteau of "microcomputer" and "software". _____ is ranked No. 30 in the 2018 Fortune 500 rankings of the largest United States corporations by total revenue.

Exam Probability: **Medium**

2. *Answer choices:*

(see index for correct answer)

- a. imperative
- b. hierarchical perspective
- c. personal values
- d. Microsoft

*Guidance:* level 1

---

:: ::

A _____ is monetary compensation paid by an employer to an employee in exchange for work done. Payment may be calculated as a fixed amount for each task completed, or at an hourly or daily rate, or based on an easily measured quantity of work done.

Exam Probability: **High**

3. *Answer choices:*

(see index for correct answer)

- a. information systems assessment
- b. imperative
- c. open system
- d. levels of analysis

*Guidance:* level 1

:: E-commerce ::

_____ Inc. was an electronic money corporation founded by David Chaum in 1989. _____ transactions were unique in that they were anonymous due to a number of cryptographic protocols developed by its founder. _____ declared bankruptcy in 1998, and subsequently sold its assets to eCash Technologies, another digital currency company, which was acquired by InfoSpace on Feb. 19, 2002.

Exam Probability: **High**

4. *Answer choices:*

(see index for correct answer)

- a. Ashley Ebner
- b. Cyberservices
- c. Optimize Capital Markets
- d. Friend-to-friend

*Guidance:* level 1

:: ::

_____ is the collection of techniques, skills, methods, and processes used in the production of goods or services or in the accomplishment of objectives, such as scientific investigation. _____ can be the knowledge of techniques, processes, and the like, or it can be embedded in machines to allow for operation without detailed knowledge of their workings. Systems applying _____ by taking an input, changing it according to the system's use, and then producing an outcome are referred to as _____ systems or technological systems.

Exam Probability: **Low**

5. *Answer choices:*

(see index for correct answer)

- a. hierarchical perspective
- b. Technology
- c. Sarbanes-Oxley act of 2002
- d. open system

*Guidance:* level 1

:: Information technology management ::

B2B is often contrasted with business-to-consumer. In B2B commerce, it is often the case that the parties to the relationship have comparable negotiating power, and even when they do not, each party typically involves professional staff and legal counsel in the negotiation of terms, whereas B2C is shaped to a far greater degree by economic implications of information asymmetry. However, within a B2B context, large companies may have many commercial, resource and information advantages over smaller businesses. The United Kingdom government, for example, created the post of Small Business Commissioner under the Enterprise Act 2016 to "enable small businesses to resolve disputes" and "consider complaints by small business suppliers about payment issues with larger businesses that they supply."

Exam Probability: **Low**

6. *Answer choices:*

(see index for correct answer)

- a. Prolifics
- b. Pop-up ad
- c. Customer intelligence
- d. Business-to-business

*Guidance:* level 1

:: Accounting source documents ::

An _____, bill or tab is a commercial document issued by a seller to a buyer, relating to a sale transaction and indicating the products, quantities, and agreed prices for products or services the seller had provided the buyer.

Exam Probability: **High**

7. *Answer choices:*

(see index for correct answer)

- a. Bank statement
- b. Invoice
- c. Parcel audit
- d. Purchase order

*Guidance:* level 1

:: Quality management ::

_____ ensures that an organization, product or service is consistent. It has four main components: quality planning, quality assurance, quality control and quality improvement. _____ is focused not only on product and service quality, but also on the means to achieve it. _____ , therefore, uses quality assurance and control of processes as well as products to achieve more consistent quality. What a customer wants and is willing to pay for it determines quality. It is written or unwritten commitment to a known or unknown consumer in the market . Thus, quality can be defined as fitness for intended use or, in other words, how well the product performs its intended function

Exam Probability: **Low**

8. *Answer choices:*

(see index for correct answer)

- a. Dana Ulery
- b. Quality Management Maturity Grid
- c. Quality management
- d. Management by wandering around

*Guidance:* level 1

:: Payment systems ::

Amazon Pay is an online payments processing service that is owned by Amazon. Launched in 2007, Amazon Pay uses the consumer base of Amazon.com and focuses on giving users the option to pay with their Amazon accounts on external merchant websites. As of January 2019 the service is available in Austria, Belgium, Cyprus, Germany, Denmark, Spain, France, Hungary, Luxembourg, Republic of Ireland, India, Italy, Japan, Netherlands, Portugal, Sweden, United Kingdom, United States.

Exam Probability: **Low**

9. *Answer choices:*

(see index for correct answer)

- a. Amazon Payments
- b. Mefo bills
- c. Certified check
- d. Euronet Pakistan

*Guidance:* level 1

:: Marketing ::

_____ is a concept introduced in a book of the same name in 1999 by marketing expert Seth Godin. _____ is a non-traditional marketing technique that advertises goods and services when advance consent is given.

Exam Probability: **Medium**

10. *Answer choices:*
(see index for correct answer)

- a. Gladvertising
- b. Permission marketing
- c. Mobile marketing research
- d. Configurator

*Guidance:* level 1

:: Auctioneering ::

A _____ is one of several similar kinds of auctions. Most commonly, it means an auction in which the auctioneer begins with a high asking price, and lowers it until some participant accepts the price, or it reaches a predetermined reserve price. This has also been called a clock auction or open-outcry descending-price auction. This type of auction is good for auctioning goods quickly, since a sale never requires more than one bid. Strategically, it's similar to a first-price sealed-bid auction.

Exam Probability: **High**

11. *Answer choices:*
(see index for correct answer)

- a. Auctionata
- b. Auction school
- c. Dutch auction
- d. Chinese auction

*Guidance:* level 1

:: Auctioneering ::

A _____ is a type of sealed-bid auction. Bidders submit written bids without knowing the bid of the other people in the auction. The highest bidder wins but the price paid is the second-highest bid. This type of auction is strategically similar to an English auction and gives bidders an incentive to bid their true value. The auction was first described academically by Columbia University professor William Vickrey in 1961 though it had been used by stamp collectors since 1893. In 1797 Johann Wolfgang von Goethe sold a manuscript using a sealed-bid, second-price auction.

Exam Probability: **Medium**

12. *Answer choices:*

(see index for correct answer)

- a. Vickrey auction
- b. Auction chant
- c. Auction catalog
- d. How Much Wood Would a Woodchuck Chuck

*Guidance:* level 1

:: Stochastic processes ::

_____ in its modern meaning is a "new idea, creative thoughts, new imaginations in form of device or method". _____ is often also viewed as the application of better solutions that meet new requirements, unarticulated needs, or existing market needs. Such _____ takes place through the provision of more-effective products, processes, services, technologies, or business models that are made available to markets, governments and society. An _____ is something original and more effective and, as a consequence, new, that "breaks into" the market or society. _____ is related to, but not the same as, invention, as _____ is more apt to involve the practical implementation of an invention to make a meaningful impact in the market or society, and not all _____ s require an invention. _____ often manifests itself via the engineering process, when the problem being solved is of a technical or scientific nature. The opposite of _____ is exnovation.

Exam Probability: **High**

13. *Answer choices:*

(see index for correct answer)

- a. Markov kernel
- b. Girsanov theorem
- c. Innovation
- d. Brownian meander

*Guidance:* level 1

:: ::

A _____ is a sworn body of people convened to render an impartial verdict officially submitted to them by a court, or to set a penalty or judgment. Modern juries tend to be found in courts to ascertain the guilt or lack thereof in a crime. In Anglophone jurisdictions, the verdict may be guilty or not guilty. The old institution of grand juries still exists in some places, particularly the United States, to investigate whether enough evidence of a crime exists to bring someone to trial.

Exam Probability: **Low**

14. *Answer choices:*

(see index for correct answer)

- a. Jury
- b. Character
- c. process perspective
- d. information systems assessment

*Guidance:* level 1

:: E-commerce ::

A _____ is a financial transaction involving a very small sum of money and usually one that occurs online. A number of _____ systems were proposed and developed in the mid-to-late 1990s, all of which were ultimately unsuccessful. A second generation of _____ systems emerged in the 2010s.

Exam Probability: **Medium**

15. *Answer choices:*

(see index for correct answer)

- a. Presumed security
- b. E-commerce payment system
- c. Public eProcurement
- d. Micropayment

*Guidance:* level 1

:: Production economics ::

In economics, _____ is the change in the total cost that arises when the quantity produced is incremented by one unit; that is, it is the cost of producing one more unit of a good. Intuitively, _____ at each level of production includes the cost of any additional inputs required to produce the next unit. At each level of production and time period being considered, _____ s include all costs that vary with the level of production, whereas other costs that do not vary with production are fixed and thus have no _____ . For example, the _____ of producing an automobile will generally include the costs of labor and parts needed for the additional automobile but not the fixed costs of the factory that have already been incurred. In practice, marginal analysis is segregated into short and long-run cases, so that, over the long run, all costs become marginal. Where there are economies of scale, prices set at _____ will fail to cover total costs, thus requiring a subsidy. _____ pricing is not a matter of merely lowering the general level of prices with the aid of a subsidy; with or without subsidy it calls for a drastic restructuring of pricing practices, with opportunities for very substantial improvements in efficiency at critical points.

Exam Probability: **High**

16. *Answer choices:*
(see index for correct answer)

- a. Factor price
- b. Average fixed cost
- c. Post-Fordism
- d. Marginal rate of technical substitution

*Guidance:* level 1

:: ::

_____ is a term frequently used in marketing. It is a measure of how products and services supplied by a company meet or surpass customer expectation. _____ is defined as "the number of customers, or percentage of total customers, whose reported experience with a firm, its products, or its services exceeds specified satisfaction goals."

Exam Probability: **Medium**

17. *Answer choices:*
(see index for correct answer)

- a. co-culture
- b. deep-level diversity
- c. information systems assessment
- d. Customer satisfaction

*Guidance:* level 1

:: International trade ::

_____ involves the transfer of goods or services from one person or entity to another, often in exchange for money. A system or network that allows _____ is called a market.

Exam Probability: **Low**

18. *Answer choices:*
(see index for correct answer)

- a. European Union Customs Union
- b. Special drawing rights
- c. National Trade Estimate Report
- d. Reimportation

*Guidance:* level 1

:: ::

A _____ is a professional who provides expert advice in a particular area such as security, management, education, accountancy, law, human resources, marketing, finance, engineering, science or any of many other specialized fields.

Exam Probability: **Medium**

19. *Answer choices:*

(see index for correct answer)

- a. Character
- b. Consultant
- c. cultural
- d. similarity-attraction theory

*Guidance:* level 1

:: Stock market ::

_____ is freedom from, or resilience against, potential harm caused by others. Beneficiaries of _____ may be of persons and social groups, objects and institutions, ecosystems or any other entity or phenomenon vulnerable to unwanted change by its environment.

Exam Probability: **High**

20. *Answer choices:*

(see index for correct answer)

- a. Security
- b. Bear raid
- c. Big boy letter
- d. Microcap

*Guidance:* level 1

:: E-commerce ::

_____ is the activity of buying or selling of products on online services or over the Internet. Electronic commerce draws on technologies such as mobile commerce, electronic funds transfer, supply chain management, Internet marketing, online transaction processing, electronic data interchange , inventory management systems, and automated data collection systems.

Exam Probability: **Medium**

21. *Answer choices:*

(see index for correct answer)

- a. Internet Marketing Conference
- b. NopCommerce

- c. Superdistribution
- d. Extended Validation Certificate

Guidance: level 1

:: ::

_____ is getting a diploma or academic degree or the ceremony that is sometimes associated with it, in which students become graduates. The date of _____ is often called _____ day. The _____ ceremony itself is also called commencement, convocation or invocation.

Exam Probability: **Medium**

22. *Answer choices:*
(see index for correct answer)

- a. surface-level diversity
- b. Graduation
- c. information systems assessment
- d. hierarchical

Guidance: level 1

:: Materials ::

A _____, also known as a feedstock, unprocessed material, or primary commodity, is a basic material that is used to produce goods, finished products, energy, or intermediate materials which are feedstock for future finished products. As feedstock, the term connotes these materials are bottleneck assets and are highly important with regard to producing other products. An example of this is crude oil, which is a _____ and a feedstock used in the production of industrial chemicals, fuels, plastics, and pharmaceutical goods; lumber is a _____ used to produce a variety of products including all types of furniture. The term "_____" denotes materials in minimally processed or unprocessed in states; e.g., raw latex, crude oil, cotton, coal, raw biomass, iron ore, air, logs, or water i.e. "...any product of agriculture, forestry, fishing and any other mineral that is in its natural form or which has undergone the transformation required to prepare it for internationally marketing in substantial volumes."

Exam Probability: **Low**

23. *Answer choices:*

(see index for correct answer)

- a. Raw material
- b. Ice substitute
- c. Saturated-surface-dry
- d. Materials World

*Guidance:* level 1

---

:: Evaluation ::

_____ is a way of preventing mistakes and defects in manufactured products and avoiding problems when delivering products or services to customers; which ISO 9000 defines as "part of quality management focused on providing confidence that quality requirements will be fulfilled". This defect prevention in _____ differs subtly from defect detection and rejection in quality control and has been referred to as a shift left since it focuses on quality earlier in the process.

Exam Probability: **Low**

24. *Answer choices:*

(see index for correct answer)

- a. Quality assurance
- b. Knowledge survey
- c. Program evaluation
- d. Princeton Application Repository for Shared-Memory Computers

*Guidance:* level 1

---

:: Scientific method ::

In the social sciences and life sciences, a _____ is a research method involving an up-close, in-depth, and detailed examination of a subject of study, as well as its related contextual conditions.

Exam Probability: **Medium**

25. *Answer choices:*

(see index for correct answer)

- a. Preference test
- b. Causal research

- c. Case study
- d. explanatory research

*Guidance:* level 1

---

:: ::

An _____ is the production of goods or related services within an economy. The major source of revenue of a group or company is the indicator of its relevant _____ . When a large group has multiple sources of revenue generation, it is considered to be working in different industries. Manufacturing _____ became a key sector of production and labour in European and North American countries during the Industrial Revolution, upsetting previous mercantile and feudal economies. This came through many successive rapid advances in technology, such as the production of steel and coal.

Exam Probability: **Low**

26. *Answer choices:*
(see index for correct answer)

- a. functional perspective
- b. empathy
- c. Industry
- d. imperative

*Guidance:* level 1

---

:: Data interchange standards ::

_____ is the concept of businesses electronically communicating information that was traditionally communicated on paper, such as purchase orders and invoices. Technical standards for EDI exist to facilitate parties transacting such instruments without having to make special arrangements.

Exam Probability: **Medium**

27. *Answer choices:*
(see index for correct answer)

- a. Data Interchange Standards Association
- b. ASC X12
- c. Interaction protocol

- d. Electronic data interchange

*Guidance:* level 1

---

:: Industrial Revolution ::

The _____ , now also known as the First _____ , was the transition to new manufacturing processes in Europe and the US, in the period from about 1760 to sometime between 1820 and 1840. This transition included going from hand production methods to machines, new chemical manufacturing and iron production processes, the increasing use of steam power and water power, the development of machine tools and the rise of the mechanized factory system. The _____ also led to an unprecedented rise in the rate of population growth.

Exam Probability: **Medium**

28. *Answer choices:*

(see index for correct answer)

- a. Industrial Revolution
- b. Water frame
- c. Sykes Bleaching Company
- d. Stott

*Guidance:* level 1

---

:: ::

Senior management, executive management, upper management, or a _____ is generally a team of individuals at the highest level of management of an organization who have the day-to-day tasks of managing that organization — sometimes a company or a corporation.

Exam Probability: **Medium**

29. *Answer choices:*

(see index for correct answer)

- a. hierarchical perspective
- b. similarity-attraction theory
- c. Management team
- d. process perspective

*Guidance:* level 1

_____ is an emotion involving pleasure, , or anxiety in considering or awaiting an expected event.

Exam Probability: **Medium**

30. *Answer choices:*

(see index for correct answer)

- a. Character
- b. open system
- c. Anticipation
- d. empathy

*Guidance:* level 1

:: Export and import control ::

" _____ " means the Government Service which is responsible for the administration of _____ law and the collection of duties and taxes and which also has the responsibility for the application of other laws and regulations relating to the importation, exportation, movement or storage of goods.

Exam Probability: **Low**

31. *Answer choices:*

(see index for correct answer)

- a. Canadian Export and Import Controls Bureau
- b. International Traffic in Arms Regulations
- c. GOST R Conformity Declaration
- d. Wassenaar Arrangement

*Guidance:* level 1

In Western musical notation, the staff or stave is a set of five horizontal lines and four spaces that each represent a different musical pitch or in the case of a percussion staff, different percussion instruments. Appropriate music symbols, depending on the intended effect, are placed on the staff according to their corresponding pitch or function. Musical notes are placed by pitch, percussion notes are placed by instrument, and rests and other symbols are placed by convention.

Exam Probability: **High**

32. *Answer choices:*

(see index for correct answer)

- a. open system
- b. Sarbanes-Oxley act of 2002
- c. similarity-attraction theory
- d. imperative

*Guidance:* level 1

:: Commercial item transport and distribution ::

Wholesaling or distributing is the sale of goods or merchandise to retailers; to industrial, commercial, institutional, or other professional business users; or to other _____rs and related subordinated services. In general, it is the sale of goods to anyone other than a standard consumer.

Exam Probability: **Low**

33. *Answer choices:*

(see index for correct answer)

- a. Wholesale
- b. Hold
- c. Tanker
- d. Supply chain management

*Guidance:* level 1

:: ::

A _____ is an individual or institution that legally owns one or more shares of stock in a public or private corporation. _____ s may be referred to as members of a corporation. Legally, a person is not a _____ in a corporation until their name and other details are entered in the corporation's register of _____ s or members.

Exam Probability: **High**

34. *Answer choices:*

(see index for correct answer)

- a. process perspective
- b. corporate values
- c. hierarchical
- d. information systems assessment

*Guidance:* level 1

---

:: Statutory law ::

_____ or statute law is written law set down by a body of legislature or by a singular legislator. This is as opposed to oral or customary law; or regulatory law promulgated by the executive or common law of the judiciary. Statutes may originate with national, state legislatures or local municipalities.

Exam Probability: **Medium**

35. *Answer choices:*

(see index for correct answer)

- a. Statutory law
- b. statute law
- c. ratification
- d. incorporation by reference

*Guidance:* level 1

---

:: Dot-com bubble ::

_____, Inc., is a web search engine and web portal established in 1994, spun out of Carnegie Mellon University. _____ also encompasses a network of email, webhosting, social networking, and entertainment websites. The company is based in Waltham, Massachusetts, and is currently a subsidiary of Kakao.

Exam Probability: **Medium**

36. *Answer choices:*
(see index for correct answer)

- a. Irrational exuberance
- b. Beenz
- c. Lycos
- d. Epidemic Marketing

*Guidance:* level 1

:: Management ::

In business, a _____ is the attribute that allows an organization to outperform its competitors. A _____ may include access to natural resources, such as high-grade ores or a low-cost power source, highly skilled labor, geographic location, high entry barriers, and access to new technology.

Exam Probability: **Low**

37. *Answer choices:*
(see index for correct answer)

- a. Design management
- b. Mobile sales enablement
- c. Community management
- d. Top development

*Guidance:* level 1

:: Consumer theory ::

A _____ is a technical term in psychology, economics and philosophy usually used in relation to choosing between alternatives. For example, someone prefers A over B if they would rather choose A than B.

Exam Probability: **High**

38. *Answer choices:*

(see index for correct answer)

- a. Hicksian demand function
- b. Consumer choice
- c. Revealed preference
- d. Expenditure function

*Guidance:* level 1

:: Price fixing convictions ::

_____ AG is a German multinational conglomerate company headquartered in Berlin and Munich and the largest industrial manufacturing company in Europe with branch offices abroad.

Exam Probability: **High**

39. *Answer choices:*

(see index for correct answer)

- a. YKK Group
- b. Northwest Airlines
- c. Heineken International
- d. SK Foods

*Guidance:* level 1

:: ::

_____ is the practice of deliberately managing the spread of information between an individual or an organization and the public. _____ may include an organization or individual gaining exposure to their audiences using topics of public interest and news items that do not require direct payment. This differentiates it from advertising as a form of marketing communications. _____ is the idea of creating coverage for clients for free, rather than marketing or advertising. But now, advertising is also a part of greater PR Activities. An example of good _____ would be generating an article featuring a client, rather than paying for the client to be advertised next to the article. The aim of _____ is to inform the public, prospective customers, investors, partners, employees, and other stakeholders and ultimately persuade them to maintain a positive or favorable view about the organization, its leadership, products, or political decisions. _____ professionals typically work for PR and marketing firms, businesses and companies, government, and public officials as PIOs and nongovernmental organizations, and nonprofit organizations. Jobs central to _____ include account coordinator, account executive, account supervisor, and media relations manager.

Exam Probability: **High**

40. *Answer choices:*

<small>(see index for correct answer)</small>

- a. co-culture
- b. personal values
- c. hierarchical
- d. levels of analysis

<small>*Guidance:* level 1</small>

---

:: Logistics ::

_____ is generally the detailed organization and implementation of a complex operation. In a general business sense, _____ is the management of the flow of things between the point of origin and the point of consumption in order to meet requirements of customers or corporations. The resources managed in _____ may include tangible goods such as materials, equipment, and supplies, as well as food and other consumable items. The _____ of physical items usually involves the integration of information flow, materials handling, production, packaging, inventory, transportation, warehousing, and often security.

Exam Probability: **Low**

41. *Answer choices:*

(see index for correct answer)

- a. Distribution resource planning
- b. Waybill
- c. Center for Transportation and Logistics Neuer Adler
- d. Logistics

*Guidance:* level 1

:: ::

_____ is an abstract concept of management of complex systems according to a set of rules and trends. In systems theory, these types of rules exist in various fields of biology and society, but the term has slightly different meanings according to context. For example.

Exam Probability: **High**

42. *Answer choices:*

(see index for correct answer)

- a. cultural
- b. personal values
- c. empathy
- d. Regulation

*Guidance:* level 1

:: Business models ::

A _____ is "an autonomous association of persons united voluntarily to meet their common economic, social, and cultural needs and aspirations through a jointly-owned and democratically-controlled enterprise". _____ s may include.

Exam Probability: **Medium**

43. *Answer choices:*
(see index for correct answer)

- a. Professional open source
- b. Component business model
- c. Volatility, uncertainty, complexity and ambiguity
- d. InnovationXchange

*Guidance:* level 1

:: Meetings ::

A _____ is a body of one or more persons that is subordinate to a deliberative assembly. Usually, the assembly sends matters into a _____ as a way to explore them more fully than would be possible if the assembly itself were considering them. _____ s may have different functions and their type of work differ depending on the type of the organization and its needs.

Exam Probability: **Medium**

44. *Answer choices:*
(see index for correct answer)

- a. Committee
- b. Over the Air
- c. Code Camp
- d. 2006 Russian March

*Guidance:* level 1

:: Market structure and pricing ::

_____ has historically emerged in two separate types of discussions in economics, that of Adam Smith on the one hand, and that of Karl Marx on the other hand. Adam Smith in his writing on economics stressed the importance of laissez-faire principles outlining the operation of the market in the absence of dominant political mechanisms of control, while Karl Marx discussed the working of the market in the presence of a controlled economy sometimes referred to as a command economy in the literature. Both types of _____ have been in historical evidence throughout the twentieth century and twenty-first century.

Exam Probability: **High**

45. *Answer choices:*
(see index for correct answer)

- a. Market structure
- b. industry concentration
- c. Liberalization
- d. Installed base

*Guidance:* level 1

:: Information retrieval ::

_____ is a technique used by recommender systems. _____ has two senses, a narrow one and a more general one.

Exam Probability: **Medium**

46. *Answer choices:*
(see index for correct answer)

- a. Collaborative filtering
- b. Greenpilot
- c. Literature-based discovery
- d. Champion list

*Guidance:* level 1

:: Marketing techniques ::

_____ is the activity of dividing a broad consumer or business market, normally consisting of existing and potential customers, into sub-groups of consumers based on some type of shared characteristics. In dividing or segmenting markets, researchers typically look for common characteristics such as shared needs, common interests, similar lifestyles or even similar demographic profiles. The overall aim of segmentation is to identify high yield segments – that is, those segments that are likely to be the most profitable or that have growth potential – so that these can be selected for special attention .

Exam Probability: **High**

47. *Answer choices:*

(see index for correct answer)

- a. Horizontal marketing system
- b. Appeal to fear
- c. Precision marketing
- d. Market segmentation

*Guidance:* level 1

:: ::

_____ s and acquisitions are transactions in which the ownership of companies, other business organizations, or their operating units are transferred or consolidated with other entities. As an aspect of strategic management, M&A can allow enterprises to grow or downsize, and change the nature of their business or competitive position.

Exam Probability: **High**

48. *Answer choices:*

(see index for correct answer)

- a. Merger
- b. Sarbanes-Oxley act of 2002
- c. information systems assessment
- d. corporate values

*Guidance:* level 1

:: ::

_____ is an American restaurant chain and international franchise which was founded in 1958 by Dan and Frank Carney. The company is known for its Italian-American cuisine menu, including pizza and pasta, as well as side dishes and desserts. _____ has 18,431 restaurants worldwide as of December 31, 2018, making it the world's largest pizza chain in terms of locations. It is a subsidiary of Yum! Brands, Inc., one of the world's largest restaurant companies.

Exam Probability: **High**

49. *Answer choices:*
(see index for correct answer)

- a. functional perspective
- b. Pizza Hut
- c. hierarchical
- d. empathy

*Guidance:* level 1

:: ::

_____ is the amount of time someone works beyond normal working hours. The term is also used for the pay received for this time. Normal hours may be determined in several ways.

Exam Probability: **High**

50. *Answer choices:*
(see index for correct answer)

- a. process perspective
- b. Character
- c. similarity-attraction theory
- d. Overtime

*Guidance:* level 1

:: E-commerce ::

_____ is the business-to-business or business-to-consumer or business-to-government purchase and sale of supplies, work, and services through the Internet as well as other information and networking systems, such as electronic data interchange and enterprise resource planning.

Exam Probability: **Low**

51. *Answer choices:*
(see index for correct answer)

- a. E-procurement
- b. Product finder
- c. Postback
- d. Plantify

*Guidance:* level 1

:: Banking ::

A _____ is a financial institution that accepts deposits from the public and creates credit. Lending activities can be performed either directly or indirectly through capital markets. Due to their importance in the financial stability of a country, _____ s are highly regulated in most countries. Most nations have institutionalized a system known as fractional reserve _____ ing under which _____ s hold liquid assets equal to only a portion of their current liabilities. In addition to other regulations intended to ensure liquidity, _____ s are generally subject to minimum capital requirements based on an international set of capital standards, known as the Basel Accords.

Exam Probability: **Low**

52. *Answer choices:*
(see index for correct answer)

- a. Common equity
- b. Bank
- c. Refinancing risk
- d. Transactional account

*Guidance:* level 1

:: Management occupations ::

_____ ship is the process of designing, launching and running a new business, which is often initially a small business. The people who create these businesses are called _____ s.

Exam Probability: **High**

53. *Answer choices:*

(see index for correct answer)

- a. County administrator
- b. General counsel
- c. Chief diversity officer
- d. Comprador

*Guidance:* level 1

:: Industry ::

A _____ is a set of sequential operations established in a factory where materials are put through a refining process to produce an end-product that is suitable for onward consumption; or components are assembled to make a finished article.

Exam Probability: **High**

54. *Answer choices:*

(see index for correct answer)

- a. Primary sector of the economy
- b. Industrial archaeology
- c. Production line
- d. Industrial region

*Guidance:* level 1

:: ::

Competition arises whenever at least two parties strive for a goal which cannot be shared: where one's gain is the other's loss .

Exam Probability: **High**

55. *Answer choices:*

(see index for correct answer)

- a. Competitor
- b. cultural
- c. functional perspective
- d. imperative

*Guidance:* level 1

:: ::

_____ is the production of products for use or sale using labour and machines, tools, chemical and biological processing, or formulation. The term may refer to a range of human activity, from handicraft to high tech, but is most commonly applied to industrial design, in which raw materials are transformed into finished goods on a large scale. Such finished goods may be sold to other manufacturers for the production of other, more complex products, such as aircraft, household appliances, furniture, sports equipment or automobiles, or sold to wholesalers, who in turn sell them to retailers, who then sell them to end users and consumers.

Exam Probability: **Medium**

56. *Answer choices:*

(see index for correct answer)

- a. corporate values
- b. Manufacturing
- c. co-culture
- d. levels of analysis

*Guidance:* level 1

:: ::

_____ or standardisation is the process of implementing and developing technical standards based on the consensus of different parties that include firms, users, interest groups, standards organizations and governments. _____ can help maximize compatibility, interoperability, safety, repeatability, or quality. It can also facilitate commoditization of formerly custom processes. In social sciences, including economics, the idea of _____ is close to the solution for a coordination problem, a situation in which all parties can realize mutual gains, but only by making mutually consistent decisions. This view includes the case of "spontaneous _____ processes", to produce de facto standards.

Exam Probability: **High**

57. *Answer choices:*

(see index for correct answer)

- a. Standardization
- b. similarity-attraction theory
- c. personal values
- d. hierarchical perspective

*Guidance:* level 1

:: ::

_____ is the exchange of capital, goods, and services across international borders or territories.

Exam Probability: **Medium**

58. *Answer choices:*

(see index for correct answer)

- a. Character
- b. International trade
- c. co-culture
- d. empathy

*Guidance:* level 1

:: International trade ::

An _____ is a good brought into a jurisdiction, especially across a national border, from an external source. The party bringing in the good is called an _____er. An _____ in the receiving country is an export from the sending country. _____ation and exportation are the defining financial transactions of international trade.

Exam Probability: **High**

59. *Answer choices:*

(see index for correct answer)

- a. Trading nation
- b. Denied trade screening
- c. Import
- d. Harberger-Laursen-Metzler effect

*Guidance:* level 1

**Business ethics**

Business ethics (also known as corporate ethics) is a form of applied ethics or professional ethics, that examines ethical principles and moral or ethical problems that can arise in a business environment. It applies to all aspects of business conduct and is relevant to the conduct of individuals and entire organizations. These ethics originate from individuals, organizational statements or from the legal system. These norms, values, ethical, and unethical practices are what is used to guide business. They help those businesses maintain a better connection with their stakeholders.

---

:: Financial markets ::

The _____ is a United States federal government organization, established by Title I of the Dodd–Frank Wall Street Reform and Consumer Protection Act, which was signed into law by President Barack Obama on July 21, 2010. The Office of Financial Research is intended to provide support to the council.

Exam Probability: **Low**

1. *Answer choices:*
(see index for correct answer)

- a. Secondary market
- b. Global Industry Classification Standard
- c. Exchange of futures for physicals
- d. Market depth

*Guidance:* level 1

---

:: ::

_____ is a bundle of characteristics, including ways of thinking, feeling, and acting, which humans are said to have naturally. The term is often regarded as capturing what it is to be human, or the essence of humanity. The term is controversial because it is disputed whether or not such an essence exists. Arguments about _____ have been a mainstay of philosophy for centuries and the concept continues to provoke lively philosophical debate. The concept also continues to play a role in science, with neuroscientists, psychologists and social scientists sometimes claiming that their results have yielded insight into _____. _____ is traditionally contrasted with characteristics that vary among humans, such as characteristics associated with specific cultures. Debates about _____ are related to, although not the same as, debates about the comparative importance of genes and environment in development.

Exam Probability: **Medium**

2. *Answer choices:*
(see index for correct answer)

- a. levels of analysis
- b. Human nature
- c. imperative
- d. co-culture

*Guidance:* level 1

:: Business ::

_____, or built-in obsolescence, in industrial design and economics is a policy of planning or designing a product with an artificially limited useful life, so that it becomes obsolete after a certain period of time. The rationale behind this strategy is to generate long-term sales volume by reducing the time between repeat purchases.

Exam Probability: **Medium**

3. *Answer choices:*
(see index for correct answer)

- a. Procurement PunchOut
- b. Business service management
- c. Planned obsolescence
- d. Citizenship for life

*Guidance:* level 1

:: Agricultural labor ::

The _____ of America, or more commonly just _____, is a labor union for farmworkers in the United States. It originated from the merger of two workers' rights organizations, the Agricultural Workers Organizing Committee led by organizer Larry Itliong, and the National Farm Workers Association led by César Chávez and Dolores Huerta. They became allied and transformed from workers' rights organizations into a union as a result of a series of strikes in 1965, when the mostly Filipino farmworkers of the AWOC in Delano, California initiated a grape strike, and the NFWA went on strike in support. As a result of the commonality in goals and methods, the NFWA and the AWOC formed the _____ Organizing Committee on August 22, 1966. This organization was accepted into the AFL-CIO in 1972 and changed its name to the _____ Union.

Exam Probability: **Low**

4. *Answer choices:*

(see index for correct answer)

- a. United Farm Workers
- b. Kolkhoz
- c. Farm Labor Organizing Committee
- d. Agricultural gang

*Guidance:* level 1

:: Electronic feedback ::

_____ occurs when outputs of a system are routed back as inputs as part of a chain of cause-and-effect that forms a circuit or loop. The system can then be said to feed back into itself. The notion of cause-and-effect has to be handled carefully when applied to _____ systems.

Exam Probability: **High**

5. *Answer choices:*

(see index for correct answer)

- a. Feedback
- b. feedback loop

*Guidance:* level 1

:: Progressive Era in the United States ::

The Clayton Antitrust Act of 1914, was a part of United States antitrust law with the goal of adding further substance to the U.S. antitrust law regime; the _____ sought to prevent anticompetitive practices in their incipiency. That regime started with the Sherman Antitrust Act of 1890, the first Federal law outlawing practices considered harmful to consumers. The _____ specified particular prohibited conduct, the three-level enforcement scheme, the exemptions, and the remedial measures.

Exam Probability: **High**

6. *Answer choices:*

(see index for correct answer)

- a. pragmatism
- b. Clayton Act
- c. Clayton Antitrust Act

*Guidance:* level 1

:: ::

A _____ is a problem offering two possibilities, neither of which is unambiguously acceptable or preferable. The possibilities are termed the horns of the _____, a clichéd usage, but distinguishing the _____ from other kinds of predicament as a matter of usage.

Exam Probability: **Low**

7. *Answer choices:*

(see index for correct answer)

- a. Character
- b. open system
- c. Dilemma
- d. information systems assessment

*Guidance:* level 1

:: United States federal trade legislation ::

The _____ of 1914 established the Federal Trade Commission. The Act, signed into law by Woodrow Wilson in 1914, outlaws unfair methods of competition and outlaws unfair acts or practices that affect commerce.

Exam Probability: **High**

8. *Answer choices:*

(see index for correct answer)

- a. Force Bill
- b. Tariff of 1833
- c. Tariff of 1883
- d. Federal Trade Commission Act

*Guidance:* level 1

:: ::

Bernard Lawrence _____ is an American former market maker, investment advisor, financier, fraudster, and convicted felon, who is currently serving a federal prison sentence for offenses related to a massive Ponzi scheme. He is the former non-executive chairman of the NASDAQ stock market, the confessed operator of the largest Ponzi scheme in world history, and the largest financial fraud in U.S. history. Prosecutors estimated the fraud to be worth $64.8 billion based on the amounts in the accounts of _____ 's 4,800 clients as of November 30, 2008.

Exam Probability: **Medium**

9. *Answer choices:*

(see index for correct answer)

- a. similarity-attraction theory
- b. hierarchical perspective
- c. functional perspective
- d. Madoff

*Guidance:* level 1

:: ::

An _____ is the release of a liquid petroleum hydrocarbon into the environment, especially the marine ecosystem, due to human activity, and is a form of pollution. The term is usually given to marine _____ s, where oil is released into the ocean or coastal waters, but spills may also occur on land. _____ s may be due to releases of crude oil from tankers, offshore platforms, drilling rigs and wells, as well as spills of refined petroleum products and their by-products, heavier fuels used by large ships such as bunker fuel, or the spill of any oily refuse or waste oil.

Exam Probability: **Medium**

10. *Answer choices:*

(see index for correct answer)

- a. information systems assessment
- b. hierarchical
- c. empathy
- d. Oil spill

*Guidance:* level 1

---

:: Human resource management ::

_____ encompasses values and behaviors that contribute to the unique social and psychological environment of a business. The _____ influences the way people interact, the context within which knowledge is created, the resistance they will have towards certain changes, and ultimately the way they share knowledge. _____ represents the collective values, beliefs and principles of organizational members and is a product of factors such as history, product, market, technology, strategy, type of employees, management style, and national culture; culture includes the organization's vision, values, norms, systems, symbols, language, assumptions, environment, location, beliefs and habits.

Exam Probability: **High**

11. *Answer choices:*

(see index for correct answer)

- a. Job description management
- b. TPI-theory
- c. Workplace mentoring
- d. Organizational culture

:: ::

_____ is an eight-block-long street running roughly northwest to southeast from Broadway to South Street, at the East River, in the Financial District of Lower Manhattan in New York City. Over time, the term has become a metonym for the financial markets of the United States as a whole, the American financial services industry, or New York–based financial interests.

Exam Probability: **Medium**

12. *Answer choices:*

(see index for correct answer)

- a. levels of analysis
- b. personal values
- c. imperative
- d. Wall Street

*Guidance:* level 1

:: ::

_____ is the means to see, hear, or become aware of something or someone through our fundamental senses. The term _____ derives from the Latin word perceptio, and is the organization, identification, and interpretation of sensory information in order to represent and understand the presented information, or the environment.

Exam Probability: **Medium**

13. *Answer choices:*

(see index for correct answer)

- a. personal values
- b. Perception
- c. Sarbanes-Oxley act of 2002
- d. hierarchical perspective

*Guidance:* level 1

:: Minimum wage ::

The _____ are working people whose incomes fall below a given poverty line due to lack of work hours and/or low wages. Largely because they are earning such low wages, the _____ face numerous obstacles that make it difficult for many of them to find and keep a job, save up money, and maintain a sense of self-worth.

Exam Probability: **High**

14. *Answer choices:*

(see index for correct answer)

- a. Minimum wage
- b. Guaranteed minimum income
- c. Working poor
- d. Minimum wage in Taiwan

*Guidance:* level 1

:: United Kingdom labour law ::

The _____ was a series of programs, public work projects, financial reforms, and regulations enacted by President Franklin D. Roosevelt in the United States between 1933 and 1936. It responded to needs for relief, reform, and recovery from the Great Depression. Major federal programs included the Civilian Conservation Corps, the Civil Works Administration, the Farm Security Administration, the National Industrial Recovery Act of 1933 and the Social Security Administration. They provided support for farmers, the unemployed, youth and the elderly. The _____ included new constraints and safeguards on the banking industry and efforts to re-inflate the economy after prices had fallen sharply. _____ programs included both laws passed by Congress as well as presidential executive orders during the first term of the presidency of Franklin D. Roosevelt.

Exam Probability: **Medium**

15. *Answer choices:*

(see index for correct answer)

- a. Collective laissez faire
- b. New Deal
- c. Labour Exchanges Act 1909
- d. Transparency of Lobbying, Non-party Campaigning and Trade Union Administration Bill

*Guidance:* level 1

:: Anti-competitive behaviour ::

_____ is a secret cooperation or deceitful agreement in order to deceive others, although not necessarily illegal, as a conspiracy. A secret agreement between two or more parties to limit open competition by deceiving, misleading, or defrauding others of their legal rights, or to obtain an objective forbidden by law typically by defrauding or gaining an unfair market advantage is an example of _____ . It is an agreement among firms or individuals to divide a market, set prices, limit production or limit opportunities. It can involve "unions, wage fixing, kickbacks, or misrepresenting the independence of the relationship between the colluding parties". In legal terms, all acts effected by _____ are considered void.

Exam Probability: **Medium**

16. *Answer choices:*

(see index for correct answer)

- a. Angelgate
- b. Collusion
- c. Coase conjecture
- d. Field-of-use limitation

*Guidance:* level 1

:: Monopoly (economics) ::

A _____ is a form of intellectual property that gives its owner the legal right to exclude others from making, using, selling, and importing an invention for a limited period of years, in exchange for publishing an enabling public disclosure of the invention. In most countries _____ rights fall under civil law and the _____ holder needs to sue someone infringing the _____ in order to enforce his or her rights. In some industries _____ s are an essential form of competitive advantage; in others they are irrelevant.

Exam Probability: **Medium**

17. *Answer choices:*

(see index for correct answer)

- a. Patent
- b. Market concentration
- c. Contestable market
- d. Coercive monopoly

*Guidance:* level 1

:: Professional ethics ::

In the mental health field, a _____ is a situation where multiple roles exist between a therapist, or other mental health practitioner, and a client. _____ s are also referred to as multiple relationships, and these two terms are used interchangeably in the research literature. The American Psychological Association Ethical Principles of Psychologists and Code of Conduct is a resource that outlines ethical standards and principles to which practitioners are expected to adhere. Standard 3.05 of the APA ethics code outlines the definition of multiple relationships. Dual or multiple relationships occur when.

Exam Probability: **High**

18. *Answer choices:*
(see index for correct answer)

- a. Dual relationship
- b. professional conduct
- c. Continuous professional development

*Guidance:* level 1

:: ::

_____ is a private Dominican liberal arts college in Madison, Wisconsin. The college occupies a 55 acres campus overlooking the shores of Lake Wingra.

Exam Probability: **Medium**

19. *Answer choices:*
(see index for correct answer)

- a. functional perspective
- b. levels of analysis
- c. personal values
- d. Edgewood College

:: ::

A _____ service is an online platform which people use to build social networks or social relationship with other people who share similar personal or career interests, activities, backgrounds or real-life connections.

Exam Probability: **Medium**

20. *Answer choices:*

(see index for correct answer)

- a. imperative
- b. similarity-attraction theory
- c. empathy
- d. interpersonal communication

*Guidance:* level 1

:: Reputation management ::

_____ or image of a social entity is an opinion about that entity, typically as a result of social evaluation on a set of criteria.

Exam Probability: **Medium**

21. *Answer choices:*

(see index for correct answer)

- a. Lithium Technologies
- b. Infamy
- c. Reputation
- d. Star

*Guidance:* level 1

:: Culture ::

_____ is a society which is characterized by individualism, which is the prioritization or emphasis, of the individual over the entire group. _____s are oriented around the self, being independent instead of identifying with a group mentality. They see each other as only loosely linked, and value personal goals over group interests. _____s tend to have a more diverse population and are characterized with emphasis on personal achievements, and a rational assessment of both the beneficial and detrimental aspects of relationships with others. _____s have such unique aspects of communication as being a low power-distance culture and having a low-context communication style. The United States, Australia, Great Britain, Canada, the Netherlands, and New Zealand have been identified as highly _____s.

Exam Probability: **Low**

22. *Answer choices:*

(see index for correct answer)

- a. High-context
- b. cultural framework
- c. Intracultural
- d. Individualistic culture

*Guidance:* level 1

:: ::

Cannabis, also known as _____ among other names, is a psychoactive drug from the Cannabis plant used for medical or recreational purposes. The main psychoactive part of cannabis is tetrahydrocannabinol, one of 483 known compounds in the plant, including at least 65 other cannabinoids. Cannabis can be used by smoking, vaporizing, within food, or as an extract.

Exam Probability: **High**

23. *Answer choices:*

(see index for correct answer)

- a. Marijuana
- b. cultural
- c. Sarbanes-Oxley act of 2002
- d. process perspective

*Guidance:* level 1

:: Euthenics ::

_____ is an ethical framework and suggests that an entity, be it an organization or individual, has an obligation to act for the benefit of society at large. _____ is a duty every individual has to perform so as to maintain a balance between the economy and the ecosystems. A trade-off may exist between economic development, in the material sense, and the welfare of the society and environment, though this has been challenged by many reports over the past decade. _____ means sustaining the equilibrium between the two. It pertains not only to business organizations but also to everyone whose any action impacts the environment. This responsibility can be passive, by avoiding engaging in socially harmful acts, or active, by performing activities that directly advance social goals. _____ must be intergenerational since the actions of one generation have consequences on those following.

Exam Probability: **Low**

24. *Answer choices:*

(see index for correct answer)

- a. Euthenics
- b. Social responsibility
- c. Family and consumer science
- d. Home economics

*Guidance:* level 1

:: United States law ::

The ABA _____, created by the American Bar Association, are a set of rules that prescribe baseline standards of legal ethics and professional responsibility for lawyers in the United States. They were promulgated by the ABA House of Delegates upon the recommendation of the Kutak Commission in 1983. The rules are merely recommendations, or models, and are not themselves binding. However, having a common set of Model Rules facilitates a common discourse on legal ethics, and simplifies professional responsibility training as well as the day-to-day application of such rules. As of 2015, 49 states and four territories have adopted the rules in whole or in part, of which the most recent to do so was the Commonwealth of the Northern Mariana Islands in March 2015. California is the only state that has not adopted the ABA Model Rules, while Puerto Rico is the only U.S. jurisdiction outside of confederation has not adopted them but instead has its own Código de Ética Profesional.

Exam Probability: **High**

25. *Answer choices:*
(see index for correct answer)

- a. Model Rules of Professional Conduct
- b. judgment notwithstanding the verdict

*Guidance:* level 1

:: ::

_____ism is a form of government characterized by strong central power and limited political freedoms. Individual freedoms are subordinate to the state and there is no constitutional accountability and rule of law under an _____ regime. _____ regimes can be autocratic with power concentrated in one person or it can be more spread out between multiple officials and government institutions. Juan Linz's influential 1964 description of _____ism characterized _____ political systems by four qualities.

Exam Probability: **High**

26. *Answer choices:*
(see index for correct answer)

- a. Authoritarian
- b. deep-level diversity

- c. levels of analysis
- d. information systems assessment

*Guidance:* level 1

---

:: ::

The _____ of 1973 serves as the enacting legislation to carry out the provisions outlined in The Convention on International Trade in Endangered Species of Wild Fauna and Flora . Designed to protect critically imperiled species from extinction as a "consequence of economic growth and development untempered by adequate concern and conservation", the ESA was signed into law by President Richard Nixon on December 28, 1973. The law requires federal agencies to consult with the Fish and Wildlife Service &/or the NOAA Fisheries Service to ensure their actions are not likely to jeopardize the continued existence of any listed species or result in the destruction or adverse modification of designated critical habitat of such species. The U.S. Supreme Court found that "the plain intent of Congress in enacting" the ESA "was to halt and reverse the trend toward species extinction, whatever the cost." The Act is administered by two federal agencies, the United States Fish and Wildlife Service and the National Marine Fisheries Service .

Exam Probability: **Medium**

27. *Answer choices:*
(see index for correct answer)

- a. empathy
- b. cultural
- c. information systems assessment
- d. imperative

*Guidance:* level 1

---

:: Management ::

_____ is the identification, evaluation, and prioritization of risks followed by coordinated and economical application of resources to minimize, monitor, and control the probability or impact of unfortunate events or to maximize the realization of opportunities.

Exam Probability: **High**

28. *Answer choices:*

(see index for correct answer)

- a. Clean-sheet review
- b. Managerial economics
- c. Risk management
- d. Board of governors

*Guidance:* level 1

:: ::

Sustainability is the process of people maintaining change in a balanced environment, in which the exploitation of resources, the direction of investments, the orientation of technological development and institutional change are all in harmony and enhance both current and future potential to meet human needs and aspirations. For many in the field, sustainability is defined through the following interconnected domains or pillars: environment, economic and social, which according to Fritjof Capra is based on the principles of Systems Thinking. Sub-domains of _____ development have been considered also: cultural, technological and political. While _____ development may be the organizing principle for sustainability for some, for others, the two terms are paradoxical. _____ development is the development that meets the needs of the present without compromising the ability of future generations to meet their own needs. Brundtland Report for the World Commission on Environment and Development introduced the term of _____ development.

Exam Probability: **Medium**

29. *Answer choices:*

(see index for correct answer)

- a. functional perspective
- b. surface-level diversity
- c. open system
- d. Sustainable

*Guidance:* level 1

:: ::

The _____ is an institution of the European Union, responsible for proposing legislation, implementing decisions, upholding the EU treaties and managing the day-to-day business of the EU. Commissioners swear an oath at the European Court of Justice in Luxembourg City, pledging to respect the treaties and to be completely independent in carrying out their duties during their mandate. Unlike in the Council of the European Union, where members are directly and indirectly elected, and the European Parliament, where members are directly elected, the Commissioners are proposed by the Council of the European Union, on the basis of suggestions made by the national governments, and then appointed by the European Council after the approval of the European Parliament.

Exam Probability: **Medium**

30. *Answer choices:*
(see index for correct answer)

- a. European Commission
- b. interpersonal communication
- c. cultural
- d. open system

*Guidance:* level 1

---

:: Cultural appropriation ::

_____ is a social and economic order that encourages the acquisition of goods and services in ever-increasing amounts. With the industrial revolution, but particularly in the 20th century, mass production led to an economic crisis: there was overproduction—the supply of goods would grow beyond consumer demand, and so manufacturers turned to planned obsolescence and advertising to manipulate consumer spending. In 1899, a book on _____ published by Thorstein Veblen, called The Theory of the Leisure Class, examined the widespread values and economic institutions emerging along with the widespread "leisure time" in the beginning of the 20th century. In it Veblen "views the activities and spending habits of this leisure class in terms of conspicuous and vicarious consumption and waste. Both are related to the display of status and not to functionality or usefulness."

Exam Probability: **High**

31. *Answer choices:*

(see index for correct answer)

- a. Consumerism
- b. Plastic Brit
- c. Blackface
- d. Washington Redskins Original Americans Foundation

*Guidance:* level 1

:: Monopoly (economics) ::

The _____ of 1890 was a United States antitrust law that regulates competition among enterprises, which was passed by Congress under the presidency of Benjamin Harrison.

Exam Probability: **High**

32. *Answer choices:*

(see index for correct answer)

- a. Privatization
- b. History of monopoly
- c. Legal monopoly
- d. Sherman Antitrust Act

*Guidance:* level 1

:: Carbon finance ::

The _____ is an international treaty which extends the 1992 United Nations Framework Convention on Climate Change that commits state parties to reduce greenhouse gas emissions, based on the scientific consensus that global warming is occurring and it is extremely likely that human-made CO2 emissions have predominantly caused it. The _____ was adopted in Kyoto, Japan on 11 December 1997 and entered into force on 16 February 2005. There are currently 192 parties to the Protocol.

Exam Probability: **Medium**

33. *Answer choices:*

(see index for correct answer)

- a. carbon trading
- b. Kyoto Protocol

- c. Western Climate Initiative
- d. Element Markets

*Guidance:* level 1

---

:: Corporate scandals ::

Exxon Mobil Corporation, doing business as _____ , is an American multinational oil and gas corporation headquartered in Irving, Texas. It is the largest direct descendant of John D. Rockefeller's Standard Oil Company, and was formed on November 30, 1999 by the merger of Exxon and Mobil. _____ 's primary brands are Exxon, Mobil, Esso, and _____ Chemical.

Exam Probability: **Low**

34. *Answer choices:*
(see index for correct answer)

- a. Cash for comment affair
- b. Mongstad scandal
- c. ExxonMobil
- d. S-Chips Scandals

*Guidance:* level 1

---

:: Marketing ::

_____ is the marketing of products that are presumed to be environmentally safe. It incorporates a broad range of activities, including product modification, changes to the production process, sustainable packaging, as well as modifying advertising. Yet defining _____ is not a simple task where several meanings intersect and contradict each other; an example of this will be the existence of varying social, environmental and retail definitions attached to this term. Other similar terms used are environmental marketing and ecological marketing.

Exam Probability: **Low**

35. *Answer choices:*
(see index for correct answer)

- a. Configurator
- b. Gift suite
- c. Marketing in schools

- d. Green marketing

*Guidance:* level 1

---

:: Production and manufacturing ::

_____ is a set of techniques and tools for process improvement. Though as a shortened form it may be found written as 6S, it should not be confused with the methodology known as 6S .

Exam Probability: **Low**

36. *Answer choices:*
(see index for correct answer)

- a. Continuous production
- b. Capacity planning
- c. Six Sigma
- d. Remanufacturing

*Guidance:* level 1

---

:: ::

_____ is a product prepared from the leaves of the _____ plant by curing them. The plant is part of the genus Nicotiana and of the Solanaceae family. While more than 70 species of _____ are known, the chief commercial crop is N. tabacum. The more potent variant N. rustica is also used around the world.

Exam Probability: **High**

37. *Answer choices:*
(see index for correct answer)

- a. Character
- b. Tobacco
- c. similarity-attraction theory
- d. imperative

*Guidance:* level 1

---

:: Globalization-related theories ::

_____ is an economic system based on the private ownership of the means of production and their operation for profit. Characteristics central to _____ include private property, capital accumulation, wage labor, voluntary exchange, a price system, and competitive markets. In a capitalist market economy, decision-making and investment are determined by every owner of wealth, property or production ability in financial and capital markets, whereas prices and the distribution of goods and services are mainly determined by competition in goods and services markets.

Exam Probability: **High**

38. *Answer choices:*
(see index for correct answer)

- a. Capitalism
- b. Economic Development
- c. post-industrial

*Guidance:* level 1

:: Confidence tricks ::

A _____ is a business model that recruits members via a promise of payments or services for enrolling others into the scheme, rather than supplying investments or sale of products. As recruiting multiplies, recruiting becomes quickly impossible, and most members are unable to profit; as such, _____ s are unsustainable and often illegal.

Exam Probability: **Medium**

39. *Answer choices:*
(see index for correct answer)

- a. Pigeon drop
- b. Pyramid scheme
- c. Sick baby hoax
- d. Patent safe

*Guidance:* level 1

:: ::

_____ in the United States is a federal and state program that helps with medical costs for some people with limited income and resources. _____ also offers benefits not normally covered by Medicare, including nursing home care and personal care services. The Health Insurance Association of America describes _____ as "a government insurance program for persons of all ages whose income and resources are insufficient to pay for health care." _____ is the largest source of funding for medical and health-related services for people with low income in the United States, providing free health insurance to 74 million low-income and disabled people as of 2017. It is a means-tested program that is jointly funded by the state and federal governments and managed by the states, with each state currently having broad leeway to determine who is eligible for its implementation of the program. States are not required to participate in the program, although all have since 1982. _____ recipients must be U.S. citizens or qualified non-citizens, and may include low-income adults, their children, and people with certain disabilities. Poverty alone does not necessarily qualify someone for _____ .

Exam Probability: **Medium**

40. *Answer choices:*

(see index for correct answer)

- a. empathy
- b. imperative
- c. cultural
- d. Medicaid

*Guidance:* level 1

:: Television terminology ::

A _____ organization , also known as a non-business entity, not-for-profit organization, or _____ institution, is dedicated to furthering a particular social cause or advocating for a shared point of view. In economic terms, it is an organization that uses its surplus of the revenues to further achieve its ultimate objective, rather than distributing its income to the organization's shareholders, leaders, or members. _____ s are tax exempt or charitable, meaning they do not pay income tax on the money that they receive for their organization. They can operate in religious, scientific, research, or educational settings.

Exam Probability: **High**

41. *Answer choices:*
(see index for correct answer)

- a. not-for-profit
- b. Nonprofit
- c. multiplexing
- d. Satellite television

*Guidance:* level 1

:: Dutch inventions ::

The Fairtrade certification initiative was created to form a new method for economic trade. This method takes an ethical standpoint, and considers the producers first.

Exam Probability: **Low**

42. *Answer choices:*
(see index for correct answer)

- a. Fair Trade Certified
- b. Dijkstra's algorithm

*Guidance:* level 1

:: ::

_____ is the introduction of contaminants into the natural environment that cause adverse change. _____ can take the form of chemical substances or energy, such as noise, heat or light. Pollutants, the components of _____, can be either foreign substances/energies or naturally occurring contaminants. _____ is often classed as point source or nonpoint source _____. In 2015, _____ killed 9 million people in the world.

Exam Probability: **Medium**

43. *Answer choices:*

(see index for correct answer)

- a. Sarbanes-Oxley act of 2002
- b. corporate values
- c. open system
- d. Pollution

*Guidance:* level 1

---

:: Business law ::

A _____ is an arrangement where parties, known as partners, agree to cooperate to advance their mutual interests. The partners in a _____ may be individuals, businesses, interest-based organizations, schools, governments or combinations. Organizations may partner to increase the likelihood of each achieving their mission and to amplify their reach. A _____ may result in issuing and holding equity or may be only governed by a contract.

Exam Probability: **Medium**

44. *Answer choices:*

(see index for correct answer)

- a. Partnership
- b. Forged endorsement
- c. Apparent authority
- d. Industrial relations

*Guidance:* level 1

---

:: Price fixing convictions ::

_____ AG is a German multinational conglomerate company headquartered in Berlin and Munich and the largest industrial manufacturing company in Europe with branch offices abroad.

Exam Probability: **Low**

45. *Answer choices:*

(see index for correct answer)

- a. Hoffmann-La Roche
- b. Siemens
- c. YKK Group
- d. British Airways

*Guidance:* level 1

:: ::

The _____ to Fight AIDS, Tuberculosis and Malaria is an international financing organization that aims to "attract, leverage and invest additional resources to end the epidemics of HIV/AIDS, tuberculosis and malaria to support attainment of the Sustainable Development Goals established by the United Nations." A public-private partnership, the organization maintains its secretariat in Geneva, Switzerland. The organization began operations in January 2002. Microsoft founder Bill Gates was one of the first private foundations among many bilateral donors to provide seed money for the partnership.

Exam Probability: **Low**

46. *Answer choices:*

(see index for correct answer)

- a. surface-level diversity
- b. levels of analysis
- c. corporate values
- d. similarity-attraction theory

*Guidance:* level 1

:: United States federal labor legislation ::

The _____ of 1988 is a United States federal law that generally prevents employers from using polygraph tests, either for pre-employment screening or during the course of employment, with certain exemptions.

Exam Probability: **Medium**

47. *Answer choices:*

(see index for correct answer)

- a. Federal Employers Liability Act
- b. Alien Contract Labor Law
- c. Workforce Investment Act of 1998
- d. Employee Polygraph Protection Act

*Guidance:* level 1

:: ::

_____ is a non-governmental environmental organization with offices in over 39 countries and an international coordinating body in Amsterdam, the Netherlands. _____ was founded in 1971 by Irving Stowe, and Dorothy Stowe, Canadian and US ex-pat environmental activists. _____ states its goal is to "ensure the ability of the Earth to nurture life in all its diversity" and focuses its campaigning on worldwide issues such as climate change, deforestation, overfishing, commercial whaling, genetic engineering, and anti-nuclear issues. It uses direct action, lobbying, research, and ecotage to achieve its goals. The global organization does not accept funding from governments, corporations, or political parties, relying on three million individual supporters and foundation grants. _____ has a general consultative status with the United Nations Economic and Social Council and is a founding member of the INGO Accountability Charter, an international non-governmental organization that intends to foster accountability and transparency of non-governmental organizations.

Exam Probability: **Medium**

48. *Answer choices:*

(see index for correct answer)

- a. open system
- b. personal values
- c. Greenpeace
- d. corporate values

*Guidance:* level 1

:: ::

_____ , O.S.A. was a German professor of theology, composer, priest, monk, and a seminal figure in the Protestant Reformation.

Exam Probability: **Medium**

49. *Answer choices:*
(see index for correct answer)

- a. Character
- b. Martin Luther
- c. Sarbanes-Oxley act of 2002
- d. corporate values

*Guidance:* level 1

:: ::

In ecology, a _____ is the type of natural environment in which a particular species of organism lives. It is characterized by both physical and biological features. A species' _____ is those places where it can find food, shelter, protection and mates for reproduction.

Exam Probability: **Medium**

50. *Answer choices:*
(see index for correct answer)

- a. personal values
- b. Sarbanes-Oxley act of 2002
- c. Habitat
- d. imperative

*Guidance:* level 1

:: ::

Revenge is a form of justice enacted in the absence or defiance of the norms of formal law and jurisprudence. Often, revenge is defined as being a harmful action against a person or group in response to a grievance, be it real or perceived. It is used to punish a wrong by going outside the law. Francis Bacon described revenge as a kind of "wild justice" that "does... offend the law [and] putteth the law out of office." Primitive justice or retributive justice is often differentiated from more formal and refined forms of justice such as distributive justice and divine judgment.

Exam Probability: **Low**

51. *Answer choices:*

(see index for correct answer)

- a. hierarchical
- b. Sarbanes-Oxley act of 2002
- c. Retaliation
- d. deep-level diversity

*Guidance:* level 1

:: Renewable energy ::

_____ is the conversion of energy from sunlight into electricity, either directly using photovoltaics, indirectly using concentrated _____, or a combination. Concentrated _____ systems use lenses or mirrors and tracking systems to focus a large area of sunlight into a small beam. Photovoltaic cells convert light into an electric current using the photovoltaic effect.

Exam Probability: **High**

52. *Answer choices:*

(see index for correct answer)

- a. Crosswind kite power
- b. Yield co
- c. Carbon Recycling International
- d. Solar power

*Guidance:* level 1

:: Anti-capitalism ::

_____ is a range of economic and social systems characterised by social ownership of the means of production and workers' self-management, as well as the political theories and movements associated with them. Social ownership can be public, collective or cooperative ownership, or citizen ownership of equity. There are many varieties of _____ and there is no single definition encapsulating all of them, with social ownership being the common element shared by its various forms.

Exam Probability: **Medium**

53. *Answer choices:*
(see index for correct answer)

- a. Left anarchism
- b. Anarchist communism
- c. Queer Mutiny
- d. Feminist Theory: From Margin to Center

*Guidance:* level 1

:: United States federal defense and national security legislation ::

The USA _____ is an Act of the U.S. Congress that was signed into law by President George W. Bush on October 26, 2001. The title of the Act is a contrived three letter initialism preceding a seven letter acronym, which in combination stand for Uniting and Strengthening America by Providing Appropriate Tools Required to Intercept and Obstruct Terrorism Act of 2001. The acronym was created by a 23 year old Congressional staffer, Chris Kyle.

Exam Probability: **Low**

54. *Answer choices:*
(see index for correct answer)

- a. Export Administration Act
- b. Patriot Act

*Guidance:* level 1

:: Natural gas ::

_____ is a naturally occurring hydrocarbon gas mixture consisting primarily of methane, but commonly including varying amounts of other higher alkanes, and sometimes a small percentage of carbon dioxide, nitrogen, hydrogen sulfide, or helium. It is formed when layers of decomposing plant and animal matter are exposed to intense heat and pressure under the surface of the Earth over millions of years. The energy that the plants originally obtained from the sun is stored in the form of chemical bonds in the gas.

Exam Probability: **Medium**

55. *Answer choices:*

(see index for correct answer)

- a. Gas Safe Register
- b. Natural gas
- c. Wet gas
- d. Renewable natural gas

*Guidance:* level 1

:: ::

_____ was a philosopher during the Classical period in Ancient Greece, the founder of the Lyceum and the Peripatetic school of philosophy and Aristotelian tradition. Along with his teacher Plato, he is considered the "Father of Western Philosophy". His writings cover many subjects – including physics, biology, zoology, metaphysics, logic, ethics, aesthetics, poetry, theatre, music, rhetoric, psychology, linguistics, economics, politics and government. _____ provided a complex synthesis of the various philosophies existing prior to him, and it was above all from his teachings that the West inherited its intellectual lexicon, as well as problems and methods of inquiry. As a result, his philosophy has exerted a unique influence on almost every form of knowledge in the West and it continues to be a subject of contemporary philosophical discussion.

Exam Probability: **Medium**

56. *Answer choices:*

(see index for correct answer)

- a. imperative
- b. Aristotle
- c. co-culture

- d. deep-level diversity

*Guidance:* level 1

---

:: Employment compensation ::

A _____ is the minimum income necessary for a worker to meet their basic needs. Needs are defined to include food, housing, and other essential needs such as clothing. The goal of a _____ is to allow a worker to afford a basic but decent standard of living. Due to the flexible nature of the term "needs", there is not one universally accepted measure of what a _____ is and as such it varies by location and household type.

Exam Probability: **Medium**

57. *Answer choices:*

(see index for correct answer)

- a. Living wage
- b. Health Reimbursement Account
- c. Total Reward
- d. Pay-for-Performance

*Guidance:* level 1

---

:: Fraud ::

In law, _____ is intentional deception to secure unfair or unlawful gain, or to deprive a victim of a legal right. _____ can violate civil law, a criminal law, or it may cause no loss of money, property or legal right but still be an element of another civil or criminal wrong. The purpose of _____ may be monetary gain or other benefits, for example by obtaining a passport, travel document, or driver's license, or mortgage _____, where the perpetrator may attempt to qualify for a mortgage by way of false statements.

Exam Probability: **Low**

58. *Answer choices:*

(see index for correct answer)

- a. Fraud
- b. Unconscious fraud
- c. Wangiri

- d. Statute of frauds

*Guidance:* level 1

---

:: Power (social and political) ::

_____ is a form of reverence gained by a leader who has strong interpersonal relationship skills. _____, as an aspect of personal power, becomes particularly important as organizational leadership becomes increasingly about collaboration and influence, rather than command and control.

Exam Probability: **Medium**

59. *Answer choices:*
(see index for correct answer)

- a. Hard power
- b. Referent power
- c. Expert power

*Guidance:* level 1

## Accounting

Accounting or accountancy is the measurement, processing, and communication of financial information about economic entities such as businesses and corporations. The modern field was established by the Italian mathematician Luca Pacioli in 1494. Accounting, which has been called the "language of business", measures the results of an organization's economic activities and conveys this information to a variety of users, including investors, creditors, management, and regulators.

---

:: Management accounting ::

_____ is a managerial accounting cost concept. Under this method, manufacturing overhead is incurred in the period that a product is produced. This addresses the issue of absorption costing that allows income to rise as production rises. Under an absorption cost method, management can push forward costs to the next period when products are sold. This artificially inflates profits in the period of production by incurring less cost than would be incurred under a _____ system. _____ is generally not used for external reporting purposes. Under the Tax Reform Act of 1986, income statements must use absorption costing to comply with GAAP.

Exam Probability: **Medium**

1. *Answer choices:*
(see index for correct answer)

- a. Variable Costing
- b. Net present value
- c. Hedge accounting
- d. Financial statement analysis

*Guidance:* level 1

:: ::

An _____ is a comprehensive report on a company's activities throughout the preceding year. _____ s are intended to give shareholders and other interested people information about the company's activities and financial performance. They may be considered as grey literature. Most jurisdictions require companies to prepare and disclose _____ s, and many require the _____ to be filed at the company's registry. Companies listed on a stock exchange are also required to report at more frequent intervals.

Exam Probability: **Medium**

2. *Answer choices:*
(see index for correct answer)

- a. similarity-attraction theory
- b. Annual report
- c. levels of analysis
- d. deep-level diversity

*Guidance:* level 1

:: Generally Accepted Accounting Principles ::

The _____ principle is a cornerstone of accrual accounting together with the matching principle. They both determine the accounting period in which revenues and expenses are recognized. According to the principle, revenues are recognized when they are realized or realizable, and are earned, no matter when cash is received. In cash accounting – in contrast – revenues are recognized when cash is received no matter when goods or services are sold.

Exam Probability: **High**

3. *Answer choices:*
(see index for correct answer)

- a. Earnings before interest, taxes, depreciation, and amortization
- b. Operating income
- c. Vendor-specific objective evidence
- d. Net income

*Guidance:* level 1

:: Business law ::

A _____ is a business entity created by two or more parties, generally characterized by shared ownership, shared returns and risks, and shared governance. Companies typically pursue _____ s for one of four reasons: to access a new market, particularly emerging markets; to gain scale efficiencies by combining assets and operations; to share risk for major investments or projects; or to access skills and capabilities.

Exam Probability: **High**

4. *Answer choices:*
(see index for correct answer)

- a. Jurisdictional strike
- b. Closed shop
- c. Secret rebate
- d. Turnkey

*Guidance:* level 1

---

:: Financial ratios ::

Earnings per share is the monetary value of earnings per outstanding share of common stock for a company.

Exam Probability: **Low**

5. *Answer choices:*
(see index for correct answer)

- a. EV/EBITDA
- b. Beta
- c. Rate of return on a portfolio
- d. Asset turnover

*Guidance:* level 1

---

:: ::

A _____ , in the word's original meaning, is a sheet of paper on which one performs work. They come in many forms, most commonly associated with children's school work assignments, tax forms, and accounting or other business environments. Software is increasingly taking over the paper-based _____ .

Exam Probability: **Medium**

6. *Answer choices:*

(see index for correct answer)

- a. surface-level diversity
- b. hierarchical
- c. Worksheet
- d. Sarbanes-Oxley act of 2002

*Guidance:* level 1

:: Accounting in the United States ::

The _____ is the source of generally accepted accounting principles used by state and local governments in the United States. As with most of the entities involved in creating GAAP in the United States, it is a private, non-governmental organization.

Exam Probability: **High**

7. *Answer choices:*

(see index for correct answer)

- a. The Wheat Committee
- b. Other postemployment benefits
- c. Public Company Accounting Oversight Board
- d. Governmental Accounting Standards Board

*Guidance:* level 1

:: Inventory ::

It requires a detailed physical count, so that the company knows exactly how many of each goods brought on specific dates remained at year end inventory. When this information is found, the amount of goods are multiplied by their purchase cost at their purchase date, to get a number for the ending inventory cost.

Exam Probability: **Medium**

8. *Answer choices:*

(see index for correct answer)

- a. LIFO
- b. Stock demands

- c. Ending inventory
- d. Cost of goods available for sale

*Guidance:* level 1

---

:: Pricing ::

_____ is a pricing strategy in which the selling price is determined by adding a specific amount markup to a product's unit cost. An alternative pricing method is value-based pricing.

Exam Probability: **Low**

9. *Answer choices:*
(see index for correct answer)

- a. Hedonic index
- b. Power purchase agreement
- c. Cost-plus pricing
- d. Value-based

*Guidance:* level 1

---

:: Asset ::

_____ s, also known as tangible assets or property, plant and equipment , is a term used in accounting for assets and property that cannot easily be converted into cash. This can be compared with current assets such as cash or bank accounts, described as liquid assets. In most cases, only tangible assets are referred to as fixed. IAS 16 defines _____ s as assets whose future economic benefit is probable to flow into the entity, whose cost can be measured reliably. _____ s belong to one of 2 types:"Freehold Assets" – assets which are purchased with legal right of ownership and used,and "Leasehold Assets" – assets used by owner without legal right for a particular period of time.

Exam Probability: **Medium**

10. *Answer choices:*
(see index for correct answer)

- a. Fixed asset
- b. Current asset

*Guidance:* level 1

:: Generally Accepted Accounting Principles ::

_____ s is an accounting term that refers to groups of accounts serving to express the cost of goods and service allocatable within a business or manufacturing organization. The principle behind the pool is to correlate direct and indirect costs with a specified cost driver, so to find out the total sum of expenses related to the manufacture of a product.

Exam Probability: **Medium**

11. *Answer choices:*

(see index for correct answer)

- a. Net profit
- b. Cash method of accounting
- c. French generally accepted accounting principles
- d. Cost pool

*Guidance:* level 1

:: ::

The _____ or just chief executive, is the most senior corporate, executive, or administrative officer in charge of managing an organization especially an independent legal entity such as a company or nonprofit institution. CEOs lead a range of organizations, including public and private corporations, non-profit organizations and even some government organizations. The CEO of a corporation or company typically reports to the board of directors and is charged with maximizing the value of the entity, which may include maximizing the share price, market share, revenues or another element. In the non-profit and government sector, CEOs typically aim at achieving outcomes related to the organization's mission, such as reducing poverty, increasing literacy, etc.

Exam Probability: **Low**

12. *Answer choices:*

(see index for correct answer)

- a. cultural
- b. Chief executive officer

- c. hierarchical
- d. process perspective

*Guidance:* level 1

:: Taxation ::

_____ refers to instances where a taxpayer can delay paying taxes to some future period. In theory, the net taxes paid should be the same. Taxes can sometimes be deferred indefinitely, or may be taxed at a lower rate in the future, particularly for deferral of income taxes.

Exam Probability: **Low**

13. *Answer choices:*
(see index for correct answer)

- a. Bracket creep
- b. Lindahl tax
- c. Tax and spend
- d. Tax deferral

*Guidance:* level 1

:: Accounting ::

_____ examines how accounting is used by individuals, organizations and government as well as the consequences that these practices have. Starting from the assumption that accounting both measures and makes visible certain economic events, _____ has studied the roles of accounting in organizations and society and the consequences that these practices have for individuals, organizations, governments and capital markets. It encompasses a broad range of topics including financial _____ , management _____ , auditing research, capital market research, accountability research, social responsibility research and taxation research.

Exam Probability: **Low**

14. *Answer choices:*
(see index for correct answer)

- a. amortisation
- b. Accounting research
- c. Professional services networks

- d. Bookkeeping

*Guidance: level 1*

---

:: Generally Accepted Accounting Principles ::

_____ is a measure of a fixed or current asset's worth when held in inventory, in the field of accounting. NRV is part of the Generally Accepted Accounting Principles and International Financial Reporting Standards that apply to valuing inventory, so as to not overstate or understate the value of inventory goods. _____ is generally equal to the selling price of the inventory goods less the selling costs. Therefore, it is expected sales price less selling costs. NRV prevents overstating or understating of an assets value. NRV is the price cap when using the Lower of Cost or Market Rule.

Exam Probability: **High**

15. *Answer choices:*
(see index for correct answer)

- a. Consolidation
- b. Treasury stock
- c. Revenue
- d. Net realizable value

*Guidance: level 1*

---

:: Pharmaceutical industry ::

A _____ is a document in which data collected for a clinical trial is first recorded. This data is usually later entered in the case report form. The International Conference on Harmonisation of Technical Requirements for Registration of Pharmaceuticals for Human Use guidelines define _____ s as "original documents, data, and records." _____ s contain source data, which is defined as "all information in original records and certified copies of original records of clinical findings, observations, or other activities in a clinical trial necessary for the reconstruction and evaluation of the trial."

Exam Probability: **Medium**

16. *Answer choices:*
(see index for correct answer)

- a. Source document
- b. Critical Path Institute
- c. Healthy Skepticism
- d. Approved drug

*Guidance:* level 1

---

:: Financial ratios ::

_____ is a financial ratio that indicates the percentage of a company's assets that are provided via debt. It is the ratio of total debt and total assets .

Exam Probability: **Low**

17. *Answer choices:*
(see index for correct answer)

- a. Debt ratio
- b. Accounting liquidity
- c. Sharpe ratio
- d. Average propensity to save

*Guidance:* level 1

---

:: Management accounting ::

_____ is an accounting methodology that traces and accumulates direct costs, and allocates indirect costs of a manufacturing process. Costs are assigned to products, usually in a large batch, which might include an entire month's production. Eventually, costs have to be allocated to individual units of product. It assigns average costs to each unit, and is the opposite extreme of Job costing which attempts to measure individual costs of production of each unit. _____ is usually a significant chapter. It is a method of assigning costs to units of production in companies producing large quantities of homogeneous products..

Exam Probability: **Low**

18. *Answer choices:*
(see index for correct answer)

- a. Process costing
- b. activity based costing
- c. Managerial risk accounting

- d. Holding cost

*Guidance:* level 1

---

:: United States Generally Accepted Accounting Principles ::

In a companies' financial reporting, _____ "includes all changes in equity during a period except those resulting from investments by owners and distributions to owners". Because that use excludes the effects of changing ownership interest, an economic measure of _____ is necessary for financial analysis from the shareholders' point of view

Exam Probability: **High**

19. *Answer choices:*

(see index for correct answer)

- a. Available for sale
- b. Comprehensive annual financial report
- c. Asset retirement obligation
- d. Accounting for leases in the United States

*Guidance:* level 1

---

:: Generally Accepted Accounting Principles ::

The first published description of the process is found in Luca Pacioli's 1494 work Summa de arithmetica, in the section titled Particularis de Computis et Scripturis. Although he did not use the term, he essentially prescribed a technique similar to a post-closing _____.

Exam Probability: **Medium**

20. *Answer choices:*

(see index for correct answer)

- a. Engagement letter
- b. Revenue
- c. Revenue recognition
- d. Depreciation

*Guidance:* level 1

---

:: Management accounting ::

A _____ is a part of a business which is expected to make an identifiable contribution to the organization's profits.

Exam Probability: **Medium**

21. *Answer choices:*

(see index for correct answer)

- a. Grenzplankostenrechnung
- b. Profit center
- c. Extended cost
- d. Corporate travel management

*Guidance:* level 1

---

:: Basic financial concepts ::

_____ is a sustained increase in the general price level of goods and services in an economy over a period of time. When the general price level rises, each unit of currency buys fewer goods and services; consequently, _____ reflects a reduction in the purchasing power per unit of money a loss of real value in the medium of exchange and unit of account within the economy. The measure of _____ is the _____ rate, the annualized percentage change in a general price index, usually the consumer price index, over time. The opposite of _____ is deflation.

Exam Probability: **Low**

22. *Answer choices:*

(see index for correct answer)

- a. Short interest
- b. Inflation
- c. Maturity
- d. Lodgement

*Guidance:* level 1

---

:: Management accounting ::

_____ is the profit the firm makes from serving a customer or customer group over a specified period of time, specifically the difference between the revenues earned from and the costs associated with the customer relationship in a specified period. According to Philip Kotler,"a profitable customer is a person, household or a company that overtime, yields a revenue stream that exceeds by an acceptable amount the company's cost stream of attracting, selling and servicing the customer."

Exam Probability: **High**

23. *Answer choices:*

(see index for correct answer)

- a. Spend management
- b. Customer profitability
- c. Inventory valuation
- d. Chartered Cost Accountant

*Guidance:* level 1

:: Accounting in the United States ::

The _____ is the internal audit profession's most widely recognized advocate, educator, and provider of standards, guidance, and certifications. Established in 1941, the IIA today serves more than 200,000 members from more than 170 countries and territories. IIA's global headquarters are in Lake Mary, Fla., United States.

Exam Probability: **High**

24. *Answer choices:*

(see index for correct answer)

- a. Cotton Plantation Record and Account Book
- b. Comprehensive Performance Assessment
- c. Institute of Internal Auditors
- d. Adjusted basis

*Guidance:* level 1

:: Valuation (finance) ::

The _____ is one of three major groups of methodologies, called valuation approaches, used by appraisers. It is particularly common in commercial real estate appraisal and in business appraisal. The fundamental math is similar to the methods used for financial valuation, securities analysis, or bond pricing. However, there are some significant and important modifications when used in real estate or business valuation.

Exam Probability: **Medium**

25. *Answer choices:*

(see index for correct answer)

- a. Turnaround stock
- b. Dividend puzzle
- c. Appraisal Foundation
- d. Expertization

*Guidance:* level 1

:: Auditing ::

A _____, also called "Internal _____", is a term of financial audit, internal audit and Enterprise Risk Management. It means the overall attitude, awareness and actions of directors and management regarding the internal control system and its importance to the entity. They express it in management style, corporate culture, values, philosophy and operating style, the organisational structure, and human resources policies and procedures.

Exam Probability: **Medium**

26. *Answer choices:*

(see index for correct answer)

- a. Audit planning
- b. Negative assurance
- c. Control environment
- d. Performance audit

*Guidance:* level 1

:: Types of business entity ::

A _____ is a partnership in which some or all partners have limited liabilities. It therefore can exhibit elements of partnerships and corporations. In a LLP, each partner is not responsible or liable for another partner's misconduct or negligence. This is an important difference from the traditional partnership under the UK Partnership Act 1890, in which each partner has joint and several liability. In a LLP, some or all partners have a form of limited liability similar to that of the shareholders of a corporation. Unlike corporate shareholders, the partners have the right to manage the business directly. In contrast, corporate shareholders must elect a board of directors under the laws of various state charters. The board organizes itself and hires corporate officers who then have as "corporate" individuals the legal responsibility to manage the corporation in the corporation's best interest. A LLP also contains a different level of tax liability from that of a corporation.

Exam Probability: **High**

27. *Answer choices:*

(see index for correct answer)

- a. Limited liability partnership
- b. Proprietary company
- c. Proprietism
- d. Kabushiki gaisha

*Guidance:* level 1

:: Accounting in the United States ::

_____ is the title of qualified accountants in numerous countries in the English-speaking world. In the United States, the CPA is a license to provide accounting services to the public. It is awarded by each of the 50 states for practice in that state. Additionally, almost every state has passed mobility laws to allow CPAs from other states to practice in their state. State licensing requirements vary, but the minimum standard requirements include passing the Uniform _____ Examination, 150 semester units of college education, and one year of accounting related experience.

Exam Probability: **Medium**

28. *Answer choices:*

(see index for correct answer)

- a. Accounting Today
- b. Other comprehensive basis of accounting
- c. Trueblood Committee
- d. National Association of State Boards of Accountancy

*Guidance:* level 1

---

:: Legal terms ::

A _____ is a gathering of people who have been invited by a host for the purposes of socializing, conversation, recreation, or as part of a festival or other commemoration of a special occasion. A _____ will typically feature food and beverages, and often music and dancing or other forms of entertainment. In many Western countries, parties for teens and adults are associated with drinking alcohol such as beer, wine, or distilled spirits.

Exam Probability: **Medium**

29. *Answer choices:*

(see index for correct answer)

- a. Legal transplant
- b. Party
- c. Motion for leave
- d. Consent decree

*Guidance:* level 1

---

:: Financial markets ::

_____ s are monetary contracts between parties. They can be created, traded, modified and settled. They can be cash , evidence of an ownership interest in an entity , or a contractual right to receive or deliver cash .

Exam Probability: **Medium**

30. *Answer choices:*

(see index for correct answer)

- a. Block trade
- b. Financial instrument
- c. Arbitrage
- d. Shelf registration

*Guidance:* level 1

:: Management ::

Business _____ is a discipline in operations management in which people use various methods to discover, model, analyze, measure, improve, optimize, and automate business processes. BPM focuses on improving corporate performance by managing business processes. Any combination of methods used to manage a company's business processes is BPM. Processes can be structured and repeatable or unstructured and variable. Though not required, enabling technologies are often used with BPM.

Exam Probability: **Low**

31. *Answer choices:*

(see index for correct answer)

- a. Logistics management
- b. Core competency
- c. Environmental stewardship
- d. Process Management

*Guidance:* level 1

:: ::

An _____ is a contingent motivator. Traditional _____ s are extrinsic motivators which reward actions to yield a desired outcome. The effectiveness of traditional _____ s has changed as the needs of Western society have evolved. While the traditional _____ model is effective when there is a defined procedure and goal for a task, Western society started to require a higher volume of critical thinkers, so the traditional model became less effective. Institutions are now following a trend in implementing strategies that rely on intrinsic motivations rather than the extrinsic motivations that the traditional _____ s foster.

Exam Probability: **High**

32. *Answer choices:*

(see index for correct answer)

- a. personal values
- b. interpersonal communication
- c. Incentive
- d. corporate values

*Guidance:* level 1

:: Insolvency ::

_____ is the process in accounting by which a company is brought to an end in the United Kingdom, Republic of Ireland and United States. The assets and property of the company are redistributed. _____ is also sometimes referred to as winding-up or dissolution, although dissolution technically refers to the last stage of _____. The process of _____ also arises when customs, an authority or agency in a country responsible for collecting and safeguarding customs duties, determines the final computation or ascertainment of the duties or drawback accruing on an entry.

Exam Probability: **Medium**

33. *Answer choices:*
(see index for correct answer)

- a. Debt consolidation
- b. Liquidation
- c. Liquidator
- d. Official Committee of Equity Security Holders

*Guidance:* level 1

:: Accounting systems ::

In accounting, a business or an organization and its owners are treated as two separately identifiable parties. This is called the _____ . The business stands apart from other organizations as a separate economic unit. It is necessary to record the business's transactions separately, to distinguish them from the owners' personal transactions. This helps to give a correct determination of the true financial condition of the business. This concept can be extended to accounting separately for the various divisions of a business in order to ascertain the financial results for each division. Under the business _____ , a business holds separate entity and distinct from its owners. "The entity view holds the business 'enterprise to be an institution in its own right separate and distinct from the parties who furnish the funds"

Exam Probability: **High**

34. *Answer choices:*

(see index for correct answer)

- a. Entity concept
- b. Waste book
- c. Standard accounting practice
- d. control account

*Guidance:* level 1

---

:: Generally Accepted Accounting Principles ::

A _____ , in accrual accounting, is any account where the asset or liability is not realized until a future date , e.g. annuities, charges, taxes, income, etc. The deferred item may be carried, dependent on type of _____ , as either an asset or liability. See also accrual.

Exam Probability: **High**

35. *Answer choices:*
(see index for correct answer)

- a. French generally accepted accounting principles
- b. Deferral
- c. Cost pool
- d. Net profit

*Guidance:* level 1

---

:: Financial statements ::

In financial accounting, a _____ or statement of financial position or statement of financial condition is a summary of the financial balances of an individual or organization, whether it be a sole proprietorship, a business partnership, a corporation, private limited company or other organization such as Government or not-for-profit entity. Assets, liabilities and ownership equity are listed as of a specific date, such as the end of its financial year. A _____ is often described as a "snapshot of a company's financial condition". Of the four basic financial statements, the _____ is the only statement which applies to a single point in time of a business' calendar year.

Exam Probability: **High**

36. *Answer choices:*

(see index for correct answer)

- a. Consolidated financial statement
- b. PnL Explained
- c. quarterly report
- d. Emphasis of matter

*Guidance:* level 1

---

:: Generally Accepted Accounting Principles ::

_____ is the accounting classification of an account. It is part of double-entry book-keeping technique.

Exam Probability: **Low**

37. *Answer choices:*
(see index for correct answer)

- a. Fixed investment
- b. Petty cash
- c. Trial balance
- d. Normal balance

*Guidance:* level 1

---

:: E-commerce ::

A _____ is a plastic payment card that can be used instead of cash when making purchases. It is similar to a credit card, but unlike a credit card, the money is immediately transferred directly from the cardholder's bank account when performing a transaction.

Exam Probability: **Medium**

38. *Answer choices:*
(see index for correct answer)

- a. Debit card
- b. Transport Layer Security
- c. Wildcard certificate
- d. Segundamano

*Guidance:* level 1

---

:: Taxation ::

_____ is a type of tax law that allows a person to give assets to his or her spouse with reduced or no tax imposed upon the transfer. Some _____ laws even apply to transfers made postmortem. The right to receive property conveys ownership for tax purposes. A decree of divorce transfers the right to that property by reason of the marriage and is also a transfer within a marriage. It makes no difference whether the property itself or equivalent compensation is transferred before, or after the decree dissolves the marriage. There is no U.S. estate and gift tax on transfers of any amount between spouses, whether during their lifetime or at death. There is an important exceptions for non-citizens. The U.S. federal Estate and gift tax _____ is only available if the surviving spouse is a U.S. citizen. For a surviving spouse who is not a U.S. citizen a bequest through a Qualified Domestic Trust defers estate tax until principal is distributed by the trustee, a U.S. citizen or corporation who also withholds the estate tax. Income on principal distributed to the surviving spouse is taxed as individual income. If the surviving spouse becomes a U.S. citizen, principal remaining in a Qualifying Domestic Trust may then be distributed without further tax.

Exam Probability: **High**

39. *Answer choices:*

<small>(see index for correct answer)</small>

- a. Max Planck Institute for Tax Law and Public Finance
- b. Taxpayer
- c. Suits index
- d. Tax uncertainty

<small>*Guidance:* level 1</small>

---

:: Marketing ::

_____ or stock control can be broadly defined as "the activity of checking a shop's stock." However, a more focused definition takes into account the more science-based, methodical practice of not only verifying a business' inventory but also focusing on the many related facets of inventory management "within an organisation to meet the demand placed upon that business economically." Other facets of _____ include supply chain management, production control, financial flexibility, and customer satisfaction. At the root of _____ , however, is the _____ problem, which involves determining when to order, how much to order, and the logistics of those decisions.

Exam Probability: **High**

40. *Answer choices:*

(see index for correct answer)

- a. Inventory control
- b. Outsourcing relationship management
- c. Promo
- d. Fifth screen

*Guidance:* level 1

---

:: Manufacturing ::

_____ s are goods that have completed the manufacturing process but have not yet been sold or distributed to the end user.

Exam Probability: **High**

41. *Answer choices:*

(see index for correct answer)

- a. International Organization of Legal Metrology
- b. Lights out
- c. Agri-Fab, Inc.
- d. Demand flow technology

*Guidance:* level 1

---

:: Financial ratios ::

The _____ or dividend-price ratio of a share is the dividend per share, divided by the price per share. It is also a company's total annual dividend payments divided by its market capitalization, assuming the number of shares is constant. It is often expressed as a percentage.

Exam Probability: **High**

42. *Answer choices:*

(see index for correct answer)

- a. stock turnover
- b. Dividend yield
- c. Earnings yield
- d. Risk-adjusted return on capital

*Guidance:* level 1

:: ::

A tax is a compulsory financial charge or some other type of levy imposed upon a taxpayer by a governmental organization in order to fund various public expenditures. A failure to pay, along with evasion of or resistance to _____ , is punishable by law. Taxes consist of direct or indirect taxes and may be paid in money or as its labour equivalent.

Exam Probability: **Medium**

43. *Answer choices:*

(see index for correct answer)

- a. empathy
- b. similarity-attraction theory
- c. Taxation
- d. corporate values

*Guidance:* level 1

:: Financial accounting ::

_____ refers to any one of several methods by which a company, for 'financial accounting' or tax purposes, depreciates a fixed asset in such a way that the amount of depreciation taken each year is higher during the earlier years of an asset's life. For financial accounting purposes, _____ is expected to be much more productive during its early years, so that depreciation expense will more accurately represent how much of an asset's usefulness is being used up each year. For tax purposes, _____ provides a way of deferring corporate income taxes by reducing taxable income in current years, in exchange for increased taxable income in future years. This is a valuable tax incentive that encourages businesses to purchase new assets.

Exam Probability: **High**

44. *Answer choices:*
(see index for correct answer)

- a. Convenience translation
- b. Controlling interest
- c. Certified Public Accountants Association
- d. Capital account

*Guidance:* level 1

:: Television terminology ::

A nonprofit organization, also known as a non-business entity, _____ organization, or nonprofit institution, is dedicated to furthering a particular social cause or advocating for a shared point of view. In economic terms, it is an organization that uses its surplus of the revenues to further achieve its ultimate objective, rather than distributing its income to the organization's shareholders, leaders, or members. Nonprofits are tax exempt or charitable, meaning they do not pay income tax on the money that they receive for their organization. They can operate in religious, scientific, research, or educational settings.

Exam Probability: **Medium**

45. *Answer choices:*
(see index for correct answer)

- a. Satellite television
- b. Not-for-profit
- c. nonprofit

- d. multiplexing

*Guidance:* level 1

---

:: Commerce ::

Continuation of an entity as a _____ is presumed as the basis for financial reporting unless and until the entity's liquidation becomes imminent. Preparation of financial statements under this presumption is commonly referred to as the _____ basis of accounting. If and when an entity's liquidation becomes imminent, financial statements are prepared under the liquidation basis of accounting.

Exam Probability: **Medium**

46. *Answer choices:*
(see index for correct answer)

- a. Going concern
- b. Issuing bank
- c. Recommerce
- d. Agio

*Guidance:* level 1

---

:: Management accounting ::

An _____ is a classification used for business units within an enterprise. The essential element of an _____ is that it is treated as a unit which is measured against its use of capital, as opposed to a cost or profit center, which are measured against raw costs or profits.

Exam Probability: **High**

47. *Answer choices:*
(see index for correct answer)

- a. Grenzplankostenrechnung
- b. Investment center
- c. Standard cost
- d. Process costing

*Guidance:* level 1

:: Capital gains taxes ::

A _____ refers to profit that results from a sale of a capital asset, such as stock, bond or real estate, where the sale price exceeds the purchase price. The gain is the difference between a higher selling price and a lower purchase price. Conversely, a capital loss arises if the proceeds from the sale of a capital asset are less than the purchase price.

Exam Probability: **High**

48. *Answer choices:*

(see index for correct answer)

- a. Capital Cost Allowance
- b. Capital gain
- c. Capital cost tax factor

*Guidance:* level 1

:: Management accounting ::

_____ , or dollar contribution per unit, is the selling price per unit minus the variable cost per unit. "Contribution" represents the portion of sales revenue that is not consumed by variable costs and so contributes to the coverage of fixed costs. This concept is one of the key building blocks of break-even analysis.

Exam Probability: **High**

49. *Answer choices:*

(see index for correct answer)

- a. Managerial risk accounting
- b. Chartered Cost Accountant
- c. Cash and cash equivalents
- d. Contribution margin

*Guidance:* level 1

:: Business models ::

A _____ is a company that owns enough voting stock in another firm to control management and operation by influencing or electing its board of directors. The company is deemed a subsidiary of the _____ .

Exam Probability: **High**

50. *Answer choices:*
(see index for correct answer)

- a. Praenumeration
- b. Parent company
- c. InnovationXchange
- d. Trade printing

*Guidance:* level 1

:: Accounting terminology ::

In management accounting or _____ , managers use the provisions of accounting information in order to better inform themselves before they decide matters within their organizations, which aids their management and performance of control functions.

Exam Probability: **Low**

51. *Answer choices:*
(see index for correct answer)

- a. Chart of accounts
- b. Managerial accounting
- c. Accounting equation
- d. Checkoff

*Guidance:* level 1

:: Management accounting ::

_____ is the process of recording, classifying, analyzing, summarizing, and allocating costs associated with a process, after that developing various courses of action to control the costs. Its goal is to advise the management on how to optimize business practices and processes based on cost efficiency and capability. _____ provides the detailed cost information that management needs to control current operations and plan for the future.

Exam Probability: **Low**

52. *Answer choices:*
(see index for correct answer)

- a. Cost accounting
- b. Overhead
- c. Inventory valuation
- d. Certified Management Accountant

*Guidance:* level 1

:: Taxation ::

_____ is an estimate of the market value of a property, based on what a knowledgeable, willing, and unpressured buyer would probably pay to a knowledgeable, willing, and unpressured seller in the market. An estimate of _____ may be founded either on precedent or extrapolation. _____ differs from the intrinsic value that an individual may place on the same asset based on their own preferences and circumstances.

Exam Probability: **High**

53. *Answer choices:*
(see index for correct answer)

- a. Tolerance tax
- b. Hotchpot
- c. Paulette
- d. Fair market value

*Guidance:* level 1

:: Shareholders ::

A _____ is a payment made by a corporation to its shareholders, usually as a distribution of profits. When a corporation earns a profit or surplus, the corporation is able to re-invest the profit in the business and pay a proportion of the profit as a _____ to shareholders. Distribution to shareholders may be in cash or, if the corporation has a _____ reinvestment plan, the amount can be paid by the issue of further shares or share repurchase. When _____ s are paid, shareholders typically must pay income taxes, and the corporation does not receive a corporate income tax deduction for the _____ payments.

Exam Probability: **Low**

54. *Answer choices:*

(see index for correct answer)

- a. Shareholder Rights Directive
- b. Friedman doctrine
- c. Dividend
- d. Stock dilution

*Guidance:* level 1

:: ::

A _____ is a tax paid to a governing body for the sales of certain goods and services. Usually laws allow the seller to collect funds for the tax from the consumer at the point of purchase. When a tax on goods or services is paid to a governing body directly by a consumer, it is usually called a use tax. Often laws provide for the exemption of certain goods or services from sales and use tax.

Exam Probability: **High**

55. *Answer choices:*

(see index for correct answer)

- a. interpersonal communication
- b. similarity-attraction theory
- c. open system
- d. information systems assessment

*Guidance:* level 1

:: Accounting systems ::

In bookkeeping, a _____ statement is a process that explains the difference on a specified date between the bank balance shown in an organization's bank statement, as supplied by the bank and the corresponding amount shown in the organization's own accounting records.

Exam Probability: **High**

56. *Answer choices:*
(see index for correct answer)

- a. Debits and credits
- b. Substance over form
- c. Bank reconciliation
- d. Cookie jar accounting

*Guidance:* level 1

:: Debt ::

A _____ is a monetary amount owed to a creditor that is unlikely to be paid and, or which the creditor is not willing to take action to collect for various reasons, often due to the debtor not having the money to pay, for example due to a company going into liquidation or insolvency. There are various technical definitions of what constitutes a _____, depending on accounting conventions, regulatory treatment and the institution provisioning. In the USA, bank loans with more than ninety days' arrears become "problem loans". Accounting sources advise that the full amount of a _____ be written off to the profit and loss account or a provision for _____ s as soon as it is foreseen.

Exam Probability: **High**

57. *Answer choices:*
(see index for correct answer)

- a. Credit crunch
- b. Legal liability
- c. Credit cycle
- d. Bad debt

*Guidance:* level 1

:: Labour law ::

In law, _____ is to give an immediately secured right of present or future deployment. One has a vested right to an asset that cannot be taken away by any third party, even though one may not yet possess the asset. When the right, interest, or title to the present or future possession of a legal estate can be transferred to any other party, it is termed a vested interest.

Exam Probability: **High**

58. *Answer choices:*
(see index for correct answer)

- a. Negligent retention
- b. Vesting
- c. Negligent hiring
- d. Matthew W. Finkin

*Guidance:* level 1

---

:: Financial regulatory authorities of the United States ::

The _____ is the revenue service of the United States federal government. The government agency is a bureau of the Department of the Treasury, and is under the immediate direction of the Commissioner of Internal Revenue, who is appointed to a five-year term by the President of the United States. The IRS is responsible for collecting taxes and administering the Internal Revenue Code, the main body of federal statutory tax law of the United States. The duties of the IRS include providing tax assistance to taxpayers and pursuing and resolving instances of erroneous or fraudulent tax filings. The IRS has also overseen various benefits programs, and enforces portions of the Affordable Care Act.

Exam Probability: **Low**

59. *Answer choices:*
(see index for correct answer)

- a. Internal Revenue Service
- b. National Credit Union Administration
- c. Commodity Futures Trading Commission
- d. U.S. Securities and Exchange Commission

*Guidance:* level 1

## INDEX: Correct Answers

## Foundations of Business

1. : Partnership

2. b: Stock market

3. d: Meeting

4. b: Audience

5. a: Arbitration

6. a: Investment

7. b: Procurement

8. a: Import

9. : Stock exchange

10. c: Social security

11. d: Scheduling

12. : Energies

13. d: Performance

14. c: Bias

15. : System

16. : Buyer

17. d: Small business

18. : Management

19. b: Regulation

20. d: Target market

21. : Strategic planning

22. d: Competitive advantage

23. d: Specification

24. c: Recession

25. c: Marketing research

26. d: Economic Development

27. d: Sony

28. a: Raw material

29. c: Publicity

30. : Venture capital

31. c: Return on investment

32. b: Tariff

33. c: Fixed cost

34. d: Case study

35. d: Percentage

36. : Economies of scale

37. a: Globalization

38. d: Review

39. : Quality management

40. c: Life

41. a: Fraud

42. : Information technology

43. c: Authority

44. b: Alliance

45. d: Federal Trade Commission

46. a: Price

47. a: Logistics

48. d: Gross domestic product

49. a: Policy

50. a: Evaluation

51. c: Commerce

52. b: Payment

53. a: Manufacturing

54. d: Efficiency

55. a: Expense

56. c: Competitor

57. : Working capital

58. c: Strategy

59. a: Officer

---

# Management

1. a: Leadership

2. b: Cash flow

3. c: Job design

4. d: Transactional leadership

5. c: Quality control

6. b: Recruitment

7. b: Incentive

8. b: Ratio

9. : Individualism

10. c: Description

11. d: Cost leadership

12. a: Gantt chart

13. c: Quality management

14. b: Six Sigma

15. d: International trade

16. b: 360-degree feedback

17. a: Human resources

18. c: Research and development

19. c: Cooperative

20. b: Project team

21. b: Product design

22. d: Interaction

23. b: Strategic alliance

24. a: Ambiguity

25. : Inventory

26. a: Information

27. b: Human resource management

28. a: Economies of scale

29. : Delegation

30. c: Learning organization

31. : Protection

32. c: Return on investment

33. d: Operations management

34. c: Decision-making

35. : Accounting

36. c: Restructuring

37. b: Employee stock

38. a: Political risk

39. c: Small business

40. a: Resource

41. d: Market research

42. a: Criticism

43. c: Environmental protection

44. d: Fixed cost

45. a: Total cost

46. : Insurance

47. : Span of control

48. c: Board of directors

49. c: Mission statement

50. d: Subsidiary

51. b: Expert

52. d: Schedule

53. : Organization chart

54. a: Virtual team

55. a: Dilemma

56. a: Time management

57. c: Chief executive officer

58. d: Reputation

59. a: Discipline

## Business law

1. a: Puffery

2. d: Property

3. a: Commercial speech

4. a: Misrepresentation

5. a: Auction

6. : Statute of frauds

7. a: Scienter

8. d: Supreme Court

9. a: Directed verdict

10. d: Intellectual property

11. : Warehouse receipt

12. d: Commerce

13. c: Indictment

14. c: Enron

15. c: Mirror image rule

16. b: Security

17. : Implied warranty

18. d: Due diligence

19. b: Implied authority

20. d: Insurable interest

21. a: Technology

22. : Output contract

23. a: Welfare

24. c: Delegation

25. : Private law

26. a: Contract law

27. c: Economy

28. b: Precedent

29. d: Bad faith

30. d: Corporate governance

31. c: Perfect tender

32. b: Insurance

33. a: Presentment

34. a: Forgery

35. : Argument

36. b: Commercial Paper

37. c: Internal Revenue Service

38. c: Corruption

39. : Appellate Court

40. a: Reasonable person

41. d: Patent

42. d: Economic espionage

43. d: Embezzlement

44. d: Contract

45. d: Litigation

46. d: Consideration

47. : Procedural law

48. d: Exclusionary rule

49. : Inventory

50. : Unconscionability

51. a: Foreign Corrupt Practices Act

52. d: Treaty

53. c: Criminal procedure

54. c: Adoption

55. : Securities Act

56. c: Bankruptcy

57. a: Creditor

58. a: Utility

59. b: Fee simple

---

# Finance

1. a: Issuer

2. d: Corporation

3. c: Opportunity cost

4. c: Financial management

5. c: Face

6. c: Current asset

7. b: Accrual

8. : Cost allocation

9. : Conservatism

10. d: Economy

11. a: WorldCom

12. a: Investment

13. b: Operating lease

14. d: Manufacturing

15. a: Time value of money

16. a: INDEX

17. b: S corporation

18. c: Journal entry

19. c: Comprehensive income

20. c: Accounting

21. a: Financial risk

22. c: Contribution margin

23. c: Saving

24. c: Stock price

25. d: Future value

26. b: Taxation

27. b: Security

28. d: Capital budgeting

29. b: Periodic inventory

30. b: Capital expenditure

31. a: Debt

32. : Maturity date

33. c: Initial public offering

34. b: Working capital

35. b: Dividend yield

36. c: Risk management

37. a: Brand

38. a: Internal rate of return

39. a: Chart of accounts

40. a: Yield curve

41. b: Wall Street

42. d: Long-term liabilities

43. a: Bank

44. b: Budget

45. : Ending inventory

46. a: Capital structure

47. a: Risk premium

48. : Aging

49. b: Accounting method

50. b: Public Company Accounting Oversight Board

51. b: Presentation

52. : Internal Revenue Service

53. a: Book value

54. b: Tax rate

55. a: Break-even

56. b: Limited liability

57. d: Bank reconciliation

58. c: Quick ratio

59. a: Capital lease

## Human resource management

1. : Free agent

2. : Occupational Safety and Health Act

3. d: Performance

4. b: Payroll

5. c: Age Discrimination in Employment Act

6. b: Golden parachute

7. a: Cross-training

8. c: Applicant tracking system

9. a: Mission statement

10. a: Occupational Information Network

11. d: Glass ceiling

12. b: Interactional justice

13. a: Persuasion

14. c: UNITE HERE

15. a: Employment

16. c: Employee benefit

17. b: Transformational leadership

18. b: 360-degree feedback

19. : E-HRM

20. a: Individualism

21. a: Affirmative action

22. b: Cross-functional team

23. a: On-the-job training

24. a: Career management

25. : Body language

26. d: Task force

27. d: Referent power

28. a: Pension

29. d: Workforce management

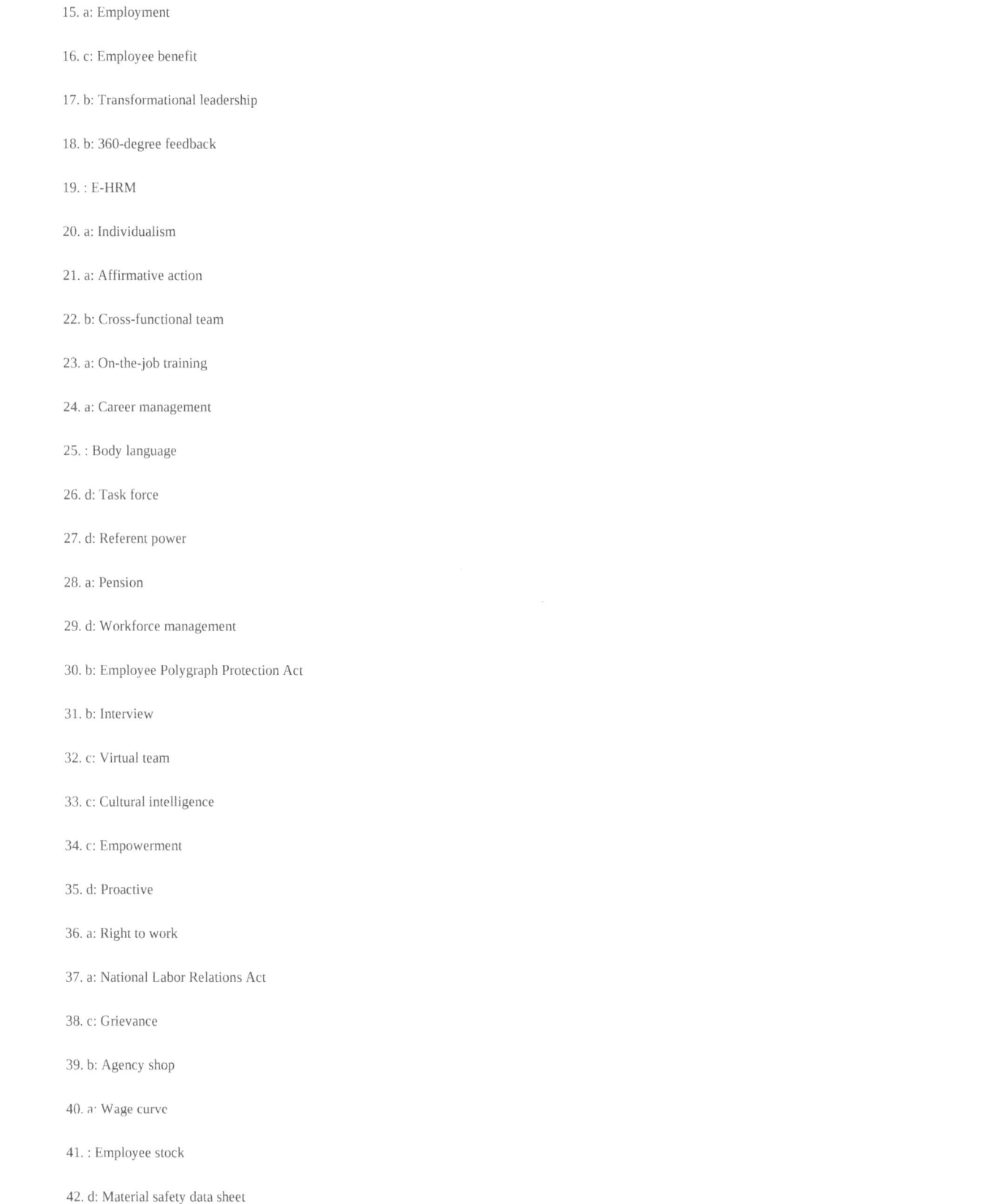

30. b: Employee Polygraph Protection Act

31. b: Interview

32. c: Virtual team

33. c: Cultural intelligence

34. c: Empowerment

35. d: Proactive

36. a: Right to work

37. a: National Labor Relations Act

38. c: Grievance

39. b: Agency shop

40. a: Wage curve

41. : Employee stock

42. d: Material safety data sheet

43. c: Industrial relations

44. : Employee retention

45. : Unemployment benefits

46. c: Employee referral

47. b: Case interview

48. c: Sweatshop

49. d: Pattern bargaining

50. a: Performance appraisal

51. : Rating scale

52. b: Kaizen

53. : Workforce

54. a: Needs analysis

55. a: Behavior modification

56. : Human resource management

57. a: National Association of Colleges and Employers

58. c: Unemployment

59. a: Action learning

## Information systems

1. a: Consumer-to-business

2. d: Information security

3. c: Data field

4. b: Computer-aided manufacturing

5. a: Documentation

6. : Mozy

7. d: Semantic Web

8. d: System software

9. c: Interactivity

10. a: Data center

11. a: Crowdsourcing

12. : Business intelligence

13. c: Census

14. : Automated teller machine

15. c: Supplier relationship management

16. a: Change control

17. c: Commercial off-the-shelf

18. b: Computer security

19. b: Top-level domain

20. d: Computer-integrated manufacturing

21. : Magnetic tape

22. d: Data visualization

23. : Google Calendar

24. c: Availability

25. d: Payment system

26. a: Information privacy

27. b: Data governance

28. : Word

29. a: Online transaction processing

30. d: Business-to-business

31. c: Zynga

32. b: Subscription

33. a: Data link

34. : PayPal

35. d: Data analysis

36. d: World Wide Web

37. d: Cookie

38. d: Decision-making

39. a: Privacy

40. a: Knowledge management

41. : ITunes

42. : Application software

43. : Statistics

44. : Google Maps

45. a: Online analytical processing

46. a: Balanced scorecard

47. : Interaction

48. a: Search engine optimization

49. a: Information technology

50. a: Data integrity

51. a: Service level

52. c: Digital rights management

53. c: Critical success factor

54. d: Global Positioning System

55. c: Enterprise information system

56. a: Trojan horse

57. c: Blog

58. a: Mobile payment

59. a: Epicor

# Marketing

1. b: Coupon

2. a: Good

3. b: Attention

4. c: Demand

5. c: Customer retention

6. c: Telemarketing

7. b: Mobile marketing

8. : Presentation

9. a: Research and development

10. d: Organizational structure

11. a: Price discrimination

12. a: Interest

13. b: Asset

14. d: Marketing

15. a: Incentive

16. : Trademark

17. : Infomercial

18. c: Marketing channel

19. c: Advertisement

20. d: Insurance

21. b: Authority

22. d: Direct selling

23. d: Standing

24. b: Sales

25. b: Census

26. d: Accounting

27. a: Global marketing

28. : Commerce

29. c: Target market

30. : Commodity

31. d: Marketing strategy

32. b: Marketing communication

33. a: Pricing strategies

34. a: Problem Solving

35. b: Brand loyalty

36. b: Public relations

37. c: Consideration

38. d: Personal selling

39. a: Strategy

40. d: Testimonial

41. a: Exchange rate

42. b: Innovation

43. b: Concept testing

44. b: Secondary data

45. b: Manager

46. d: Comparative advertising

47. d: Brand image

48. a: Information technology

49. : Reinforcement

50. a: Target audience

51. : Manufacturing

52. d: Clayton Act

53. : Partnership

54. b: Productivity

55. d: Merchant

56. a: Outsourcing

57. c: Project

58. c: Evolution

59. d: Globalization

## Manufacturing

1. : Tool

2. a: Quality management

3. a: Pareto analysis

4. b: Gantt chart

5. a: Water

6. : Sequence

7. b: Sales

8. b: Total quality management

9. d: Vendor relationship management

10. d: Control chart

11. : Pattern

12. b: E-commerce

13. a: Scientific management

14. b: Cost estimate

15. : Synergy

16. a: Quality control

17. c: Volume

18. : Value engineering

19. a: Process engineering

20. c: Material requirements planning

21. c: Process management

22. a: Strategic planning

23. d: Solution

24. c: Joint Commission

25. : ROOT

26. a: Furnace

27. : Change management

28. d: Blanket

29. c: Strategy

30. d: Ball

31. : Capacity planning

32. d: Stakeholder management

33. a: E-procurement

34. a: Natural resource

35. d: Project manager

36. : Clay

37. : Forecasting

38. : Process capital

39. : DMAIC

40. b: Authority

41. b: Process capability

42. : Steel

43. a: Voice of the customer

44. c: Project

45. b: Flowchart

46. a: Prize

47. c: Good

48. b: Supply chain management

49. : Purchase order

50. a: Economies of scope

51. d: Purchasing manager

52. b: Quality costs

53. a: Catalyst

54. : Aggregate planning

55. : Resource

56. d: Consensus

57. a: Certification

58. : Minitab

59. c: Acceptance sampling

# Commerce

1. a: Minimum wage

2. d: Microsoft

3. : Wage

4. : DigiCash

5. b: Technology

6. d: Business-to-business

7. b: Invoice

8. c: Quality management

9. a: Amazon Payments

10. b: Permission marketing

11. c: Dutch auction

12. a: Vickrey auction

13. c: Innovation

14. a: Jury

15. d: Micropayment

16. : Marginal cost

17. d: Customer satisfaction

18. : Trade

19. b: Consultant

20. a: Security

21. : E-commerce

22. b: Graduation

23. a: Raw material

24. a: Quality assurance

25. c: Case study

26. c: Industry

27. d: Electronic data interchange

28. a: Industrial Revolution

29. c: Management team

30. c: Anticipation

31. : Customs

32. : Staff position

33. a: Wholesale

34. : Shareholder

35. a: Statutory law

36. c: Lycos

37. : Competitive advantage

38. : Preference

39. : Siemens

40. : Public relations

41. d: Logistics

42. d: Regulation

43. : Cooperative

44. a: Committee

45. a: Market structure

46. a: Collaborative filtering

47. d: Market segmentation

48. a: Merger

49. b: Pizza Hut

50. d: Overtime

51. a: E-procurement

52. b: Bank

53. : Entrepreneur

54. c: Production line

55. a: Competitor

56. b: Manufacturing

57. a: Standardization

58. b: International trade

59. c: Import

# Business ethics

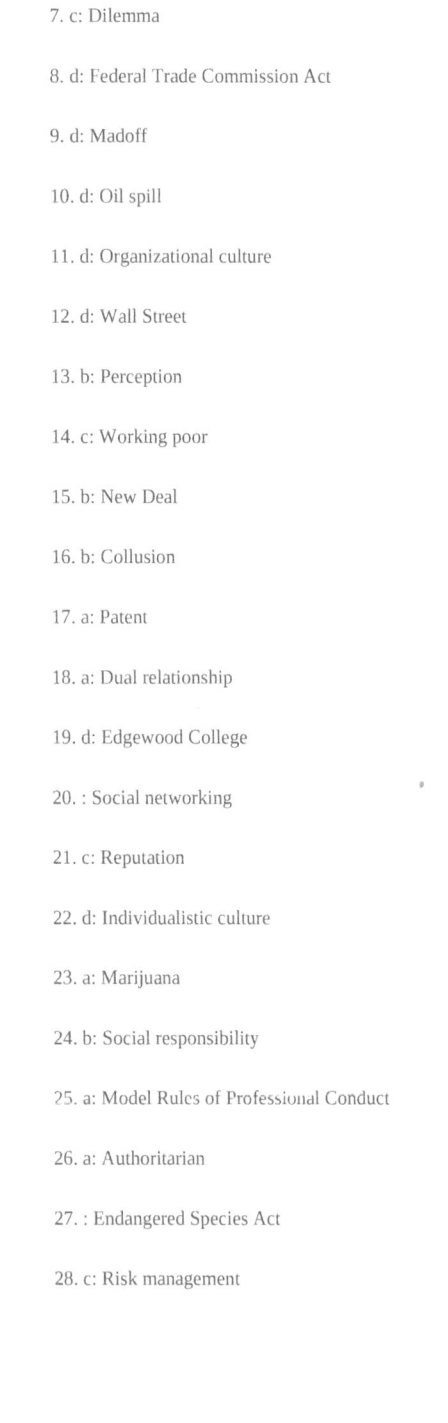

1. : Financial Stability Oversight Council

2. b: Human nature

3. c: Planned obsolescence

4. a: United Farm Workers

5. a: Feedback

6. b: Clayton Act

7. c: Dilemma

8. d: Federal Trade Commission Act

9. d: Madoff

10. d: Oil spill

11. d: Organizational culture

12. d: Wall Street

13. b: Perception

14. c: Working poor

15. b: New Deal

16. b: Collusion

17. a: Patent

18. a: Dual relationship

19. d: Edgewood College

20. : Social networking

21. c: Reputation

22. d: Individualistic culture

23. a: Marijuana

24. b: Social responsibility

25. a: Model Rules of Professional Conduct

26. a: Authoritarian

27. : Endangered Species Act

28. c: Risk management

29. d: Sustainable

30. a: European Commission

31. a: Consumerism

32. d: Sherman Antitrust Act

33. b: Kyoto Protocol

34. c: ExxonMobil

35. d: Green marketing

36. c: Six Sigma

37. b: Tobacco

38. a: Capitalism

39. b: Pyramid scheme

40. d: Medicaid

41. b: Nonprofit

42. a: Fair Trade Certified

43. d: Pollution

44. a: Partnership

45. b: Siemens

46. : Global Fund

47. d: Employee Polygraph Protection Act

48. c: Greenpeace

49. b: Martin Luther

50. c: Habitat

51. c: Retaliation

52. d: Solar power

53. : Socialism

54. b: Patriot Act

55. b: Natural gas

56. b: Aristotle

57. a: Living wage

58. a: Fraud

59. b: Referent power

## Accounting

1. a: Variable Costing

2. b: Annual report

3. : Revenue recognition

4. : Joint venture

5. : Diluted earnings per share

6. c: Worksheet

7. d: Governmental Accounting Standards Board

8. : Specific identification

9. c: Cost-plus pricing

10. a: Fixed asset

11. d: Cost pool

12. b: Chief executive officer

13. d: Tax deferral

14. b: Accounting research

15. d: Net realizable value

16. a: Source document

17. a: Debt ratio

18. a: Process costing

19. : Comprehensive income

20. : Trial balance

21. b: Profit center

22. b: Inflation

23. b: Customer profitability

24. c: Institute of Internal Auditors

25. : Income approach

26. c: Control environment

27. a: Limited liability partnership

28. : Certified Public Accountant

29. b: Party

30. b: Financial instrument

31. d: Process Management

32. c: Incentive

33. b: Liquidation

34. a: Entity concept

35. b: Deferral

36. : Balance sheet

37. d: Normal balance

38. a: Debit card

39. : Marital deduction

40. a: Inventory control

41. : Finished good

42. b: Dividend yield

43. c: Taxation

44. : Accelerated depreciation

45. b: Not-for-profit

46. a: Going concern

47. b: Investment center

48. b: Capital gain

49. d: Contribution margin

50. b: Parent company

51. b: Managerial accounting

52. a: Cost accounting

53. d: Fair market value

54. c: Dividend

55. : Sales tax

56. c: Bank reconciliation

57. d: Bad debt

58. b: Vesting

59. a: Internal Revenue Service

CPSIA information can be obtained
at www.ICGtesting.com
Printed in the USA
LVHW041328301019
635717LV00008B/1015/P